D0906576

Privatization in Four European Countries

Comparative Public Policy Analysis Series

Series Editors
Martin Rein, *Massachusetts Institute of Technology*
Lee Rainwater, *Harvard University*

PUBLIC/PRIVATE INTERPLAY IN SOCIAL PROTECTION
Martin Rein and Lee Rainwater, Editors

THE SCANDINAVIAN MODEL: WELFARE STATES AND WELFARE RESEARCH
Robert Erikson, Erik Jørgen Hansen, Stein Ringen, and Hannu Uusitalo, Editors

STAGNATION AND RENEWAL IN SOCIAL POLICY
Martin Rein, Gøsta Esping-Andersen, and Lee Rainwater, Editors

THE STUDY OF WELFARE STATE REGIMES
Jon Eivind Kolberg, Editor

BETWEEN WORK AND SOCIAL CITIZENSHIP
Jon Eivind Kolberg, Editor

THE WELFARE STATE AS EMPLOYER
Jon Eivind Kolberg, Editor

PRIVATIZATION IN FOUR EUROPEAN COUNTRIES
COMPARATIVE STUDIES IN GOVERNMENT-THIRD SECTOR RELATIONSHIPS
Ralph M. Kramer, Håkon Lorentzen, Willem Melief, Sergio Pasquinelli

Privatization in Four European Countries

Comparative Studies in Government-Third Sector Relationships

RALPH M. KRAMER
HÅKON LORENTZEN
WILLEM B. MELIEF
SERGIO PASQUINELLI

M.E. Sharpe

Armonk, New York
London, England

HV238
.P75
1993

Library of Congress Cataloging-in-Publication Data

Privatization in four European countries : comparative studies in government–third sector
relationships / Ralph M. Kramer . . . [et al.].
p. cm. — (Comparative public policy analysis series)
Includes bibliographical references and index.
ISBN 1-56324-132-3
1. Social service—Europe—Contracting out—Case studies.
2. Privatization—Europe—Case studies.
3. Nonprofit organizations—Europe—Case studies.
I. Kramer, Ralph M.
II. Series.
HV238.P75 1993
338.94—dc20
93-24985
CIP

Printed in the United States of America
The paper used in this publication meets the minimum
requirements of American National Standard for
Information Sciences—Permanence of Paper for
Printed Library Materials, ANSIZ 39.48-1984.

MV 10 9 8 7 6 5 4 3 2

Contents

Tables and Figures

Tables

Figures

Preface

This book has a dual focus: on how four countries use voluntary nonprofit organizations to provide services to the physically, mentally, and sensorially handicapped; and on the changing role of the voluntary, or "third," sector in welfare states. At the same time, it is also a comparative study of privatization in the special sense of using nongovernmental organizations to implement public policy. Most comparative studies of the welfare state have neglected this form of "indirect public administration" because researchers have usually conceived of government as monolithic and consequently overlook the frequent separation of financing from the delivery of public services.

As part of a response in Europe and North America during the late 1970s to "the crisis of the welfare state," the voluntary sector was rediscovered by both the Right and the Left in welfare states as varied as France, Italy, the United States, and Norway. Containing a bewildering diversity of nonprofit organizations, this newly defined third sector—between the state and the market—has been viewed as a less costly and more flexible alternative to the overloaded state, particularly in the social services. Of somewhat less interest is nonprofits' historical role, at least in the United States and the UK, of seeking social change through influencing public policy.

Reflecting the growing use of voluntary organizations by government, a new, interdisciplinary field of social science research has emerged, producing numerous case studies of the third sector, but very few comparative analyses of the character and role of voluntary social service organizations in different types of welfare states. In this book, therefore, the changing role of these typical third sector organizations in England, Italy, the Netherlands, and Norway is viewed comparatively for the first time in a historical and sociopolitical context. Also innovative is the comparative analysis of the organizational behavior of a cohort of twenty similar voluntary agencies in each country. By linking the sectoral (macro) and organizational (micro) levels, we sought to identify the influences of different national policies and contexts on the role and performance of voluntary social service agencies in welfare states. Although the concepts, models, and implications of the findings are based on organizations serving the handicapped, they should also be applicable to other types of voluntary organizations in other fields of service, and in different kinds of welfare states.

Our research had its origin in the first international comparative study of such organizations, which I conducted in the 1970s in the United States, England, the Netherlands, and Israel *(Voluntary Agencies in the Welfare State,* 1981). This, in turn, was based on my earlier research in the mid-1960s on the shifting relationships between government and voluntary organizations in the United States. I had planned to revisit England and the Netherlands in the fall of 1989 to update the original 1975–1977 study in the light of subsequent political developments in those countries such as the Thatcher regime's promotion of privatization and voluntarism. Because of the special interest of Sergio Pasquinelli and Håkon Lorentzen and the support of their respective social research institutes in Milan and Oslo, the scope of the comparative study was enlarged to include Italy and Norway. The Netherlands Institute of Social Welfare Research (NIMAWO) in the Hague, which had participated in the first study, had earlier assigned its senior researcher Willem Melief to the project.

During the fall of 1989, I was based at the Centre for Voluntary Organisation of the London School of Economics, where I collected the data for the case study of England, and I met with the other members of the research team in Milan, the Hague, and Oslo. We also worked together at a series of meetings during 1990–1991 in London and Berkeley.

Starting as research associates, Håkon Lorentzen, Willem Melief, and Sergio Pasquinelli became co-authors, each preparing the first draft of the case study of his country's third sector and organizational cohort, and one other chapter of the comparative analyses. This resulted in the following: Willem Melief (Chapters 3 and 6); Håkon Lorentzen (Chapters 4 and 7); Sergio Pasquinelli (Chapters 2 and 8). I prepared the Introduction and Chapters 1, 5, 9, and 10, and wrote the subsequent versions of all the other chapters.

A multi-authored volume requires multiple acknowledgments. I am grateful for the assistance of the Institute of International Studies and the Committee on Research at the University of California, Berkeley, both of which have supported my research for many years, and for a Fulbright Research Award for the Western European Region in 1989. My work in London was facilitated by David Billis and his staff at the Centre for Voluntary Organisation at LSE; by the executives of the national agencies I interviewed; and by the staff members of the National Council for Voluntary Organisations, particularly Marilyn Taylor, Richard Gutch, and Tessa Harding. In Berkeley, I benefited from the critical comments of my faculty colleagues in the School of Social Welfare—Neil Gilbert, Bart Grossman, and Paul Terrell; and in Jerusalem, Michael Shalev of the Hebrew University provided helpful technical assistance. I also want to thank my wife, Hadassah, for her care when I was indisposed, and for her patience when I was working.

Sergio Pasquinelli acknowledges with thanks the help of Costanzo Ranci, Paolo Barbetta, Dr. Piero Merzagora of LEDHA, Dr. Zaccheo Moscheni of the Milan Department of Social and Health Services, and Dr. Enzo Vaghi, Lombardy Regional Department of Social Welfare Services.

Håkon Lorentzen is grateful to Bennedichte C.R. Olsen, who did the interviewing of the Norwegian cohort, and to the Norwegian Ministry of Social Affairs, which sponsored the project.

Willem Melief appreciates the work of his research assistants Esther Plemper and Anneke Adriaansen, who collected much of the data, and thanks Ton Wijnands of NIMAWO for his support.

Earlier versions of portions of some of the chapters have been published in the following: *Voluntas* 2:1 1991; Estelle James, ed., *The Nonprofit Sector in International Perspective: Studies in Comparative Culture and Policy* (1989); Kathleen McCarthy, Virginia Hodgkinson, and Russy Sumariwalla, eds., *The Nonprofit Sector in the Global Community: Voices from Many Nations* (1992); Stein Kuhnle and Per Selle, eds., *Government and Voluntary Organizations: A Relational Perspective* (1992a). Papers based on this research have been presented at international conferences in Jerusalem, May 1989, Boston, March 1990, University of Essex, Colchester, March 1990, and Indianapolis, March 1992.

Ralph M. Kramer
January 1993

Privatization in Four European Countries

Introduction

> [T]he future of the welfare state will be the invention of institutions that
> are not private and not public.
>
> —Martin Rein (1989)

Background

During the years since the mid-1970s there has been a tremendous upsurge of
public interest in North America and Western Europe in the role of voluntary
nonprofit organizations (VNPOs) as an alternative to government in the provision of quasi-public services.[1] Even in Eastern Europe, with the dismantling of
former communist regimes, there is renewed interest in the efficacy of VNPOs as
service providers and as organizational vehicles for citizen participation. Although
the relationship between the state and voluntary associations is deeply rooted in
history and, since de Tocqueville, in political theory, there has probably been more
public discussion and research on the role of the voluntary nonprofit or third sector
since the 1970s than in the previous fifty years. For example, it is estimated that
there are over 200 researchers in forty different countries, and that a new interdisciplinary field in the social sciences has emerged (Anheier and Seibel 1990:3). Within
the last five years, a dozen or more scholarly books have been published, over
twenty new research centers have been established in the United States and at the
London School of Economics, two new scholarly journals have been launched, and
four international conferences for researchers on VNPOs have taken place.

What accounts for all this activity? Related developments in ideology and
social policy help explain this resurgence of interest as a response to the "crisis
of the welfare state" after its unprecedented expansion over the last twenty-five
years. During this time the welfare state became a "problem creator" as well as a
"problem solver" (Heidenheimer, Heclo, and Adams 1990:369). From the ideological perspective of halting the expansion of the welfare state, there has been a
rediscovery by both the Right and the Left of the civil society and the special
advantages of VNPOs. This process has occurred not only in the United States
and Britain, but also in countries differing widely in the scope of their welfare
state and political culture such as France, Italy, and Norway (Kuhnle and Selle

1

1992a). On the Right, voluntary organizations are seen as a bulwark against further governmental intervention, or at least as an alternative, if not a substitute for it. On the Left, these organizations are often viewed nostalgically, as a means of recovering a lost sense of community through voluntarism, self-help, and other forms of citizen participation (Janowitz 1976; Hadley and Hatch 1981). Hence, there are calls for privatization, partnerships, and welfare pluralism in England, and for empowerment and co-production in the United States. However, their proponents usually fail to distinguish among different types of voluntarism; between volunteers as unpaid staff and as peer self-help; between mutual aid associations and neighborhood- or community-based organizations, and service bureaucracies staffed by professionals. This confusion reflects the continuing absence of an accepted definition and typology of voluntary organizations, except perhaps as "tax-exempt entities" with a social purpose.

Another development involves the convergence of five policy streams conducive to the greater utilization of VNPOs in implementing public policy: retrenchment in public spending, governmental decentralization, debureaucratization, deregulation, and deinstitutionalization. While these trends may be perceived as putting the welfare state in retreat or at an impasse—at least its growth has slowed—an entity sometimes called "the contract state" has rapidly emerged as VNPOs have been used to deliver personal social services (PSS) to an ever-growing clientele for whom there is governmental responsibility. These include the needy elderly, mentally ill or retarded persons, the physically handicapped, and abused or neglected children who may receive PSS such as day or institutional care, counseling, or rehabilitation services, and so forth. It is the character and role of VNPOs in the personal social services in England, the Netherlands, Italy, and Norway that are the focus of this book.

Through its grants, subsidies, and fee-for-service payments, the state has everywhere become a *partner, patron,* or *purchaser* of services for VNPOs, whose number increases each year. In fact, wherever there is a substantial voluntary sector, it is dependent on governmental support to a greater or lesser degree (James 1989). In the United States, governmental funds have become a more important source of revenue for VNPOs than all private giving combined (Salamon 1987). Similarly, in England, despite the apparent cutbacks in public expenditures since 1975, statutory fees and grants have been the fastest growing source of voluntary sector income, almost doubling in amount and as a percentage of total income in the last fifteen years (Knapp and Saxon-Harrold 1989). In Italy, where the growth of VNPOs is a very recent phenomenon, there has been a striking increase in their utilization and funding by local government.

The increased interdependency of government and the voluntary sector is recognized in the popular concept of a "mixed economy of welfare," a pervasive and complex mingling of public and private funds and functions, spawning quasi-nongovernmental organizations (quangos) and para-governmental organizations (PGOs), with the consequent blurring of the traditional boundaries among the state, the market, and the "independent" or third sector (Hood and Schuppert 1988). While it may be an exaggeration that "all organizations are public" (Bozeman 1987), it is quite evident that most PSS organizations, regardless of their auspices, have become more bureaucratic, professional, political, and in the United States and England more entrepreneurial (Butler and Wilson 1990; Kramer 1987). Under these circumstances, it is strange that third sector organizations have been ignored in virtually all comparative research on the welfare state (Kuhnle and Selle 1992a:12–19). Typical studies of the welfare state (Dierkes et al. 1987; Esping-Andersen 1990; Flora and Heidenheimer 1981) generally convey the impression of government as a monolithic structure, with no significant separation between the *provision* and the *production* of public services (Kolderie 1986). Consequently, they overlook the role of other social allocational systems such as the market, voluntary organizations, and informal social systems such as families, neighbors, and friends (Miller 1990). We seek to correct this omission, and will analyze the widespread policy or practice—for which there is still no accepted term—in which government utilizes VNPOs to provide state-financed social services.

Welfare states vary considerably in the extent to which they separate public financing from service provision. The Netherlands, where VNPOs are the primary service-delivery system, and Sweden, where practically no VNPOs are used, stand at either end of a continuum. Closer to the Netherlands is West Germany, where well over half of the social services are subsidized by government but provided by VNPOs, some of which are indistinguishable from conglomerates or cartels. Other countries with similar patterns are Italy, Belgium, Switzerland, and Austria. England and Norway are closer to Sweden because of the dominance of their statutory systems, while France, Canada, and Australia stand between them and the United States, which is closer to England.

In each country, the particular division of responsibility between government and VNPOs is not formalized, but reflects a distinctive history and sociopolitical context. Yet they all share the basic perception that VNPOs are expected to be innovative and flexible, protect particularistic interests, promote citizen participation, and meet needs not met by government. More specifically, the relationship between these two coexisting systems can be summarized as follows: together with government and profit-making organizations, VNPOs may relieve, replace, or reinforce the primary social systems of family, friends, and neighbors. In the public sector, they may substitute for, influence, extend, and improve the work of government, or they may offer complementary services different in kind. VNPOs may also compete with profit-making organizations in many fields of social service (Kramer 1987:241; Wolfenden Committee 1978:26). From an organizational perspective, VNPOs also differ vastly in their size, age, purpose, locus (national or local), structure, governance, and other such aspects, with consequences that are only beginning to be understood.

Generally, there is growing interdependence between the VNPOs and central and local governmental agencies involved in fiscal and, to a lesser degree, regulatory, planning, coordinating, legal, and political relationships. At the same time, there is enormous variation in these interorganizational relationships, few of which are standardized or even formalized. The proportionate size of the governmental funds received is of much greater importance to a VNPO than to the state because such governmental payments and grants generally constitute a small percentage of the total public expenditures, although in some fields of service they can constitute 30 to 50 percent. Typically, there is coexistence and accommodation between government and VNPOs, with infrequent collaboration or partnerships, but relatively little competition or conflict. Contrary to the conventional wisdom, there seem to be few successful attempts by the state to control, regulate, monitor, evaluate, or press for greater accountability (Gidron, Kramer, and Salamon 1992).

Despite the variations in their reliance on VNPOs, all welfare states in the advanced industrial countries have encountered similar problems in their service-delivery systems: the spiraling of costs, over- or under-use, fragmentation of services, and other obstacles to access, accountability, equity, planning, and coordination (Kahn and Kamerman 1981). At the same time, curiously, the standards of quality—insofar as we have data other than expenditures—do not seem to be markedly different among the Netherlands, Sweden, West Germany, and Switzerland. This suggests that the legal "ownership" of an organization may not be as important as organizational variables such as size, structure, degree of formalization, type of technology, resource dependencies, degree of competition in the external environment, and so forth. Perhaps *how* may be more important than *who* delivers a service.

Nevertheless, advocates of privatization would insist that organizational auspices are important. Privatization, one of the leading slogans in the attack on the welfare state, has been viewed as an idea, as theory or rhetoric, and as a political practice (Starr 1989). Its multiple meanings are usually based on the assumption that government has become too big and inefficient, and that its functions and expenditures can be effectively reduced by introducing various market mechanisms (Donahue 1989). Generally proposed on grounds of cost-efficiency, privatization can refer to the divestiture of state-owned enterprises through their sale, or to the *delegation* of responsibilities for the production and delivery of public services to nongovernmental organizations. The latter function is embodied in what the Gilberts (1990) have termed the "enabling state," which is a more complete and accurate model of how the welfare state actually works: in addition to direct cash expenditures for welfare, there are numerous indirect forms of welfare transfers through tax expenditures, exemptions, and deductions, and by separating provision (financing) from production through purchase of service contracting (POSC). It is this latter form of privatization that is the subject of this book.

The expanded use of contracting by government has contributed to the blurring of the boundaries between the public and the private, but there are still no generally accepted concepts, models, or theories to describe and explain this process of interpenetration of the state by the market and the third sector (Streeck and Schmitter 1985; Hernes 1986). Instead, there are numerous metaphors such as the "new political economy," "welfare pluralism," and the "shadow state"; "third-party government," "nonprofit Federalism," the "enabling state," and the "franchise state" in the United States; "indirect public administration" in Finland, West Germany, and Denmark; or the "social economy" in France.

The proliferation of these metaphors in the 1970s reflected the dramatic increase in scholarly interest in the third sector in the United States and Europe, a subject described as "one of the fastest growing and most dynamic areas in the social sciences" (Knapp and Anheier 1990). Because of the recency of this rapid development, there is a tendency to overlook the fact that the issues pertaining to the relationship between the state and VNPOs predate the debate about the "crisis of the welfare state." While the pressures for privatization emerged with greater force during the 1970s as part of the conservative attack on the welfare state, both the use of VNPOs to implement public policy and the ideological resistance to state intervention have a long tradition in North America and Europe. When the intellectual history of this subject is written, its roots will probably be found in the century-long struggle between church and state, and the dispute over what shall belong to Caesar. Opposing theories of the state originating with Hobbes and Locke in the seventeenth century, extended by Burke, de Tocqueville, and Mill in the nineteenth century, are embedded, though not always acknowledged, in the arguments regarding privatization, or the belief that voluntary associations are necessary to ensure a democratic society (Wuthnow 1991).

There is also an unwritten history of the continual interaction between governments and VNPOs in the evolution of the modern welfare state, and the record of various attempts to formulate a theory and a set of principles for the division of responsibility between them in Britain and the United States, beginning with the Goschen Minute in 1869 relating to the English Poor Law. This was followed in 1914 when Sidney and Beatrice Webb proposed a more rational and equitable distinction between the role of the state and private charity (Owen 1964). In the United States, this topic was addressed almost every year beginning in the 1880s at the National Conference of Charities and Corrections, and the arguments for and against governmental funding of voluntary social service organizations in Amos G. Warner's *American Charities* (1894) were considered authoritative until the 1930s. In fact, the nineteenth-century controversy about government subsidies to voluntary child welfare agencies is remarkably similar to the debate during the 1980s about the use of public funds by VNPOs (Kramer 1987).

Definitions and Terminology

These considerations are a reminder of the complexities of this subject and the lack of consensus on terminology. Not only are there separate "stories" for the various types of VNPOs such as philanthropic foundations, voluntary associations, and the corporate providers of quasi-public services such as education, health, and PSS, each of these fields of service, or "industries," has its own history, institutional structure, character, and relationships to government. VNPOs and their sector have been called private, independent, voluntary, or more recently in the United States, nonprofit. The latter term, despite its specific origins in Sec. 501(c)(3) of the U.S. Internal Revenue Code, has rapidly spread to many countries in Europe, and illustrates what George Orwell once called "coca-cola-nization." The same process has also been described in another context as "the quangocratization of the world" (Hood 1991). Yet an extensive review of the research on VNPOs came to the conclusion that " 'nonprofitness' has no single trans-historical or transnational meaning; nonprofit-sector functions, origins, and behavior reflect specific legal definitions, cultural inheritances, and state policies in different national societies" (DiMaggio and Anheier 1990:137).

Despite their inherent diversity, it is possible to generalize about some of the distinctive features of VNPOs such as the following:

1. Values, ideologies, and public policies have a great influence on them while market behavior is less significant in their decision making (Hasenfeld 1983; Kramer 1987:244–48).
2. Their income is typically derived from many sources, but it has less relationship to performance than to their fund-raising capacity (Kramer 1981).
3. They tend to have multiple goals, constituencies, and income sources (Anheier and Seibel 1990:13).
4. Loosely coupled, their authority structure is an ambiguous hybrid of bureaucracy, voluntary association, and informal social systems, relying on a staffing mix of professionals, para-professionals, and volunteers (Billis 1989).
5. The relationship between the unpaid governing board and their executive director is the crucial element in policy determination and organizational maintenance (Middleton 1987; Herman and Heimovics 1989).
6. Dependent for virtually all of their resources on the external environment (Pfeffer and Salancik 1978), VNPOs have both service-providing and advocacy functions, and can be instruments of social control as well as social change (DiMaggio and Anheier 1990).

These characteristics are further analyzed in Chapter 9.

Current Theories and Research

Following the lead of DiMaggio and Anheier (1990), we can divide the research literature into studies focusing on institutional choice, and/or on organizational behavior. The first type is concerned with the question, *why* are there third sector organizations? *What* accounts for the variations in the size and scope of the sector in different countries? in the division of responsibility between the state,

the market, and VNPOs? The second group of studies is devoted to the consequences of their "voluntary" character, that is, *how* are they different from governmental and commercial organizations in their structure, governance,
performance, and other attributes?

Another form of classification is in terms of the three levels of research: the
first treats the sector as a meta-concept; the second level is focused on a sub-
sector, a field of service such as education (schools and colleges), health (hospitals and clinics), PSS (social agencies), or art and culture (museums and theaters)
and compares them with their public and/or commercial counterparts; the third
or micro level consists of studies of the character, role, and performance of
voluntary organizations, their structure, governance, management, finances, service programs, advocacy, and their interorganizational relations, particularly
with government. While there have been a growing number of studies of the third
sector in various countries (James 1989; Gidron, Kramer, and Salamon 1992;
Kuhnle and Selle 1992b; McCarthy, Hodgkinson, and Sumariwalla 1992), there has
not been a corresponding increase in empirical research on VNPOs themselves.

The first attempts to develop a theory to explain the existence of a third or
nonprofit sector began in the United States in the 1970s. Based on microeconom-
ics, the early theories all dealt with some version of institutional "failure": government, in the case of Weisbrod (1977) and Douglas (1983); the market for
Hansmann (1980); and the voluntary system itself for Salamon (1987). According to some of these theories, the inherent limitation in both the private market
and government to provide collective or merit goods explains the existence of a
third sector composed of organizations that can meet excess demand and/or
heterogeneous tastes that the state cannot satisfy. "Contract failure" can also
account for the reliance on nonprofit organizations where there is inadequate
information about their "product"—that is, they are regarded as more trustworthy
because of the nondistribution constraint whereby board members may not de-
rive any direct financial gain from their participation.

These first attempts to develop a single, microeconomic model of nonprofit
organizational roles and behavior have not been successful because their
explanatory power is weak when applied to particular sub-sectors such as the
arts, the personal social services, or health (DiMaggio 1987:204–5; Steinberg
1987:126–34). James (1989) has criticized these theories because they lack a
comparative dimension and cannot account for cross-national variations in the
size and character of the third sector. In addition, they lack empirical support and
neglect crucial historical and sociological factors (Kuhnle and Selle 1992a:19–
25). Consequently, they may have encouraged the premature development of
meta-theory while, at the same time, atheoretical studies have proliferated.

Typically, many of these studies have sought to map the third sector, and to
describe its size, scope, finances, and contribution to the economy and to the society.
Although this research has contributed to the legitimation and status of the third
sector, it does not provide knowledge about the performance of VNPOs in different

fields of service that might prove useful in the formation of social policy.

So far, few consistent factors have been found that can explain the presence, development, and change in VNPOs in widely different countries—democratic and totalitarian, highly centralized or decentralized regimes, religiously heterogeneous or homogeneous, or with a particular mix among the three sectors in different fields of service. Accordingly, it has been suggested that research would be more productive if it were directed to the development of middle-range theories based on comparison of the same field of service in countries that vary in their reliance on VNPOs and on other sociopolitical dimensions (Anheier 1988). When this has occurred as in James (1982) and Kramer (1981), it has been found that governmental use of VNPOs is better understood as a mixed product of historical, political, and pragmatic fiscal factors, rather than as a simple function of the market behavior of consumers, as implied by the microeconomic theorists.

James and Anheier are also among the few scholars who have attempted to identify the critical variables that might explain the cross-national patterns in the relationship between the state and the third sector. James (1989) has concentrated on the field of education, although her conclusions may also be relevant for health and the social services. She explains the relative size of the third sector in terms of excess and differentiated demand for public goods such as education, and the supply of religious entrepreneurship. For example, the homogeneous, egalitarian character of Sweden with a single, established church has resulted in very few VNPOs, whereas the strong religious cleavages in the Netherlands have led to virtually all nongovernmental organizations being publicly subsidized in every phase of community life.

Carrying this analysis further, Anheier (1990) emphasizes the importance of constitutional and legal elements, the type of regulatory regime, religion, and the history of the church–state relationship. Seibel (1990) explains cross-national differences in terms of state autonomy, dominant actors, and styles of linkage, similar to the administrative culture, or the structural "embeddedness" of the third sector. Salamon also rejects the economic theories that view the third sector in residual terms, as a response to the failure of either the market or government to meet social needs and the demand for public goods. He argues, on historical grounds, that a partnership between government and VNPOs in the United States has been the rule from earliest times, marked by a separation between governmental provision by legislation and financing, and service delivery by nongovernmental organizations. "Third party government" is the term coined by Salamon (1987) for this policy, which is viable because of what might be called "compensatory complementarity," whereby the strengths of one compensate for the organizational and fiscal deficiencies of the other.

Gronbjerg (1987) is one of the few scholars who has analyzed the interorganizational relationships between government and VNPOs. She has identified four characteristic patterns occurring in particular fields of service: cooperation in child welfare, accommodation in health, competition in education, and symbiosis in housing and community development. In addition, Gronbjerg has found that the strong presence of profit-making organizations in a field of service tended to make the relationship between VNPOs and government more antagonistic and opportunistic, particularly in the fields of health and education.

Cost studies in the fields of child welfare and care of the aged have been conducted by Martin Knapp and his associates at the University of Kent at Canterbury, where they found that intrasectoral differences were often more significant than cost differences between government and VNPOs. The average costs in VNPOs increased with size, although in the short run they were cheaper mainly because of low wages and the use of volunteers. James (1989) also found that the cost advantage of nongovernmental organizations diminished over time as they complied with personnel and other governmental standards. Additional studies in the United States on the differences between hospitals or nursing homes under different auspices (Weisbrod 1988) have rarely been able to overcome the formidable methodological difficulties confronting such comparisons and/or they have reported equivocal findings. Indeed, Knapp et al. (1990) concluded that it is probably not possible to make valid and reliable generalizations from such studies, that their findings are not likely to be replicated, and hence "are not transportable."

The equivocal nature of the findings regarding comparative costs and other variables influencing organizational behavior seems to challenge the validity of the sector concept. In an incisive critique, Langton (1988) concluded that it is an inadequate paradigm for research; perhaps necessary, but obviously insufficient. Questions about validity and univocality can also be raised because the sector metaphor obscures the internal diversity, the interpenetration and blurring in the mixed economy, producing hybrid organizations such as quangos and PGOs (para-governmental organizations), which have the characteristics of all three sectors. While it may be an exaggeration to claim that "all organizations are public" (Bozeman 1987), it is evident that there is a convergence in the character of most social service organizations whereby they have all become more bureaucratic, professional, political, and in the United States and England, more entrepreneurial (Butler and Wilson 1990; Kramer 1987). This convergence of the imperatives of organizational development suggests that the analog of a marble cake rather than a demarcated segment of a circle may be more appropriate.

Furthermore, it is questionable whether the fact that board members may not distribute any surplus of income over expenditures for their own purpose is a sufficient basis for classifying organizations about which empirical generalizations can be made. It has been observed that "there is no discernible common pattern in State–third sector relations" and that the greater the differentiation and complexity, the less useful is the sector concept (Anheier and Seibel, 1990:380). On the other hand, it could be argued that there is just as much diversity in government and in the economy, and in the case of the latter, the quest for profit is considered a sufficient basis on which to generalize about the market sector and its widely different types and sizes of firms.

There is undoubtedly a sense in which the third sector is largely a rhetorical device or a "strategic artifact" in which evidence of its extensive size and scope of public benefits is used to justify its tax exemption and other benefits in the United States. There is also a vested, ideological interest in the concept by those seeking to reduce the role of the state through such alternative mechanisms as privatization, decentralization, debureaucratization, deprofessionalization, and deregulation. This is not to mention social scientists and other researchers who also have a professional interest in studying this newly discovered sector!

Yet even if the metaphor is obsolete or of questionable validity, social policy decisions must still be made regarding *who* will finance and/or provide what service. These considerations underlie the concept of "institutional choice" in which the sectors are essentially proxies for systems of resource allocation in the society (Streeck and Schmitter 1985). Consequently, it would be desirable to have a more rational and empirical basis for such policy decisions, based more on what can realistically be expected from VNPOs, instead of the ideological or impressionistic judgments that usually prevail.

First, it is necessary to clarify the terminology that will be used. Because of the blurring of boundaries, the lack of consensus regarding definitions, and even the absence of public recognition in many countries of its existence, the term "sector" is best used as a "guiding metaphor" (Wuthnow 1991:26) to refer to a collection of highly diverse organizations in between the state and the market, but sharing characteristics of both. Accordingly, the "third sector" will be used as a shorthand term—a convenient summary expression—for many different types of organizations that are: formal; legally separate from government; self-governing; non–profit distributing; with some degree of voluntarism and philanthropy; and expected to produce a public benefit in the fields of health care, education, social welfare, the arts, culture, leisure time, the environment, and so forth. This would exclude many other types of nonprofit organizations often considered part of the civil society, such as religious and political bodies, trade unions, professional and trade associations, and other interest groups (Salamon and Anheier 1992).

More specifically, most of our generalizations will pertain mainly to the sub-sector of the personal social services (PSS), which is also part of the context for our study of the voluntary organizations (VNPOs) in four countries serving the physically, mentally, and sensorially handicapped, to be described in the next section on methodology.

Rationale for a Comparative Study of VNPOs

Despite the growing interest in VNPOs, there is a paucity of policy-oriented, comparative research on any of the three levels that could provide a basis for distinguishing the effects of different sociopolitical contexts and public policies on the character, role, and performance of VNPOs in different types of advanced industrial democratic welfare states. This is part of the rationale for our study, which had a dual focus both on the level of the third sector in England, the Netherlands, Italy, and Norway, and on a cohort of twenty comparable organizations serving the disabled in each country.

As noted earlier, there is little empirical data on the trends and consequences in different countries of utilizing VNPOs as private, public service providers for various forms of social care (Knapp et al. 1990; Leat et al. 1986). Since VNPOs have facilitated the extension of the welfare state and are likely to assume a larger role in the provision of PSS in the future, it is important to know what can be expected from them. Answers to questions such as the following would be desirable:

- Why and how are VNPOs used to implement public policy and with what consequences?
- What explains the similarities and differences in the patterns, trends, and role of VNPOs in such countries as England, the Netherlands, Italy, and Norway?
- What are the advantages and disadvantages in governmental funding of VNPOs?
- How can they preserve their autonomy when receiving public funds?
- How can governmental agencies obtain accountability for public funds when they support voluntary organizations?

The absence of such knowledge constitutes part of the rationale for our study. As policy research, it is informed by an empirical, comparative analysis of organizational behavior in four different sociopolitical contexts. It describes and seeks to explain both the similarities and the differences among the four case studies relating to these questions:

1. What are the major historical patterns of development in the character and role of the third sector, particularly in its relationship to government?
2. What is the current status of the third sector in the country, and how has it been affected by public policy—for example, why was the third sector more visible in the 1980s than in the 1960s?
3. On the organizational level, what are the major changes in the structure and performance of VNPOs serving the disabled, and how did these come about?
4. What are the social policy implications for the future of the welfare state?

In view of the reappraisal of the state in the post–cold war era and the continuing development of the European Community, an interdisciplinary, cross-national study is particularly well suited to inform the social policy debate about privatization with some empirical data about the experience of four European countries with different relationships between government and VNPOs. For example, the Netherlands is a classic prototype of privatization with the longest post–World War II history of virtually 100 percent governmental subsidy of its almost 4,000 VNPOs, which are known as "p.i." (private initiative). Originally under the auspices of religious-political blocs *(zuilen),* p.i.'s have become increasingly professionalized, bureaucratized, secularized, and the object of governmental pressures for greater coordination, efficiency, and accountability (Brenton 1985; Idenberg 1985).

More reliance on VNPOs instead of government, or "welfare pluralism," has been urged in England where the Local Authority is the primary social services provider. Major changes in community care policy and in organizational roles are slated to occur in the 1990s when Local Authorities will be expected to contract with more VNPOs for service delivery (Gutch 1992; Taylor 1992). The Dutch experience is cited by both supporters and opponents of a greater role for VNPOs, but neither side has much evidence.

In Italy, a latecomer to these issues, the relationship between government and VNPOs has been changing rapidly, reflecting the growing number of voluntary associations, the shifting power relations between the Catholic Church and the state, and the strong desire for regional and local independence. VNPOs are seen as the basis for a new social policy in Italy, but there is concern about their capabilities and the preservation of their identity and autonomy if they become more dependent on government support (Ascoli 1992; Pasquinelli 1989). In Norway, by contrast, autonomy is not viewed as a serious problem because of the long history of the blending of the public and private sectors in a form of "integrated dependency."

In all four countries, the decade of the 1980s was one of significant change and growth in the number of VNPOs of all types and in the size of their income from governmental sources. For example, UK estimates show aggregate increases in real income of 200 percent, with statutory fees and grants constituting the fastest growing source of revenue, rising from about one-third in 1975 to two-thirds in 1987. Using a broader sample of voluntary organizations, there is a tenfold increase in grants from the Department of Health and Social Security from 1976–1977 to 1985–1986 (Knapp et al. 1990). The magnitude of growth in total and statutory income is also evident in the cohort of the twenty national agencies in the study whose payments and/or grants from government more than doubled within the decade. Similarly, in Italy there was a 40 percent growth in governmental income from 1984 to 1988 in the eight largest VNPOs in the sample that received 87 percent of their income from this source.

In these countries as in most others, it was the necessity for reducing governmental expenditures that was associated with the renewed interest in the third sector; this seemed to be the "real" reason—if there was a primary cause—with the ideology of voluntarism providing the "good" reasons. Before the growth rate of public spending on social welfare started to decline in 1976, VNPOs had prospered during the expansion of the welfare state during the 1960s and 1970s; they continued to grow in number and size even under the more restrictive economic conditions prevailing in the 1980s. In England and the Netherlands, VNPOs flourished under both Labour and Conservative governments. Contrary to widespread belief, very few of the VNPOs in our sample were affected by any retrenchment in governmental spending (Brown 1988:3–28).

A second notable trend was an ongoing policy debate reevaluating the respective roles of government and VNPOs. In contrast to the 1970s, when national commissions in the United States, Canada, and the Netherlands reviewed the prevailing division of responsibility between government and VNPOs, the process in the last decade was more related to new public fiscal policies and the election of conservative governments. Hence the promotion of the virtues of the market, degovernmentalization, and privatization, as well as the search for greater efficiency and accountability. In England this took the form of support for "welfare pluralism," a belief in the superiority of VNPOs as service deliverers and the preference for contracting instead of grant-aids (Johnson 1987). In the Netherlands, where the social services were already privatized, the emphasis was on greater efficiency, with some decentralization and deregulation. In Italy, where the VNPOs were proliferating, there was interest in their serving as an alternative or substitute for government and not just as a supplement. This coincided with the development of a research interest in voluntary organizations for the first time (Pasquinelli 1992). Similarly, in Norway the first national report on the possibility of VNPOs as an alternative to government was published in 1988.

Research Design and Methods

The research in this book combined case study methods with a historical approach; in the case of the British VNPOs, a life-cycle model was also used. Case studies were completed in 1989 of a cohort of twenty comparable VNPOs serving the physically, mentally, and sensorially handicapped in England, the Netherlands, Italy, and Norway, representing four different types of welfare states and societies. In England and the Netherlands, the agencies studied were the same ones included in the first international comparative analysis of such organizations conducted in the mid-1970s (Kramer 1981). Comparable agencies in Norway and Italy were selected by the co-authors in consultation with their respective institutes for social research; in Italy, the sample was drawn only from the Lombardy region because there were very few national voluntary organizations providing social services to the disabled comparable to their counterparts in the other three countries. Norway and Italy were included in the study because the recency of their "discovery" of the third sector contrasts with the long tradition of use of VNPOs in England and the Netherlands. In addition, Norway represents the Scandinavian welfare state that has relied mainly on state provision of the PSS, while in Italy an unplanned "contract state" is rapidly developing.

In each country, the purposive sample included different types of agencies. There were organizations both *of* and *for* the blind, deaf, and other handicapped groups; "health agencies," such as those for cancer, heart disease, and arthritis; and the counterparts of organizations serving the mentally handicapped (developmentally disabled) and victims of such neuromuscular conditions as poliomyelitis, cerebral palsy, muscular dystrophy, and multiple sclerosis. The VNPOs varied by age, size, scope, and degree of emphasis on services and/or advocacy. They differed in the extent to which they operated institutions for residential care or supported research, and perhaps most significantly, the extent to which they relied on governmental funds for their operations.

Data were collected about each agency from documents and from extensive, structured interviews with the executive director conducted by the co-authors in their respective countries. This provided information about the changes and continuities in organizational structure, governance, management, program, finances, and interorganizational relationships, particularly with government. On the macro level, information was obtained in each country about the dominant social policy trends affecting the third sector such as the pressures for privatization, as well as public fiscal policy and ideology relating to VNPOs. Other aspects of the sociopolitical context identified were the type of political regime and extent of decentralization, the role of religion in the society, and the civic culture.

Essentially, this is a study of social policy and organizational behavior, not an evaluation of service programs for the disabled. While the generalizations are drawn from this particular field of service, their implications are applicable to other types of voluntary organizations and fields of service.

Plan of the Book

The book consists of three parts. Part I contains four chapters, each devoted to a national case study of the third sector in either England, Italy, the Netherlands, or Norway—its history, scope, and relationship to the government—and selected findings from the study of organizations serving the physically, sensorially, and mentally handicapped—their structure, income sources, governance and administration, and interorganizational relationships.

Part II presents a comparative analysis of both the sectoral and the organizational data from the four countries. The similarities and differences in their sociocultural patterns and trends are summarized in Chapter 5 in historical and structural terms. These include the role of church–state relationships, the degree of centralization in government, the type of political regime, civic culture, and the character of the welfare state.

The next three chapters in Part II are devoted to a comparative analysis of the five dimensions of the cohort of VNPOs in each of the countries: their income, structure, governance and administration, and interorganizational relations. Similarities and differences are explained in terms of the distinctive internal and external environment of voluntary organizations. Trends toward bureaucratization, professionalization, and corporatism are compared, as is the adaptive capacity of older, traditional charities such as those in England. The changing organizational cultures in England and the Netherlands, with their respective emphases on "business-like" efficiency and "no-nonsense" rationality, are contrasted with the patterns in Norway and Italy. The "contract culture" in England, a new conservative paradigm of the welfare state, is compared with the recent restructuring of "private initiative" by central government in the Netherlands, which relies on increasing control of an array of nonprofit organizations for the delivery of virtually all public services.

Chapter 9 in Part II contains a synthesis of the previous comparative analysis of the five organizational dimensions. The voluntary organization is viewed holistically, rather than in terms of discrete factors, as a hybrid of a bureaucracy, a voluntary association, and informal social relations. Utilizing related research in various countries, this leads to a series of generalizations about the distinctive character of the voluntary agency, its possibilities and constraints. Social science theories of public choice, institutional failure, neocorporatism, and isomorphism are drawn upon in analyzing the common properties of voluntary organizations.

We conclude the book with a final chapter that summarizes the study's implications for social policy and the future of the welfare state in Europe and the United States.

Note

1. Originating in the United States in the early 1970s, the term "nonprofit organization" is increasingly used in other countries to refer to an extraordinarily diverse collection of organizations between the state and the market, sharing some of the characteristics of each. They are also known variously as nongovernmental, voluntary, private, intermediary (Ware 1989a), or as mediating (Berger and Neuhaus 1977) between citizen and state. Essentially, they are formal bodies, self-governing, non–profit distributing, usually characterized by some degree of voluntarism and/or philanthropy, and expected to produce a public benefit (Brenton 1985:9; Knapp and Kendall 1990).

Because different countries also use different terms to refer to what is called the nonprofit sector in the United States, it is more useful for comparative purposes, as Seibel (1990:58) has suggested, to call it the third sector.

Part I

Four National Case Studies

1

England: Statutory Alternative

Introduction

The decade of the 1980s may well be regarded in retrospect as the beginning of a new era for VNPOs in England. More likely, however, it will be remembered as the period during which Margaret Thatcher served as prime minister of a Conservative government that promised to "roll back the frontiers of the state" by reducing statutory responsibility, promoting privatization, and expanding the role of the market, voluntarism, and the informal sector (Gamble 1988). As a revival of nineteenth-century liberalism and a Victorian ethos, this New Right ideology represented a reversal of the historical process in Britain whereby many social services pioneered by voluntary organizations were eventually taken over and provided by government. Conservatives regarded this policy as having contributed to the fiscal crisis of the overloaded welfare state, and consequently, they sought the divestiture of many public functions and their privatization (Ware 1989a).

The new conservative paradigm of the British welfare state implied a considerably expanded role for VNPOs, which, however, was viewed by many of their leaders with considerable anxiety. Only a few years before, during the 1970s, there was much concern about the declining role of VNPOs as Local Authority Social Service Departments (LASSDs) began implementing the Seebohm Report, which sought to strengthen the local statutory services; the most that VNPOs could expect then was to continue as "the junior partner in the welfare firm" (Owen 1964:528). The public image of British charities changed gradually, and they were less likely to be regarded as a marginal appendage to the welfare state, or fillers of gaps in the statutory services (Ware 1989b:26). From their traditional role as a supplementer to the statutory services, they came to be viewed in the Thatcher era as an alternative if not a substitute for the Local Authority.

Within a few years, there had occurred one of those "shifting involvements between public and private" (Hirschman 1982; Paci 1987) that has characterized the changing relationship between the state and the voluntary sector. The concept of the Fabian State of Lord Beveridge was to be replaced by the Enabling State with its separation of the financing and production of public services and a partnership with the market, voluntary organizations, and the family. There is a remarkable continuity in British history of statutory-voluntary relationships beginning in 1601 with passage of the Statute of Charitable Uses. Representing "the starting point of the modern British Law of Charities, it was adopted in the same year as the Elizabethan Poor Law. From that time, the pattern of development of the British welfare state can be viewed as two parallel streams of governmental and voluntary effort, occasionally intersecting and generally affecting each other's course" (Rooff 1957). In reviewing this history, it was concluded that "for centuries, charities in Britain have been used as agents of public policy" (Ware 1989b:15).

Although parishes were empowered by the Poor Law to provide a modicum of education and to care for the disabled if their families were unable to do so, relatively little was done, and for the next three hundred years, religious and philanthropic organizations were almost alone in the social services (Owen 1964).

The nineteenth century was marked by the expansion of private philanthropy and the founding of numerous charities that pioneered in the care of the handicapped, the poor, and the sick. The tradition of voluntarism, which is deeply embedded in the British and American civic culture, was also expressed in the Victorian movements for social reform, mutual aid, and friendly societies, as well as in campaigns to improve public education, prisons, and hospitals.

Around the turn of the century, statutory responsibility began to be assumed for pensions, school meals and medical services, and unemployment and health insurance for selected portions of the population, but voluntary organizations continued to provide most of the personal social services, particularly for children and the handicapped. Both sectors had developed sufficiently by 1912 for the Webbs to propose a set of principles for a functional division of responsibility that is still widely regarded as valid. They rejected the "Parallel Bars" theory of 1869 of two mutually exclusive sectors in which private charity was more highly valued. Instead, they advocated the "Extension Ladder" theory in which VNPOs supplement the basic statutory services that provide a minimum standard of living for all. This was the origin of what later became known as the "partnership" concept of statutory-voluntary relationships (Kramer 1981:39).

In the period between the two world wars, the state gradually took responsibility for additional welfare services, but because of the prior existence of VNPOs, it reimbursed them for services rendered to various handicapped groups both in and out of institutions. This practice continued until the postwar period beginning with 1946, which marked the start of the rapid growth and consolidation of the welfare state. While the social philosophy behind the implementation of the Beveridge Report was Fabian in its commitment to the superiority of governmental responsibility and provision over charity, Beveridge (1948) himself was opposed to a state monopoly of welfare and stressed the vital role of voluntary action.

Although there was considerable anxiety that private philanthropy and voluntary organizations would be displaced by the cradle-to-the-grave legislation,

VNPOs not only flourished, but new types were established, such as those concerned with a single disability whose constituency consisted of the victims themselves and their families. These peer self-help groups, rooted in the tradition of mutual aid, also became articulate pressure groups for persons suffering from a specific disability.

During the "takeoff" of the welfare state in the 1960s, VNPOs continued to increase in number and importance, often because of the gap between statutory responsibility and resources. For example, almost three-fourths of the Local Authorities used VNPOs for some services to the disabled, mainly because their rates of reimbursement were considerably below the costs. This era was also characterized by a rapid increase in community-based organizations providing information, advice, and advocacy, as well as other forms of citizen and consumer participation.

The 1970s saw increasing dissatisfaction with the welfare state in Britain and many other countries. Based on economic growth and relatively full employment, the postwar consensus on the welfare state was seriously weakened in the face of persistent "stagflation"—rising inflation and unemployment. There was mounting resistance to the increased taxes required by the sevenfold growth in expenditures for the personal social services from 1961 to 1976. Statutory services were criticized not only for their costs, but also for their standardization, bureaucratic insensitivity, and rigidity. It was also feared that the ever-widening scope of statutory power would overshadow and weaken the viability of the voluntary sector. In assessing the future of the voluntary sector in 1978, the Wolfenden Committee recommended a more balanced partnership with government, but also increased statutory funding.

Shortly afterward, the perception of voluntary organizations as alternatives to governmental service delivery was more widely discussed as the core of "welfare pluralism," which was promoted as the best means of coping with the inherent deficiencies of statutory services (Gladstone 1979). This was part of the growing ideological opposition to the welfare state which, together with an economic recession, rising unemployment, and a series of crippling public sector strikes, contributed to the election of a Conservative government in 1979 (Johnson 1987).

Beginning in 1979, the Thatcher government sought to limit state responsibility for the social services and to favor more use of nongovernmental organizations as part of an effort to promote an "enterprise culture" (Humble and Walker 1990). The primary strategies to reduce statutory ownership and provision were degovernmentalization (denationalization and privatization of former state-owned industries and public utilities), permitting the "opting out" of schools and hospitals from statutory control, and requiring the contracting out of many of the functions of local government. The neoconservative ideology underlying these changes stressed the values of the competitive market, individual responsibility ("there is no such thing as society"), voluntarism, "value for money," as well as greater consumer choice and participation (Brenton 1985; Johnson 1986; Taylor 1992).

In the course of a prolonged and dramatic struggle for power between central and local government, voluntary organizations were caught in the middle, with the larger national agencies seemingly beneficiaries, and local, community-based organizations as likely losers. Ten major initiatives affecting the social services were undertaken in rapid succession beginning in 1985; they were unprecedented in their speed and scope, and were regarded by many as the most significant changes in social policy since the end of World War II (Glennerster et al. 1991).

Despite Conservative rhetoric to the contrary, a political outcome of the Thatcher legacy, setting the stage for the next decade in the social services, was a greater concentration of power in central government, which would exercise even more control over local government taxing, spending, and operations as a result of fifty pieces of legislation restricting local government since 1979 (Pickvance 1987). LASSDs were more limited in their direct service functions because of reduced allocations from central government and the pressures to contract. Confined to an "enabling" role in which they finance, arrange, and coordinate, but do not directly provide the personal social services, they will be "purchasers of care and not monolithic providers" (Griffiths 1988:6). Originally planned for 1991, implementation of the *White Paper on Community Care* (HMSO 1989), in which these policy changes were proposed, was phased in over a three-year period.

Government also tried to strengthen voluntarism by stimulating charitable giving of individuals and corporations through authorization of payroll deductions, more liberal income tax deductions, and by lifting the thirty-four-year-old ban on advertising by charities on independent radio and TV. These measures have evidently had little impact on increased philanthropic giving (Saxon-Harrold 1992) despite the vastly increased attention given to the voluntary sector by the mass media. Although the government stressed the importance of voluntary contributions as the "only proper foundation for a vigorous independent voluntary movement" (Charities Aid Foundation 1982:7), it consistently refused to exempt their income from sales of goods and services from the 15 percent VAT.

Numerous government reports and white papers have appeared, signifying the growing importance of the voluntary sector. One of the most significant of these, the *Efficiency Scrutiny of the Government Funding of the Voluntary Sector* (Home Office 1990), acknowledged the value of the more than £2 billion allocated in 1988–1989 to upwards of 10,000 voluntary organizations by the thirty-four departments and quangos of central government. Health and the personal social services, however, received only 2.4 percent of this sum; half of the £2 billion went to housing associations, and another 25 percent to employment training. Consequently, generalizations about the size of the income of the voluntary sector in England must be tempered by the absence of any clear delineation of its boundaries, which include an exceptionally diverse array of organizations such as housing, cultural and arts associations, hospitals, schools, universities, and religious institutions that account for most of its fee income (Lee 1989). Many if not most of the latter types of organizations are included in the 170,000 registered charities whose combined income more than doubled

Table 1.1

Trends in the Income of Registered Charities, 1975–1990

Current prices

	1975		1980		1985		1990		Annual average growth rate (%)	
	£m	%	£m	%	£m	%	£m	%	1985–90	1975–90
Donations	683.6	28.4	890.6	12.2	1,925.3	15.2	3,224.3	19.9	13.5	24.8
Fees & charges	821.5	34.1	4,802.6	65.9	7,672.3	60.7	8,650.8	53.5	2.6	63.5
Rents & investments	523.3	21.7	886.3	12.2	1,398.4	11.0	2,485.8	15.4	15.6	25.0
Government grants	175.2	7.3	576.9	7.9	1,375.7	10.9	996.5	6.2	−5.5	31.3
Other income	205.8	8.5	135.2	1.8	278.4	2.2	817.9	5.0	38.8	19.8
Totals	2,409.4	100.0	7,291.6	100.0	12,650.1	100.0	16,175.3	100.0	5.6	38.1
No. of registered charities (000)	120.0		136.0		154.1		171.4		2.2	2.9
Mean income per charity (£000)	20.078		53.615		82.090		94.372		3.0	24.7

Constant prices (1975 = 100)

	1975 (£m)	1980 (£m)	1985 (£m)	1990 (£m)	Annual average growth rate (%)	
					1985–90	1975–90
Donations	683.6	455.3	695.0	873.8	5.1	1.9
Fees & charges	821.5	2,455.0	2,772.0	2,344.4	−3.1	12.4
Rents & investments	523.3	453.0	505.2	673.7	6.7	1.9
Government grants	175.2	295.0	497.0	270.0	−9.1	3.6
Other income	205.8	69.0	100.6	221.7	24.1	0.5
Totals	2,409.4	3,727.3	4,569.8	4,383.6	−0.8	5.5
Mean income per charity (£000)	20.078	27.407	29.655	25.575	−2.8	1.8

Source: Posnett 1992:12.

during the 1980s, to a total of over £16 billion at current prices, which is equivalent to 3.4 percent GNP (see Table 1.1).

Similarly, much attention has been given to the growth of the voluntary sector in terms of numbers of organizations (27 percent increase in the last decade at the rate of 3,000–4,000 per annum), and the almost doubling of its income from statutory fees and grants even in the face of a slowdown and cutback in government spending from 1976 to 1987 (Knapp and Saxon-Harrold 1989). Again, there is insufficient awareness that these statistics regarding the voluntary sector are at best gross "guesstimates" because of the absence of definitions and reliable, standardized accounting procedures. Consequently, there are serious limits to a macro perspective of "trends in the voluntary sector" if it is used for extrapolation to a specific field such as the personal social services, or to a particular type of voluntary organization.

The Sample of British Voluntary Agencies

As part of one of the early efforts to develop a more empirical basis for social policy decisions regarding voluntary agencies as public service providers, a group of twenty large national agencies in Britain serving the physically, mentally, and sensorially handicapped were included in a four-country study completed in the mid-1970s (Kramer 1981). The purposive sample, selected with the aid of experts, represented the majority of the agencies in this field. Based in the greater London area, they included typical small, medium, and large organizations, with some distribution among organizations of and for the disabled. The agencies selected also differed in age, size, and structural character. (For more details, see Kramer 1981:293–304.) While all of them also had local affiliates, they differed mainly in the degree to which they provided social care services directly to handicapped persons in the local community or in one of their national institutions. All of the agencies engaged in various forms of advocacy, public education and information, and fund-raising, with many also supporting research on the disability with which they were concerned. (See the agencies listed in Table 1.2.) A further division of the sample into two cohorts based on size and extent of statutory funding is described in the first section of the findings that follows.

The same twenty national agencies were revisited in the fall of 1989 for interviews with their chief executives and for a review of various documents since 1976. In the ensuing years, their environment had become more turbulent and competitive in the mixed economy of welfare that had evolved and had resulted in greater pressures for reduced public spending and more utilization of voluntary organizations. While not designed as a replication of the earlier study, the research in 1989 focused mainly on changes and continuity in six aspects of organizational performance: (1) sources of income (to 1987); (2) structure; (3) governance; (4) management; (5) program operations; and (6) interorganizational relations, particularly with government.

Table 1.2

Income and Staffing Levels of Twenty British Charities, 1976 and 1987

	Income (at 1976 prices)			No. of staff	
	1976 £000	1987 £000	% change	1976	1987
Top nine charities					
Cheshire Homes	6,662	10,939	+64	2,017	3,045
Invalid Children's Aid Association	773	1,203	+56	245	448
Jewish Blind Society	814	2,018	+148	65	238
Mencap	1,568	3,726	+138	343	776
National Society for Autistic Children	447	1,360	+204	158	358
Royal National Institute for the Blind	8,857	12,060	+36	1,595	1,700
Royal National Institute for the Deaf	1,500	2,292	+53	40	530
Shaftesbury Society	997	1,929	+93	390	650
Spastics Society	9,729	15,706	+61	1,874	3,000
Total	31,307	51,233	+63	6,727	10,745
Eleven other charities					
Arthritis Care	357	1,084	+203	38	78
Association for Spina Bifida	314	407	+30	27	105
British Association for the Hard of Hearing	35	25	−29	1	6
British Polio Foundation	185	335	+81	21	28
Chest, Heart and Stroke Association	399	1,130	+183	25	38
Multiple Sclerosis Society	1,104	3,139	+184	19	30
Muscular Dystrophy Group	773	1,139	+47	20	28
National Deaf Children's Society	96	259	+170	6	28
National Society for Cancer Relief	1,609	4,029	+150	40	66
Royal Association in Aid of Deaf People	216	261	+21	58	69
Spinal Injuries Association	35	63	+80	1	19
Total	5,138	12,065	+135	258	495

Source: Kramer 1990:37. Reprinted courtesy of Manchester University Press.

In the first section, the main findings under these six rubrics are summarized, followed by the development of a model based on an analysis of the sources of the changes and continuities found in the cohort. The chapter concludes with a discussion of statutory funding and its effects, and the future of the "contract culture" in the British welfare state of the 1990s.

Figure 1.1. **Growth of Real Income of Top Nine Charities, 1976–1987**

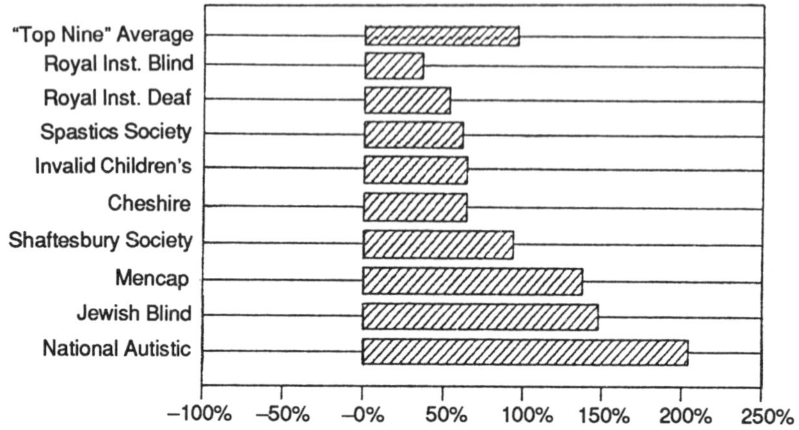

Sources of Income

The cohort was divided into two groups: the "top nine," consisting of the large, direct service national agencies with an average of 50 percent of their income from statutory fees and grants, mainly from local government, for residential and community care; and the "other eleven," smaller agencies that received less than 5 percent of their income from governmental sources. The latter group, with one exception, generally supported research and public information and provided minimal social care services. Their staff accounted for only 2 percent of the total number, although their agency income constituted 19 percent of the total income of the cohort in 1988.

Despite the marked differences in size, function, and degree of dependency on statutory funding, the growth rate of the two sub-groups was about the same as shown in Figures 1.1 and 1.2.

Fiscal data collected for 1976, 1981, and 1987–1988 showed *an increase in combined real income* (in 1976 constant £) from 1976 to 1987 of 74 percent for the entire cohort, with most of the gains during the 1980s. On average, however, agencies doubled their real income during this period, due in large part to the reduction in the rate of inflation by 50 percent from 1982 to 1987. (The income of the affiliates is not shown because it is generally not available to the national organization). Income growth uncorrected for inflation, which is the way it is usually cited by the agencies, showed an average of a more than fivefold increase in total income for 1976–1987. This represented an increase of total real income from £36,445 in 1976 to £63,298 in 1987, or an annual average increase of approximately 6 percent over inflation. Most of the increased income was used for additional staff, which, as noted earlier, grew by 61 percent during this period.

Figure 1.2. **Growth of Real Income in Other Eleven Charities, 1976–1987**

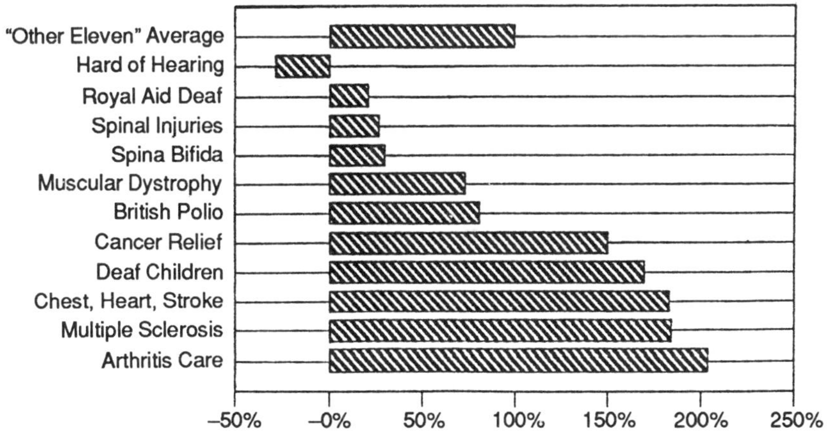

Statutory Funding

There are considerable differences in the purposes, forms, and levels of statutory funding. Core grants for basic administrative costs are provided by both central and local government, with special demonstration and research projects usually sponsored by central government. Fees and payments for personal services and care are generally made by the Local Authority Social Service Department (Judge and Smith 1982). The following data is based on the experience of national agencies whose relationship to the Local Authority differs from that of most community-based organizations that do not usually provide a direct service to a population for whom there is a public responsibility. The latter may receive an annual grant for their administrative and/or local program expenses, although such allocations may be substantially reduced in the future, while the national agencies in our sample operate a wide variety of service programs for the disabled in many localities throughout the country. Hence, it is important to restrict generalizations from this data to similar types of voluntary organizations, and not to the sector as a whole. One further caveat: because there is no standardized system of accounts for voluntary organizations in England, it has been necessary to use judgment and discretion in interpreting the financial statements issued by the agencies. For example, income from statutory sources was not always designated clearly; sometimes it was included in "other," as "general income," or even as part of contributions. It is noteworthy that it was not until 1983 that the Charities Aid Foundation listed income from statutory sources as a separate item in its annual survey of charitable income and expenditures.

Total statutory income for the nine larger agencies, as shown in Figure 1.3,

Figure 1.3. **Percentage of Income from Government in Top Nine Charities**

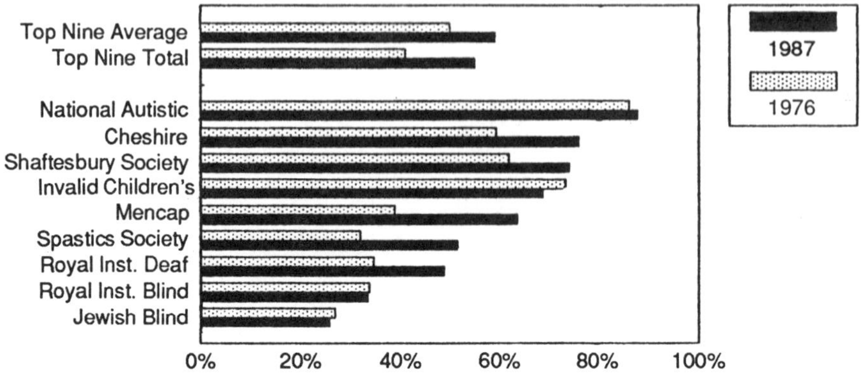

increased by 133 percent in real terms during the eleven-year period, despite the slowdown and cutbacks in public spending, from a total of approximately £13,000 to £28,000.

As a proportion of total income, however, statutory fees and grants grew by 34 percent—from 41 percent to 55 percent of the agency budgets—predominately after 1981, with an average annual growth of a little over 1 percent. Much of the growth in statutory fee income in the early 1980s was due to a halving of the rate of inflation from 1976 to 1982, and changes in the government's social security policies, which precipitated an unprecedented and unintended expansion in residential care—mainly those facilities under commercial auspices—for the elderly, and physically and mentally handicapped (Royal College of Physicians 1986; Day and Klein 1987). In contrast to a widely held view, therefore, there was no dramatic "takeoff" in statutory income over the decade: the average percentage of statutory funding only increased from 50 percent to 55 percent of respective budgets. Five of the largest agencies, however, received more than two-thirds of their revenue from statutory payments for services, mainly for residential care. One of these agencies, for example, made a strong defense in its annual report of its continuing need for contributions, despite its receipt of 78 percent of its income from statutory fees. This pattern may contribute to the belief that "to a surprisingly large extent, the British formal system of voluntary social services is another way of spending public money" (Pinker 1985:106).

Yet these sums rarely met the "actual" costs of care to the voluntary agencies that had to use capital and other contributed funds to cover their annual deficits, in addition to raising their fees. For example, Chesire Homes, which received 76 percent of its income from statutory fees, referred to its £2.8 million deficit—met largely by using capital funds contributed for the construction of new institutions—as its "subsidy" of the statutory sector.

While there were substantial increases in the agency's real income, there was

Figure 1.4. **Total Sources of Income of Top Nine Charities, 1976–1987**

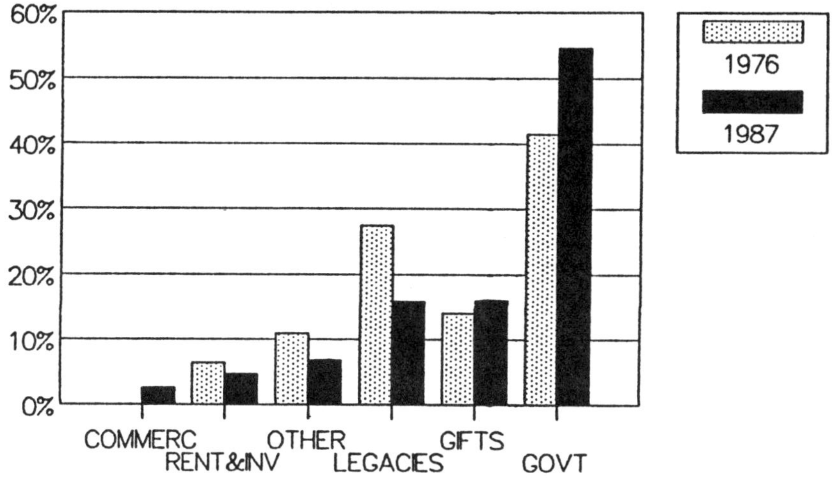

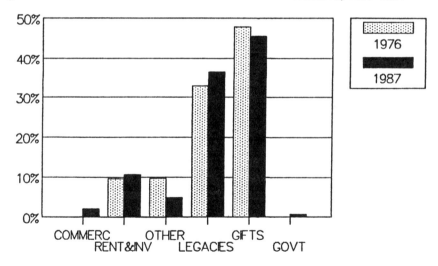

Figure 1.5. **Total Sources of Income of Other Eleven Charities, 1976–1987**

relatively *little change in the proportion of income derived from the five major sources.* (See Figures 1.4 and 1.5.)

For example, there were only 3 percentage points difference in the amount received from legacies and from commercial sales by the eleven smaller agencies in 1987. This statistic tends, however, to obscure great variation among the agencies in their ability to obtain revenue from the sale of goods and services, principally through their wholly owned subsidiaries such as charity shops. While the overall growth in income from commercial sources of the eleven smaller agencies was 30 percent, several of them almost doubled their income from the sale of Christmas cards, used clothing, and furniture. One agency, with a budget of almost £3 million, derived over 40 percent of its income from the sale of goods, which represented a sevenfold increase over a five-year period. Under these circumstances, it is understandable why the voluntary agencies have continued to fight for their exemption from payment of VAT on their commercial income, and why they regard it as an indirect tax on charity.

While much of the increased value of legacy property was due to the high rate of inflation, income from this source dropped by 41 percent—from 27 percent to 16 percent of the revenue of the nine larger agencies during the same period. In general, legacies and deeds of covenant—a special gift in which the charity rather than the contributor receives the tax benefit—are perceived as among the more erratic sources of revenue by voluntary organizations, whereas statutory payments for care are regarded to be the most reliable, even if they are invariably considered inadequate.

Yet statistics alone do not convey the ubiquitous centrality and diversity of voluntary organization funding in England where, like the United States and only a few other countries, philanthropic contributions still play an important role (D. Wilson 1989). For example, voluntary organizations compete for a wide array of contributions from: deeds of covenant, legacies, endowments and bequests; gifts from individual donors, companies, trusts, and foundations obtained via personal solicitation, fund-raising events, and telethons; and "trading" or sales of goods and services. This is in addition to rents and investments, user fees and statutory grants, payments, various indirect forms of assistance such as tax exemptions and reductions, and in-kind transfers of statutory personnel, facilities, and equipment.

Some of the major trends in funding from 1976 to 1989 can therefore be summarized as follows: an increase in income from government, trading, and fees; the rapid professionalization of fund-raising with its extensive use of marketing techniques; the growth in competition for public attention and contributions as expressed in the more extensive use of advertising and TV.

Structural Changes

Four types of structural changes were found: formalization, bureaucratization, administrative reorganizations (departmentalization and decentralization), and "spin-offs" and mergers.

All the organizations have the typical bureaucratic structure of a national organization with a headquarters office in London consisting of various functional units responsible for the operation of its programs, obtaining funds, managing its affairs, and relating to its membership constituencies in affiliated chapters throughout the country.

In response to the growth in the size of their income, membership, and ultimately staff and programs, virtually all organizations, large and small, undertook various structural changes during 1976–1988. For example, in addition to the growth in the size of their budgets described in the previous section, membership in their locally affiliated branches also expanded: the average number of such affiliates increased by almost one-third, from 134 to 174 per organization. As a result, the number of national organizations with more than 40,000 members grew from 12 to 14 of the 20. While the national-local relationship is very loose, as will be seen in the section on governance, nevertheless, eight organizations had assigned additional regional staff to assist the expanding number of affiliates: for example, in one organization, Arthritis Care, the number of local affiliates grew from 250 to 450 within a five-year period.

The total number of employed staff in the twenty agencies grew from 6,727 in 1976 to 10,745 in 1988—an increase of 61 percent (see Table 1.2). The eleven smaller agencies in the sub-group increased their staff, mainly in the national office, from a total of 258 to 495, or by 92 percent, but they constituted only 2 percent of the total number of employed persons. The total number of agency staff ranged from 6 to 3,000, averaging 1,194 for the 9 larger agencies and 45 for the 11 smaller ones, with the proportion of part-time staff constituting at least 15–20 percent. These figures do not include paid staff employed by the local affiliates of these national organizations; this information was generally not known in the London headquarters because of the highly independent nature of the local associations. Staff growth took place both in the headquarters and in the field where the various service units of the larger national organizations are located. By 1988 the headquarters staff size varied from 120 to 160 for the 4 largest organizations, up to 80 for 5 organizations, and 40 or less for the other smaller 11 organizations. The smaller organizations almost doubled the size of their staff during this period, but many of them had only 5 to 10 employees in 1976.

Both types of organizations, large and small, became more formalized, that is, work norms were made more explicit, more bureaucratic and professional. This was evident in: (1) the development of more elaborate and complex tables of organization, including new divisional structures; (2) the adoption of service and personnel policy manuals in thirteen agencies compared to only five that had them in 1976; (3) the computerized management information systems that were introduced in eleven agencies that did not have them in the 1970s. Similar trends have been reported in other studies of local voluntary organizations (Billis and Harris 1992a).

Professionalization also proceeded apace, and agencies expressed great pride in the increasing number of their staff members, particularly those working in residential care, who had obtained various degrees and other credentials certifying to their qualifications.

Significantly, management consultants were used by virtually all organizations (eighteen out of twenty), usually as part of a comprehensive review of their administrative structure, which led in twelve cases to a major reorganization of their headquarters, and in eight of them to some decentralization. These reorganizations were usually long overdue. The incremental growth in income and staff had occurred without much change in organizational structure, and this resulted in numerous fiscal and management problems that will be discussed in the section on management.

The structure of the six largest organizations came to resemble a quasi-public bureaucracy or a "mini-conglomerate" because of the growing number, diversity, and complexity of their administrative divisions and service programs. While some appeared to be more of a confederation, particularly because of the large number of independent branches or local chapters, they nevertheless operated as highly centralized, professionalized service bureaucracies.

During the same period of time, other structural changes took place such as the establishment of wholly owned subsidiaries for the sale of goods and services, and/or property management by three agencies with interlocking boards of directors to keep control of their agency resources and to obtain tax benefits. One large agency benefited from the central government's policy of financing housing for elderly and handicapped persons as part of its campaign to reduce the role of Local Authorities in this field. Virtually all of the capital investment was made by the government, and the agency acquired a very large number of residential facilities as part of its Housing Association, for which it established a separate charitable trust. Three other agencies transferred some of their program staff to other voluntary organizations, and in one case, the National Health Service assumed financial responsibility for a Volunteer Stroke Scheme pioneered by the Chest, Heart, and Stroke Association as part of an agreement.

Several other organizations changed their legal structure from a registered charity to one more appropriate for their multifarious nonprofit and for-profit activities, thus providing themselves with more flexibility in the use of internally generated income. Only one merger was reported involving an agency that had been in existence 134 years, and it required an Act of Parliament before it could be finally approved.

Management Changes

Perhaps the most notable finding was the high rate of turnover of the organizations' executives since 1985: fourteen out of the twenty agencies replaced their chief executives. Ten of the executives had been with their agency less than 4 years, four less than 18 months, three for 13 to 16 years, and three for 5 to 8 years. New directors were appointed in seven of the nine agencies that received substantial statutory fees and grants, and in seven of the eleven organizations that were dependent mainly on contributed funds. All but two of the fourteen new executives came from outside the organization, but most of them had previously been employed in the voluntary sector or in the social services. Two notable exceptions were a former British admiral retired from NATO and an ex–flight surgeon; another executive had a successful stage career as an actor and theater manager, but he had been previously active in the organization as a volunteer. Most of their predecessors had been in office ten to twenty-five years and had reached retirement age or had decided to resign; others were replaced because of a fiscal crisis and/or recognition that the organization was drifting, declining, or endangered. In two instances, the board president was also forced to resign when the trustees became aware of the precarious state of the organization's finances.

Four of these new executives led their agencies through a period of extensive reorganization and, ultimately, revitalization by means of a process that has been called "transformational executive succession" (Bass 1985). In the largest one, the Spastics Society, with over 3,000 staff members, a completely new top management cadre was appointed. These organizations, which included some of the oldest, most traditional British charities, had considerably expanded the scale of their income, staff, and programs during the 1980s, and they had confronted serious managerial and fiscal crises with which the incumbent executive was unable to cope. For example, in one case, the board of directors learned that in the course of a few years, the organization had acquired a deficit amounting to 20 percent of the budget of £4.5 million. Typically, following recognition of the problem, a management consultant was called in for recommendations. In two agencies the trustees took over the administration of the agency themselves, in one case for over two and one-half years while a management consultant conducted a study. In another, the twelve top staff members rebelled against the successor to their previous executive who had served for twenty-five years. The board then transformed itself into a Management Committee for the first time, and administered one of the largest voluntary agencies for almost a year until an acceptable replacement was found (Rix 1989).

Contrasting strategies were employed by the new executives who sought to "turn around" these organizations in trouble. In the Royal National Institute for the Deaf (RNID), the board apparently gave the new general manager the authority to institute whatever changes he deemed necessary, and, in the course of a few months, he prepared plans for rejuvenating the agency that were implemented over a three-year period. In another, much larger and more complex organization, the new executive of the Royal National Institute for the Blind (RNIB) also prepared a series of recommended changes, but he then proceeded to involve the entire board and staff in a series of discussions over an eighteen-month period before a plan was adopted to restructure and modernize the entire organization. Thirty areas of potential development were identified in this process, and it resulted in a major turnaround of the organization (Butler and Wilson 1990:116–30).

In the larger organizations, which had grown incrementally without stopping to assess the adequacy of their administrative arrangements, the executive was generally unaccustomed to delegating authority. As a result, it was not uncommon for dozens of employees to report directly to the executive. As part of the reorganization, the executive's span of control was substantially reduced, in several instances from twenty to seven staff members. In addition, departmentalization and a greater measure of decentralization, together with strategic planning, were introduced in seven of the agencies.

The increasingly complex character of administration in these agencies is revealed in the larger size of their headquarters staff, which expanded from three- to eightfold in individual agencies, and gave them somewhat more influence over their local affiliates. Additional staff members were also assigned to fund-raising—the Spastics Society alone hired seventy new persons over a two-year period—for advocacy, and for the coordination of the growing number of their local affiliates. For example, from 1982 to 1988, Arthritis Care had a spectacular expansion in the number of its branches—from 240 to 440—and its membership—from 24,000 to 44,000. An almost threefold increase in its nominal income during this period made it possible for the headquarters staff to grow from 30 to 41 and its regional staff from 15 to 37.

These changes were paralleled by the growing bureaucratization and professionalization of the service provision staff and management in all agencies. Management presented itself as more "businesslike" and professional, as evident in the new titles and the more corporate style of its leadership. The former secretary generals or executive directors acquired new titles as manager, director general, or chief executive officer, and an Association of the Chief Executives of National Voluntary Organizations was established in 1987. Even the smallest agencies became more modernized, and several reported that, to their regret, they had become more secular in their approach. On the other hand, one of the largest agencies, the Shaftsbury Society, claimed that its increased formalization and efficiency helped make its Christian mission more successful.

There was also a greater emphasis in most agencies on the use of marketing both in fund-raising and service programs, and on more extensive involvement of public relations consultants in an effort to change their public image. As part of the expansion of fund-raising, there was more use of paid advertising; the largest agency's expenditure for advertising in 1988 was the same as the total budget for one of the medium-sized voluntary organizations, approximately £1 million.

It was claimed that many of these trends reflected the growing influence of the market and the "enterprise culture" fostered by the Thatcher government that served as the sociopolitical context for voluntary organizations in Britain during the 1980s (Johnson 1989; Taylor 1992). For example, the National Council for Voluntary Organisations responded to the growing concern for more efficiency and effectiveness in the voluntary sector by initiating a Working Party headed by Lord Nathan. At about the same time, the government launched its own Efficiency Scrutiny of voluntary organizations, which revealed the scope and some of the complexities of their statutory funding.

Governance Patterns

The distinctive governance system of these organizations can be viewed as a product of their hybrid character, which combines in one structure three seemingly incompatible elements: a service bureaucracy, a voluntary membership association, and a pattern of informal social relationships (Billis 1989). In addition, there are two concurrent lines of authority: between board and staff, and between professionals and volunteers (Kramer 1985; Slavin 1978).

While the terms referring to the members of the governing board have changed during the last decade—from Trustees to Management Committees or Councils—their function has remained the same: to legitimate the agency, adopt policy, employ the executive, and receive and allocate funds that they are prohibited from distributing among themselves. In contrast to their counterparts in the United States, board members in England were generally not responsible for raising funds for their agencies' budgets.

Voluntary agencies are still governed by two bodies: a large Management Council averaging twenty-seven persons (up from an average of twenty-four in 1976) that meets two to three times a year, and an Executive Committee that continues to average seven members and is convened every month or two. The lack of congruence between the size of the organization and its governing board was still evident. For example, the largest agency, the Spastics Society, which claims over 125,000 volunteers, has only fifteen board members—five each of parents, professionals, and consumers—but smaller organizations with less than one-fifth of its income have two to three times as many trustees.

While the average percentage of women on the boards has decreased from 33 percent to 25 percent, consumer representation has increased somewhat in many of the agencies. In the RNIB, one of the largest organizations, there has been a fivefold increase in the number of blind persons, who constitute over 50 percent of its governing body.

All boards continue to share one basic characteristic in common: self-selection and self-perpetuation, with very little turnover. It is not unusual for board members to serve uninterrupted for ten to fifteen years, with some acting as trustees for upwards of forty years. The lack of rotation of board members in these "private governments" was regarded as a problem by only three chief executives. In one agency, the executive was only able to overcome the presence of "dead wood" on the board, which could not be removed, by persuading them to increase their number from thirty to fifty in order to add more active persons. In addition, this agency became one of the very few to limit the president's term to a maximum of six years. It is expected that the reforms in the Charity Law beginning in 1991 may result in trustees having more accountability and responsibility (Home Office 1989).

Another continuity was the persistence of power struggles in the delegate assemblies of the agencies, where representatives of their local affiliates may even have a veto power over the actions of the national governing board. More characteristic is the franchise character of their relationships, which are "loosely coupled," and generally reflect their top-down origin and authority structure. It is still exceptional for the autonomous local affiliates to have any significant fund-raising responsibility for the national organization, or for the latter to have systematic information about its affiliates in their headquarters offices. Typically, the national office is staffed by paid employees, while volunteers predominate in the affiliates, although those located in the larger urban centers often operate service programs funded by the Local Authority. Basic policy and program decisions are made centrally, however, and there is considerable variation in the extent to which local affiliates are encouraged to sponsor service programs.

There may also be a potential for more intraorganizational conflict in the future when both the national organization and its affiliates could compete for contracts to serve the disabled in the local community. On the other hand, those affiliates that are not able to undertake service provision could lose the grant support of the Local Authority for their information and advocacy functions as statutory funds become more scarce.

As described in the previous section, six of the governing boards had to face serious management and fiscal crises that culminated in the replacement of their chief executives, and in several instances, the president. After usually muddling through, the trustees would belatedly recognize the nature of the crisis and only then would they call in a management consultant. The new managers who were subsequently appointed provided fresh leadership in reorganizing and rejuvenating the agency. Three of the boards were also deeply involved in this process of organizational renewal and participated in the inauguration of strategic planning in their agency.

Apart from the exceptional circumstances of crisis management, the prevailing pattern of board activity was generally one of policy ratification. The working relationship between the board and the executive director continues to be one of the most critical factors in the governance and management of these voluntary organizations (Leduc and Block 1985; Herman 1990). Generally, there is a balance of power between the two, with the executive tending to dominate; in only one agency was the executive clearly subordinated to the board members, who were each responsible for overseeing five of their institutions. This pattern was due in great measure to the continuing board leadership role of the person who founded the organization forty years before.

In contrast to the trends found in the financing of these organizations, in their structure and management, there were fewer changes evident in their governance—in the character of the boards of directors, and national-local relationships—where essentially the same patterns prevailed as those noted in the 1970s (Kramer 1981:114–27).

Program Operations

There was an increased number of new and improved service programs reported by most agencies, which were characterized by their greater diversity, complexity, and specialization. Two of the largest agencies expanded their services during the decade to over fifty programs each, at forty and ninety different sites, respectively. There was a notable growth in residential care and other special purpose facilities as a result of successful capital fund campaigns, but the expansion was also fueled by increased statutory fees and grants.

At the same time, public policy on dehospitalization reinforced the trend toward more community care, described in a newspaper editorial as "the underdeveloped, underfunded and uncoordinated Cinderella services for the mentally ill, mentally handicapped and the elderly" (*Guardian* 1989; Higgins 1989). Considerable flexibility and capacity for adaptation were shown by some of the larger organizations in developing more community-based service programs that should make it easier for them to operate in the "contract culture" expected to prevail in the 1990s (Kunz et al. 1989; National Council for Voluntary Organizations [NCVO] 1989). The gradual shift from residential care to various forms of community care by several agencies stemmed from changes in professional philosophy and public opinion, difficulties in complying with the new, more costly, and tighter regulations pertaining to institutional care after 1984, and, in some instances, a decreasing number of referrals for institutional care. The most extensive program changes were announced by the largest agency, the Spastics Society, which, after a complete reorganization instituted by its new executive in 1988, planned to sell or lease back all of its institutions over the next ten years and to use the funds to rehouse 650 of their 850 residents in various forms of family care. This ambitious program also involved a fund-raising campaign for over £50 million to promote a new set of independent living arrangements for clientele over the next three years.

There were several notable examples of goal succession and transfers of programs to other voluntary organizations, although few were transferred to LASSDs. Agencies reacted differentially to the decreasing incidence of a disability, such as spina bifida and/or the aging of their original clientele, with responses ranging from organizational decline, upgrading and refinement of existing services, to identifying a new niche or domain. For example, an agency facing increasing competition in its traditional domain of cardiac and respiratory diseases adopted stroke victims as a new field of service in order to change its public image and appear more distinctive.

Most of the "new programs" were reported by the nine larger agencies receiving statutory funds, but very few of these were truly "innovative"; rather, they were essentially extensions or improvements of existing programs. This was not true, however, of the majority of the ten new programs initiated by the RNIB over a ten-year period. Respite care, facilities for independent living, and family support programs were among the most frequently reported new programs. Both the expanded and the more innovative programs were hindered in several agencies by the shortage of specialized staff. This is a particularly serious problem in working with the deaf, where there are over 100 organizations.

Despite the proliferation and modernization of services during the 1980s, there is still very little use made of program evaluation. Because funding may be more scarce in the face of greater demand for the personal social services in the next decade, there will probably be additional pressures on these organizations to produce more evaluative information about the effectiveness of their service programs.

Interorganizational Relations

As the medium through which resources are obtained from the environment, interorganizational relationships have increased in importance for all agencies (Pfeffer and Salancik 1978). Resources are both tangible—funds, clients, volunteers, and staff—and intangible—information, reputation, and experience. They are interconnected with all of the operating systems of an organization: its finances, governance, management, and service delivery. Interorganizational relations exist on the national and on the local levels, among voluntary organizations and between them and statutory ones. Regarding the former, both more competition and more collaboration, particularly in advocacy, were reported with other voluntary organizations. Competition has grown among these national agencies in fund-raising and staff recruitment, for clients and public attention (Wilson 1992). This is partly due to the steadily increasing number of such organizations each year: as noted earlier, there are between three and four thousand new registered charities each year, and perhaps an equal number of other types of voluntary organizations. One of the oldest agencies, ICAN, reported that it competes with six other organizations in its field, and that as a result, it has tried to specialize in services for children with communication and language disorders. The larger, richer, and more "appealing" agencies are in a better competitive position to benefit from media attention. For example, one of the first agencies to take advantage of the removal of restrictions on TV advertising by charities, the RNID invested over £100,000 in its initial campaign, and claimed that it received three to four times its value in TV announcements.

There are four types of transactions between governmental and voluntary organizations, each of which has both a national and a local dimension: (a) *fiscal* (grants, fees, and indirect and in-kind assistance); (b) *regulatory* (standard setting and licensing); (c) *service delivery* (exchange of information, referrals, consultations, coordination and planning, contracts, and joint operations); (d) *political* (advocacy or "campaigning," as it is often known in Britain).

Many of the national agencies receive small, core grants for their administration from central government, and occasionally, grants for research and demonstration or special projects. Payments for the care of the residents in their

institutions for whom there is a statutory responsibility come from Local Authorities, with the rates generally set by negotiations with their representatives. In
addition, some of the larger affiliates operate programs in cooperation with the
Local Authority, such as providing residential care, leisure time services for
mentally handicapped persons, and/or a support group for their parents, while the
Local Authority operates a day care center and other forms of housing.

It is not unusual to find both statutory and voluntary organizations serving
the same disabled population, but with different types of services. As a result,
the various forms of interorganizational relations with government can vary
by the degree of interaction and frequency, formalization and dependency
(Leat et al. 1986; NCVO 1986). On the whole, however, most of these interorganizational relationships involve collaboration or accommodation, and rarely
competition or conflict. The relationships are, of course, influenced by the mutual attitudes and perceptions of the staff members involved, but they do not
seem to be seriously affected by the efforts of central government to reduce the
role of local government as a provider of services, and to expand the responsibilities of voluntary organizations.

Despite the continual concern expressed by their national intermediary body
(NCVO 1986, 1988, 1989), statutory-voluntary relationships were not perceived
as particularly problematic by any of the agency executives. Few voiced complaints about the fiscal and regulatory practices of LASSDs comparable to those
found in the United States (Demone and Gibelman 1989), apart from the failure
to pay the full cost of care. This is somewhat surprising because there have been
additional regulations and more costly standards established for residential care
since 1984, but these seem to have been accepted. In only one case was there a
major conflict with the government regarding the appropriate classification of
many of the Cheshire Homes in which the board of directors contested the
application of nursing home standards to its residential facilities on the grounds
that Cheshire Homes stressed self-care rather than a nursing home environment.

The paucity of problematic statutory-voluntary relationships reported can be
explained in several ways. As respondents, the executives of these national agencies may, of course, be too far removed from the Local Authority where many of
these issues arise, although there is, as we shall see, considerable interaction with
officials in the central government. Some of the agencies had up to forty joint
operating projects with LASSDs, while others were involved in extensive coordi-
native arrangements, or benefited from substantial in-kind support. This suggests
that *interdependence* may be the dominant characteristic of these statutory-
voluntary relationships, a generalization that is also supported by the rather limited
research on this subject (Leat et al. 1981, 1986). From a practical viewpoint, the
number of handicapped persons requiring the kind of specialized care provided
by these voluntary agencies is very small in any Local Authority, and would not
justify the development of special residential facilities or other forms of care for
them under statutory auspices. Consequently, the service programs of these na-

tional agencies are a valuable resource for Local Authorities that should be protected. Some of these cooperative relations, however, may change because of new policies in which direct service provision of the LASSD is expected to be reduced, and the role of voluntary organizations expanded in community care, education, and housing, a topic to be discussed in the section on the future of the contract culture.

Advocacy is still another way in which voluntary agencies relate to government. While fifteen out of the twenty organizations reported an overall increase in the amount and extent of advocacy, there were considerable differences in the degree to which voluntary agencies were active in campaigning for their constituencies in Parliament, among the departments in central government, or in local government. Only a few of the largest agencies were consistently involved in advocacy, in meeting regularly with governmental officials, participating in coalitions, and in the employment of special staff for this purpose; several reported the appointment of parliamentary officers for the first time. In supporting its claim to more advocacy in the 1980s compared to the previous decade, Mencap cited thirty pieces of legislation in which it was involved compared to only ten in the 1970s. These were also the agencies that received over half of their income from statutory sources, a fact that evidently did not inhibit their advocacy.

Other smaller agencies were, however, at pains to dissociate themselves from engaging in advocacy and declared, "we don't do that sort of thing." That such an attitude is neither typical nor necessary is suggested by an extensive survey of 191 voluntary organizations in 1989, which revealed that over 75 percent regarded advocacy as a fundamental function, although less than 25 percent committed any staff resources to this activity (NCVO 1990a). Very few reported that they had ever been criticized for campaigning on behalf of their clientele; more often they were criticized for not doing enough! For example, voluntary organizations have been singled out for their failure to lead the opposition to the cuts in local welfare spending imposed by the central government (Pickvance 1987). On the other hand, beginning in June of 1989, 250 organizations formed the Disabled Benefits Consortium in a campaign to raise the income level of 4.3 million disabled persons who are mainly dependent on their statutory income.

There is periodic concern that the government will regard the traditional advocacy role of these organizations as inappropriate for a charity, but "reasonable campaigning" has not been restricted when the issue relates to the purpose and special interest of the voluntary organization in matters that directly affect its clients. Typically, there is considerable consultation by the officials in central government with voluntary organizations, but few executives believe that their influence is particularly significant: "we may have some influence on the small type in the legislation, but not on the broader issues." Few could point to any notable successes; even the power of the RNIB was unable to prevent the National Health Service from eliminating free eye examinations, despite the evidence that thousands of persons would fail to obtain such examinations that could prevent more serious and costly vision care in the future.

Implications of the Findings: Toward a Developmental Model

Although the political landscape in Britain from 1976 to 1988 was marked by a succession of unprecedented shifts in government policy, there was, nevertheless, more continuity than change within this group of national voluntary agencies. True, virtually all of them became larger, more bureaucratized, and more professionalized, but at the same time, traditional, long-standing patterns persisted in their governance, basic organizational structure, income sources, service program operations, and advocacy.

Political factors militated against more extensive changes such as "hiving off," "load shedding," and other forms of degovernmentalization advocated by the Thatcher government, changes that could have substantially altered the way of life of many of these voluntary agencies. By 1991, a new prime minister was elected by the Conservative Party, and the end of the Thatcher era was even being described as a "failed revolution," despite the re-election of the Conservative Party in 1992. Neither the dream nor the nightmare of the contract culture was imminent, and because the implementation of the *White Paper on Community Care* proceeded very slowly, prolonging the period of uncertainty, it provided an opportunity for more thoughtful consideration of the advantages and disadvantages of contracting (Gutch 1992).

There were some noteworthy organizational changes ranging from the widespread introduction of computerized financial accounting systems to the revitalization of previously declining organizations. In addition to growth in the size of their income, staff, and programs, a trend toward more rationalized management procedures was found in virtually all of the agencies, regardless of whether their dominant mode of financing was statutory or voluntary. This suggests that the widely used resource dependency model—which says the source of financing determines organizational structure and performance—may be overly deterministic and less appropriate in explaining the behavior of these agencies than an institutional or developmental model (Billis 1991; Hasenfeld and Schmid 1989). Using a combination of two complementary models—open systems and life cycle—we can view these voluntary agencies as open systems adapting to multiple factors in their internal and external environments (Kimberly and Miles 1980; Tushman and Romanelli 1985).

The life cycle of these organizations typically evolved from an informal, small group such as a self-help organization for mutual and/or public benefit, which became more formalized as a voluntary association (Chapin and Tsouderos 1956; Katz 1960; Wolfensberger 1973). Through a process of organizational development and institutionalization, these voluntary associations usually acquired staff and became more bureaucratized and professionalized. They could then be described as voluntary *agencies,* a term that fits the cohort since the 1970s.

The model begins at the stage where the dominant organizational character of the British voluntary agency was a traditional philanthropic charity. (See Table 1.3.)

Table 1.3

Three-Stage Model of UK Voluntary Agencies*

DOMINANT ORGANIZATIONAL CHARACTER	Charity (1970s)	Corporate (1980s)	Contractor (1990 —>)
Stages in the organizational life cycle	Development/collectivity	Maturation/formalization	Elaboration of structure
Organizational image	Voluntary, philanthropic agency	"Big business"	Statutory service provider
Size	Small/medium	Medium/large	Large
Perceived environment	Stable	Changing/uncertain	Competitive
Organizational culture	Organic	Mechanistic	Mechanistic
Structure	"Loose coupling"	Bureaucratic/hierarchical	Decentralized
Major fiscal resource system	Contributions and gifts	Fees and grants	Statutory payments
Primary governance body	Trustees, including founders	Management council	Executive committee
Administrative leadership patterns	Authoritative, centralized	Formalized, institutionalized procedures of delegation	Professionalized management
Principal strategies	Reactive, defensive	Proactive	Expansion and diversification
Interorganizational relations to government	Accommodation	Collaboration	Contractual
Service programs	Specialized, complementary	Supplementary and alternatives	Substitutes, more standardized

*This descriptive model is intended to be suggestive and not deterministic, i.e., there is no intrinsic "necessity" for organizations to become more corporate or to become contractors, although this trend has been noted among many of the large national agencies. Also, the fact that many organizations retain characteristics of earlier stages of their development contributes to the hybrid character of social agencies in which elements of a bureaucracy, a voluntary association, and informal social systems are combined. This model is based on the one developed by Hasenfeld and Schmid (1989).

Source: Kramer 1990:47. Reprinted courtesy of Manchester University Press.

The next corporate phase evolved during the 1980s, and was reflected in changes in selected organizational attributes such as size, structure, strategy, and image, most of which were related to growth, formalization, bureaucratization, and professionalization. As a result of increased income, staff and programs were expanded, and in becoming more bureaucratized, many voluntary agencies became more corporate in their structure and managerial style, some of the largest ones resembling highly decentralized conglomerates. (Because "corporate" has many meanings, it is *not* used here to refer to "peak associations" as they operate in "corporatist societies"; rather, as a metaphor, it refers to a characteristic complex organizational structure associated with large commercial or industrial enterprises, with a board of directors and professional management.)

The third stage in the model is projected to the decade of the 1990s when the "contract culture" is expected to prevail, and the organizational character of the voluntary agency would be primarily influenced by expansion of its role as a provider or vendor of public services—in short, as a contractor.

Sources of Organizational Change

The transition from the charity to the corporate model has its roots in earlier trends during the 1970s in the UK when the principles of modern management were being increasingly adopted both in business and in public administration circles. For example, the Wolfenden Report of 1978—the last large-scale national study of the future of the voluntary sector—gave scant attention to management issues. Rather, it stressed the special contribution of voluntary agencies to their "partnership" with government and recommended greater statutory funding. Since then, the "cult of the manager" attracted many adherents in the voluntary sector, particularly among the larger organizations. For example, in the 1980s it was no longer sufficient for agencies to invoke the virtues of voluntarism and/or charity for their legitimation. Increasingly, as part of the "enterprise culture" espoused by the Thatcher government, it was expected that they would also be efficient, effective, and give "value for money" (Taylor 1992). Influenced by the social norms of their trustees and large donors regarding professional managerialism, voluntary organizations, as described earlier, adopted new, modern corporate names for their governing boards and their executives. In addition, trustees sought new chief executives outside their organizations who had professional expertise in management, marketing, or fund-raising that was usually obtained in other organizations or government.

Thus, while the external environment was important, the engine or driving force for the growing institutionalization and adaptation was the process of *executive succession* that occurred in fourteen out of the twenty agencies, mostly since 1985. The replacement of these agency executives by the governing boards came during a time when a new managerial ethos was taking hold, so it is not surprising that the voluntary agencies became more "corporate" in their structure and operations. Because the new executive leadership was more appropriate to the stage of development of the organization, it was able in several instances to arrest a process of stagnation or decline and to initiate a process of reorganization and revitalization. Butler and Wilson (1990), among others, also found strong evidence in their sample of thirty-one national British voluntary organizations of increased bureaucratization and professionalization, and a corporate managerial culture which they believe may be dysfunctional for the voluntary sector. They claim that corporatism, with its distinctive style of control and rationalization, could lead to value conflicts with a staff ostensibly committed to individualism, high moral codes, and autonomy. This would, however, depend on the meaning and type of "corporate culture," the extent to which it is more form than substance or is identified only with cost-accounting and a short-term profitability approach to service provision (Dartington 1989). For example, the corporate concept not only can refer to more rationalized management, but it can also mean a shared sense of identity and mission among staff and their democratic participation in organizational decision making. The latter, in the form of a human relations approach to management, may be found not only in voluntary and public organizations but also in some of the most successful business corporations (Peters and Waterman 1982).

Statutory Funding and Its Effects

While it is exceedingly difficult to disentangle the sources and consequences of organizational change, the findings suggest that the growth of formalization, bureaucratization, and professionalization associated with the corporate stage of development was not, contrary to a widely held belief, due primarily to increased statutory funding. There is a tendency among voluntary agency leaders in England and elsewhere to exaggerate somewhat the effects of governmental funding on bureaucratization. Yet there are in modern societies many different internal and external pressures on organizations to become more formalized, bureaucratic, and professional. As Salamon (1987:115) observes, "pressures for improved agency management, tighter financial control and the use of professionals in service delivery do not, after all, come solely from government."

As noted above, an incremental process of modernization or rationalization was found among both types of voluntary agencies, regardless of the degree of dependency on statutory funding. These structural changes were strongly influenced by the growth of "managerialism" in the external environment—the economy and in the public sector—as well as by a process of institutionalization within each agency. Furthermore, insofar as it was possible to ascertain, few if any of the commonly feared consequences of dependency on statutory funding were reported. There was little or no evidence of "government control," goal deflection, reduced autonomy, lessened innovation, volunteerism, or advocacy among the nine agencies that could be attributed to their reliance on statutory fees for one-half to two-thirds of their income.

In one of the few empirical studies in England (Leat et al. 1986), it was also found that, paradoxically, local voluntary organizations receiving high statutory grants were able to raise more, not less, money from the general public, and that they involved more volunteers than those receiving less or no statutory funds. While the cost of such aid was reported as a certain amount of uncertainty, this was seen as not much different than the cost of funding from other sources. Also, the minimal accountability required by the Local Authority compensated for any possible loss of "autonomy." This finding is similar to independent studies in other countries where some of the disadvantages of governmental funding were more than offset by the opportunity to extend and/or improve services for a larger clientele (Hartogs and Weber 1978). Indeed, many British agencies also believed that they had more influence on public policies because they were "on the inside and not outside," and that, consequently, their service programs did not preempt their advocacy (Knapp et al. 1990).

How to explain these findings? It seems contrary to the conventional wisdom that he who pays the piper calls the tune, but perhaps "he who calls the tune [is] tone deaf. . . . Those who dispense funds may not have complete information, nor are they always rational and consistent. They may hold values that encourage them to react . . . in other than utilitarian terms. In addition, funders are subject to the pressures of conflicting interests and reference groups" (Brager and Holloway 1978:43).

Among the factors that could have mitigated the corrupting, co-opting, or controlling elements usually ascribed to statutory funding are the following:

1. *Incremental growth.* Although the nine agencies' total increase of real income from statutory funding was 133 percent from 1976 to 1988, this more than twofold growth was essentially quite gradual—averaging a little over 1 percent per year, a total increase for the nine agencies of 14 percent. Thus, the modest scope may have blunted a more substantial impact on the organization.

2. The *form* and *purpose* of the fiscal transfer—fees and payments for residential care rather than time-limited grants or subsidies—contributed to the *quid pro quo* character of a relationship between buyer and seller (Kramer 1981:167).

3. "Autonomy" was also not seriously constrained because of the *multiplicity* of statutory income sources. "Statutory funding" is not monolithic; income was obtained from upward of eighty to one hundred different Local Authorities rather than one single source. Even in central government, there were thirty-four different allocating bodies. There is considerable agreement that dependency is inversely related to the number of income sources and that it is less an inherent property of the source itself. In fact, the relationship between statutory funder and voluntary provider is, as noted earlier, most often one of *interdependence* because government needs the services of the voluntary agency as much as the latter requires income (Saidel 1989). For government, the costs of more intrusive monitoring or "control" are generally too great fiscally, administratively, and politically. Typically, government lacks the in-

centive and the capacity to be a more effective controller of its grants, subsidies, and contracts. In addition, there is a strong British tradition favoring "arm's length" organizational relationships. As Gutch and Young concluded: "the supposed threat to the voluntary sector caused by excessive controls imposed by public agencies when purchasing services is rarely supported by any evidence" (1988:21). More often than not, insufficient accountability is more likely to be found than reduced autonomy.

Conclusions: The Future of the Contract Culture

In the decade of the 1990s, it is generally assumed that there will be continued and more likely increased use of voluntary organizations as contractors for the provision of both residential and community care, even though official implementation of the White Paper of 1989 will be delayed. Consequently, future developments may be less dramatic than a "dream" for large, national agencies or a "nightmare" for smaller, community-based organizations, as suggested by some of the publications of the National Council for Voluntary Organisations. At least some caution is indicated when generalizing about "the future of the voluntary sector" because of its enormous diversity. Voluntary organizations in England as elsewhere vary greatly in their age, size, complexity, purposes, scope of concern (national or local), degree of professionalization and bureaucratization, type of management committee, extent of service provision and advocacy, consumer participation, and the nature of their clientele and constituencies. Because these variables may influence their performance much more than does their legal status as registered charities (DiMaggio and Anheier 1990), different types of voluntary agencies will have different futures as they react in their own way to the contract culture that may emerge. For example, rate capping and the financial incentives for local authorities to divest themselves of residential facilities may be regarded as an opportunity to be seized by large national organizations, but as a dangerous threat to the survival of small, community-based organizations whose customary grant-aids may be eliminated, or who may be unable or unwilling to compete for contracts because they cannot meet the requirements for greater specificity, accountability, and compliance with regulations. These differences suggest that the contract culture may contribute further to the bifurcation of the British voluntary sector in the future.

Then, too, Local Authorities also vary greatly, and depending on their history and politics, they may not be interested in "partnerships" with voluntary agencies; they may be reluctant to invest resources in their development, if, as is often true in many communities, the voluntary agencies are too small and weak, and generally lack the capacity to serve as contractors (Hallet 1982). Under these circumstances, Local Authorities may set up their own surrogates in the form of nonprofit trusts and limited companies, or they may prefer to contract instead with commercial companies.

In whatever ways voluntary organizations view contracting, it does change their relationship to local government: from supplicant–patron to supplier–purchaser; from asking for support or generosity, to negotiating deals; from a "partner," to a party in a legal contract (Kunz et al. 1989; Mackintosh 1989).

Apart from these changes in their status and power relationships, voluntary agencies with the capacity for local social service delivery may still find that the "enabling" role proposed for Local Authorities results in unwanted "off-loading" and dumping of case responsibilities and/or even larger deficits to be financed by their other nonstatutory sources of income. While the Local Authority as the purchaser of care has the authority to delegate responsibility, it may not be able to obtain sufficient resources from central government. There is a historic pattern of the Conservative Party stressing voluntarism, but at the expense of allocating insufficient resources to the Local Authority (Sainsbury 1977:219).

Consequently, it is apparent that voluntary and statutory agencies will continue to have to adapt to numerous changes in their environments. As part of the evolving mixed economy of welfare in Britain, voluntary organizations will undoubtedly have more active interorganizational relationships with government. There is considerable variation among voluntary agencies in their ability to recognize and to deal effectively with such challenges. Some organizations are more opportunistic or risk-aversive than others, but evidently few make plans, anticipate, or prepare for change (Stone 1989; Wolch 1990). The pressures of competition, scarcity, and uncertainty in the future will place a great premium on the capacity of the leadership of voluntary organizations in the UK to analyze their situation and to respond strategically.

2

Italy: Toward an Unplanned Partnership

Introduction

In Italy, the third sector should probably be called the "first sector," as it appeared well before the late-blooming modern democratic state and also before the free, competitive market.

Over the centuries, both the state and the church discouraged spontaneous, voluntary associations because they were regarded as potential usurpers of government power. This is one of the most important differences between the Anglo-Saxon and Latin traditions. Until recently, there were few intermediate bodies between the state and civil society. The church preempted most of the participative space through its extended network of affiliated religious associations.

Italy is witnessing a historical rise in the importance of voluntary social welfare activities. The traditional division of the public domain between the state and the Catholic Church is giving way to a proliferation of new voluntary social welfare agencies. Born of the turbulent social movements of the 1970s, these new organizations are at least supplementing church-based ideas of charity with a new altruism based on secular concepts of social justice.

Some privatization of social and health services is now receiving serious consideration, and nonprofit bodies have been viewed by some as a "providential instrument for correcting the many evils of the welfare state, first among them the excessive cost of supplying services and their bureaucratization" (Ascoli 1992:37). Proponents of a revitalized third sector have also contrasted the values of voluntary action, solidarity, and altruism against the rigid bureaucratization of the state. This was a major departure from the past emphasis on a welfare system dependent on the development of a huge public apparatus. While the centrality of public responsibility continues, there are now more opportunities for collaboration between government and various types of voluntary organizations. In large part, this is a consequence of the emergence over the last twenty years of thousands of local, single-issue groups, which are focused less on the political system than on producing services and conducting advocacy activities on behalf of specific client groups.

This chapter examines the rise of the new third sector in the context of church–state relations and the structure of the Italian political system. The findings of the study of twenty social service agencies in the Milan area are then presented. The chapter concludes with a discussion of the implication of the case studies for the character of Italy's third sector and its likely future direction.

Private Philanthropy and Church–State Relations

Italian social services have traditionally been the exclusive domain of the Catholic Church. In the period between the unification of Italy in 1861 and the early 1920s, the state rarely intervened in matters of social welfare. Its nonengagement was codified by a 1862 law that put the government in charge of health services, and left the rest of the country's social services in the hands of church-dominated charitable associations. As a dense structure of national and local institutions known as *opera pie*, these associations consisted primarily of residential institutions serving the sick, the disabled, and orphans; later they grew to include educational institutions and local parish groups. In 1890, these church-sponsored organizations were formally annexed by the state and required by the Crispi Law to obtain a public charter as *Istituti Publici di Assistenza e Beneficenza* (IPAB). Though nominally transferred into the public domain, these institutions continued to function as private organizations heavily influenced by the church. While receiving most of their funds from government, they were relatively free from public control. This arrangement was consistent with the generally weak national powers of the constitutional monarchy that ruled Italy from its founding until the early 1920s.

The rise of Mussolini in 1922 did not substantially change these relationships between church and state. The twenty-year period of Fascist dictatorship saw an expansion of national welfare policies under direct state control, a further curtailment of an independent public domain, but the church retained its strong influence over the IPABs. Like the Catholic Church, Fascist rule was also hostile to the development of voluntary, nonprofit philanthropic institutions.

Further reconciliation between the government and the Catholic Church was effected in 1929 with the signing of the *Concordato*, which recognized Catholicism as the official state religion. This ended the long period of conflict that began in 1870 when the Italian state invaded Rome. Yet Church hegemony persisted until the 1960s; only then did the idea of independent social welfare organizations slowly begin to gain acceptance.

The division between public and church-sponsored welfare was typical of Latin countries, where the church dominated the intermediate space between the state and civil society. This historical legacy is an important reason why private philanthropy is less prominent in Italy than in many other Western industrial countries.

Postwar Developments

After World War II, Italy became a multiparty parliamentary constitutional republic led by the Christian Democrats. This robust "party for all seasons" has asserted its dominance over Italian politics through innumerable governments up to the present time (Pasquino 1980, 1990; LaPalombara 1987). From the 1950s to the mid-1960s, the country went through its "economic miracle." This period of transformational yet chaotic change was marked by a process of increasing secularization, together with a major shift in the state from a conservative and centralized model toward a more decentralized and welfare-oriented one. Many of the attempts at reform were, however, little more than a multiplication of bureaucratic structures accompanied by little substantive improvement (Pasquinelli 1989).

The first attempt to form a new relationship between public and private systems of service provision was in the health sector. Private hospitals and nursing homes, primarily church-managed, were the first to receive funding from the regional governments beginning in 1974.

The late 1960s witnessed the first innovative attempts, particularly in the North, to offer social services other than traditional residential care and economic assistance (David 1984). This was the beginning of an increase in welfare expenditures that almost doubled between 1960 and 1984 when it reached 30.3 percent of GNP. The social reform movements of the late 1960s and the 1970s, first involving workers, then youth and women, provided fuel for changes in social policy, including a decentralization of most social welfare functions from Rome to regions and municipalities (Tarrow 1989; Melucci 1991).

The wave of cultural renewal also sparked the beginnings of a process of deinstitutionalization and demedicalization; and of the development of innovative services to replace traditional institutions (Ferrera 1984; O. Ranci 1989). Other important changes included the establishment of a national health service, the closing of psychiatric institutions, and the expansion of kindergarten and counseling services.

Italy's welfare system has undergone a remarkable transformation in the past twenty years, during which the Catholic Church lost much of its traditional cultural and political dominance. This can be attributed to the diminishing religiosity of the population, the weakened political bond between the church and the Christian Democrat Party, and the social revolutions of the 1970s, which included the adoption of legislation granting the rights to abortion and divorce. The church's original network of social service associations was augmented by the proliferation since the 1960s of an estimated 15,000 or more secular and religious organizations of volunteers operating on both the national and local levels in the fields of health and social welfare. Studies of what has come to be called *volontariato* (Rossi and Colozzi 1985) agree on at least three points:

1. The number of organizations and volunteers has increased considerably: 56 percent of the 7,024 groups studied in a national survey were founded between 1975 and 1983; about two-thirds were established between 1981 and 1991 (Censis 1991:376), although the rate of growth seems to be slowing. The number of volunteers has grown from 6.0 percent of the population aged eighteen to seventy-four at the beginning of the 1980s to 7.2 percent in 1989.
2. Over half (56.2 percent) of the local groups of volunteers were involved in some form of social service, as well as cultural and educational activities. Youth at risk and the handicapped were among the more frequent population groups identified as the concern of these voluntary associations (Censis 1991; Ranci, De Ambrogio, and Pasquinelli 1991).
3. The range of activities broadened during the eighties as new forms of volunteerism emerged, including an increase in counseling and advocacy activities.

These changes have accompanied an evolution in values underlying voluntary service: Traditional groups were based on the idea of a moral obligation toward the poor and the oppressed. Today's less paternalistic volunteers are motivated more by the ideal of a normative right to basic services. Traditional groups consisted mostly of middle-aged women, while the new organizations include young men and women as well as older working people. They have inherited many of the skills and informal networks created during the social movements of the 1970s that resulted in greater social awareness. According to Ranci (1992), many leaders of the new volunteerism honed their activist skills in the political and reform movements of that period.

Advocacy organizations and, to a lesser extent, self-help groups, have also grown over the last fifteen years. These groups organize around social issues ranging from hospital patients' rights to consumer advocacy, and the pressure they exert is often a potent force in local political processes. Studies show that this kind of organization expresses widespread popular dissatisfaction with traditional representative organizations such as political parties. They fill a participatory space left empty after the social conflicts of the 1970s (Turnaturi 1991; Noventa, Nava, and Oliva 1990).

Social solidarity cooperatives have also multiplied significantly in recent years (Barbetta and Ranci 1990), as a means of providing social services or work opportunities for nonmembers. An extensive survey found a total of about 570 cooperatives operating in 1986 (Borzaga 1991), although this was not an exhaustive inventory. About 40 percent of the 570 organizations employed 6,000 workers, providing services to 15,000 clients. In certain types of services, such as home care for the elderly or the handicapped, social solidarity cooperatives, as de facto nonprofit organizations, may be becoming the main service providers, though they continue to receive most of their funding from the state (Borzaga 1991).

The Italian welfare state, despite its resemblance to the rest of Western Europe, is strongly characterized by "clientelism"—the use of public funds to provide benefits to certain favored interest groups (Paci 1984; Ascoli 1987). This is part of a long-standing tradition of rewarding various constituencies with social policies that benefit only them (Ferrera 1984). While political patronage and corruption have been pervasive elements in Italian life, some have seen *volontariato* as a possible antidote. Others have even regarded such associations as "an alternative that could ease the state's financial burdens of service provision and also contribute to the building of a more autonomous civil society" (Perlmutter 1991:177). There is, however, relatively little evidence that such organizations could overcome the formidable inroads already made by the Italian political and economic systems.

The growth and development of the third sector has also been constrained by the failure to support many of the new policies born of the reform movements of the 1970s (Ascoli 1992), and the slowing or reversal of many of those modernizing trends. This includes a punitive 1990 law pertaining to drug addicts, the introduction of market elements into the state-dominated health system, and possible revision of the psychiatric reforms of 1978, which had been considered some of the most advanced in the world. This retrenchment occurred at a time when new social needs were emerging, brought on by the growth of impoverished North African and Eastern European immigrant communities in many areas of Italy.

By the 1990s the Italian version of the welfare state seemed, at least outwardly, similar to that of other advanced industrial countries, especially when compared with the conditions of the preceding decades. In 1988, total social expenditures were equal to 22.9 percent of GNP, two points less than the average of EEC countries (Eurostat Statistics 1989). At the same time, Italy also had the largest public debt of any of the European countries. In addition, it should be noted that Italy's expenditure masked the great disparities between the North, where services are comparable to those of Northern Europe, and the South, where even basic services are scarce or absent.

Italian Decentralization and the Third Sector

Italian government is characterized by great inertia at the central level and considerable vitality at the local level (O. Ranci 1989; Dente 1990). This favors services, including those of voluntary organizations, that are supported almost exclusively through the country's 8,000 municipalities. Although local governments have practically no independent revenue capability, they have nearly unlimited scope in their power to shape implementation. This tension between financial dependence and programmatic independence in local government is a major feature of national-local relationships in Italy.

The national level is a paradoxical combination of governmental instability (most governments have rarely lasted more than one year) and political immobility due to the continuing dominance of the Christian Democrats. The political system has become highly fragmented, with thirteen parties now represented in Parliament. In the 1992 election, the Christian Democrats, who have generally controlled 34 percent of the seats in Parliament, dropped to 28 percent, followed by the Communist Party which fell from 26 percent to 16 percent, with the Socialists receiving 14 percent. The Lega Lombarda, a new right-wing party seeking to vest most of the governmental power in the regions, received 9 percent of the vote, up from 1 percent in 1987. Against a backdrop of financial crisis, the central government has been unable to mount effective efforts to contain the growth of public expenditures. No party or coalition of parties has felt strong enough to pay the inevitable political price for unpopular budget-cutting decisions, or to deal with the notorious widespread evasion of taxes in Italy. As a result, the public debt reached a record of 101.3 percent of GNP in 1991 (Ascoli 1992). The legendary instability of Italian governments has worsened in recent years, and the general picture is that of a government reacting to crises but totally lacking in planning capabilities.

The public financial crisis, the persistent inefficiency of the state, and the failure of many reform projects of the 1970s have contributed to the belief in some quarters that voluntary organizations could even substitute for the state. Others see a continuing central role for government, but would encourage more planning and partnerships between public and voluntary agencies (Ascoli 1992; Balbo 1984).

However, representative bodies such as parties and trade unions have lost the mobilizing force they once had. Even the feminist and other major social movements of the seventies lack a strong following today. They have been supplemented by many locally based single-issue groups, less concerned with broad political and social reform than with offering social services and some advocacy. A recent study suggests that 18.9 percent of the population are involved in some type of voluntary collective activity, of which 7.2 percent are in the field of social welfare (IREF 1990), and over one-third of these volunteers serve the handicapped.

The growth in volunteerism has occurred despite Italy's lack of any broadly accepted definition of a nongovernmental social welfare sector. Even "nonprofit" has no legal status, nor does Italian law attach any importance to the "nondistribution constraint" used to distinguish such organizations in many countries. There has been no national registry of nonprofit organizations and there is no national legislation regulating nonprofit organizations as entities distinct from commercial firms, although Italian law does differentiate between organizations on the basis of their goals such as public, private commercial, and private noncommercial (Preite 1990; Barbetta and Ranci 1990; Borzaga 1991). *Fondazioni* and *associazoni* are the two main organizational forms among voluntary organizations, and similar to the pattern in Germany, they are distinguished mainly by their public, noncommercial purpose. There are some tax exemptions favoring social service organizations included in the corporate income tax structure, in value-added taxes, and in taxes on commercial income (Weisbrod 1991).

Representing the first legislative attempt to promote voluntarism in Italy, the Voluntary Action Act of August 11, 1991, adopted as National Law 266, pertains mainly to associations of volunteers with little or no paid staff, and specifies the way in which they may receive funds from regional and local governments. For example, public funds as grants or contracts will only be available to voluntary organizations that are registered. The Act also provides for the establishment of government-funded community centers to be run by voluntary organizations. In addition, to overcome the lack of information about voluntary organizations in Italy, a "National Observatory" is to be created for the support of research and training.

Reform legislation in 1990, Law 142, further spelled out the powers and obligations of local governments and recognized the existence of other providers of public services, specifying the conditions under which they may be used: "when there are technical, financial or socially expedient reasons for it" (art. 4). In addition, as a result of abuses of the contracting system, the new legislation grants authority to local governments to impose certain criteria on the management of public services when they are delegated.

Political discourse about the third sector, however, remains general and ideological. There is no coherent public policy at the national level regarding private social welfare agencies; instead, there are various experiments with state–third sector partnerships. In the absence of a central policy, local funding mechanisms for voluntary organizations tend to multiply and to fragment the financing and delivery of services. Most social policies and programs are compromised by the high degree of personal discretion with which such funding is given to organizations. Much depends on the personal goodwill of individual politicians and local bureaucratic chiefs. Political convenience is usually the most powerful factor in determining which programs receive public support. Funding of voluntary agencies has rarely related to substantive concerns such as cost-effectiveness, accountability, or service quality, although the new legisltion seeks to change this.

Funding Mechanisms

The main form of public funding of nongovernmental organizations serving the handicapped is either the payment of a daily fee for persons recognized as a public responsibility, or direct subsidy. In Lombardy, contracting has developed mainly in fields of service were there was no early tradition of support by local government, such as the treatment of drug addicts or the handicappd. Beginning in 1976, contracts or *convenzioni* were officially authorized by the regional government, although the rules regarding their utilization by local government are very general. In practice, there is little consistency in, or regulation of, governmental contracts for service delivery by voluntary or for-profit organizations. Each municipality can decide on its own how it will allocate its block grant for all governmental purposes; it is not required to fund specific social programs, or to secure strict accountability for delegated functions.

Contracting with voluntary organizations thus represents a pragmatic solution

Table 2.1

Expenditures of Municipalities in Lombardy for Services to the Handicapped, 1985–1988 (in thousands of lire)

	1985	1986	1987	1988
Total of municipal expenditures for the handicapped	42,033,911	48,083,937	53,403,820	60,040,826
Amount allocated to VNPOs for services to the handicapped	11,173,334	4,508,032	18,643,447	21,738,848
Percentage of total municipal expenditures for the handicapped	(26.6%)	(30.3%)	(34.9%)	(36.2%)

Source: Regione Lombardia, Department of Social Welfare, 1985–1988.

to various problems faced by public agencies. These include civil service restrictions on firing staff or even changing job descriptions, and statutory restrictions on increasing budgets or staff size. For example, a strong incentive for local governments to contract is a law enacted during the early 1980s stipulating that local governments may hire one new person only if four others are released!

The trend toward contracting for services is reflected in the data on public transfers. In the Lombardy municipalities, public funding of private organizations for the handicapped increased from 26.6 percent to 36.2 percent of total expenditures on services between 1985 and 1988, as shown in Table 2.1. In Milan the same funding rose from 21.8 percent to 25.2 percent of total expenditures between 1986 and 1987. In 1989, Milan spent nearly 5 billion lire in contracts for services to the handicapped, in addition to 100 million lire given directly to such organizations for their unrestricted use. The proportion of governmental income varies, of course, according to the particular field of service, ranging from 7 to 82 percent, as shown in Table 2.2.

Subsidies are not used widely in Lombardy, and are subject to rather strict regulations; in other regions they are the most important source of public funds for voluntary agencies.

The Case Study: Voluntary Organizations for the Handicapped

Twenty diverse Milan-based agencies for the handicapped were selected to represent four common types of nonprofits as shown in Table 2.3. The four types can be described as follows:

1. *Community care* includes organizations whose services are geographically decentralized and primarily social service–oriented.

Table 2.2

**Average Percentage of Sources of 1000 Income of
126 VNPOs in Milan, Six Fields of Service**

	Health care	Residential care/ hospitals	Advocacy	Scientific research	Mental handicap	Drug treatment
Government	11	82	13	7	17	59
Private donations	38	0	26	46	4	17
Clients	0	18	7	0	4	5
Internal sources	6	0	4	16	37	8
Members	45	0	50	31	38	11
Total	100	100	100	100	100	100

Source: Istituto per la Ricerca Sociale 1990:86.

2. *Institutional care* refers to agencies whose activities are housed in a shared complex of buildings, and which carry out a range of health and social services.
3. *Advocacy* includes agencies whose aims are to generate support for people with a specific disability.
4. *Sheltered workshops* (described earlier as social solidarity cooperatives) provide skills training and job placement services for the disabled.

The following are examples of each of these four types of agencies.

Community Care

Six community care organizations were included in this study, three of which are affiliated with national organizations. The average staff has twenty-nine paid employees and eight volunteers. The National Association of Families of Disabled Youth and Adults (ANFFAS), one of the few nationally affiliated organizations, is typical of the whole group of six. ANFFAS, which primarily serves mentally handicapped children and adults, was founded in the 1950s as part of a worldwide movement at the time, and the Milan branch was established in 1966. Today, ANFFAS has 12 branches in Milan Provincia alone, and 165 throughout Italy. Its members are parents of the handicapped, although its services are not restricted to members or their children.

ANFFAS participated in the cultural movements of the late 1970s, and in the rapid expansion of voluntary social services that followed, which was related to the policy of deinstitutionalization. In 1982, ANFFAS in Milan had only 22

Table 2.3

Four Types of Voluntary Organizations in Lombardy

	Community care	Institutional care	Advocacy	Sheltered workshop cooperatives
	ANFFAS (*)	Don Gnocchi	ANMIC (*)	Sommozzatori
	AIAS (*)	Don Calabria	ENS (*)	della Terra
	Coop. Lotta	La Nostra	AISM (*)	Il Ponte
	Contro	Famiglia	UILDM (*)	Spazio Aperto
	l'Emarginazione	La Sacra	UIC (*)	Francis Today
	ENAIP (*)	Famiglia		
	Coop. Il Papiro	Istituto dei		
	Polisportiva	Ciechi		
	Milano			
Average number per organization of:				
Paid staff	29	338	3	18
Volunteers	8	45	14	2
Clients	127	389	320	25

(*) Local sections affiliated to national organizations.

full-time paid staff, but today, with 108 paid staff augmented by 30 volunteers, and 650 members, it is the largest community care organization in Italy. In 1984, ANFFAS had a budget of 1.9 billion lire, of which 86 percent was provided by public agencies. In 1988, the budget reached 4.2 billion lire (corrected for inflation of 27 percent since 1984), of which 93 percent were public funds.

ANFFAS serves 268 clients in Milan through eleven different types of programs; 175 of these clients receive services through contracts with public bodies. Outside Milan, ANFFAS conducts a professional training center for the handicapped under a 1986 contract with the Regione Lombardia. ANFFAS also provides leisure time and supportive services such as a library and a sports club.

Today ANFFAS is primarily engaged in developing innovative residential homes for the mentally handicapped. During 1981–1983 ANFFAS entered into contracts with the Municipality of Milan for four day care centers serving 105 handicapped children and for a fifteen-client residential home. More recently, ANFFAS received a contract to operate two apartment houses for the handicapped. In 1989 ANFFAS received 3.2 billion lire from the municipality just to operate these three programs.

Institutional Care

The residential care system for the handicapped is dominated by the two largest nongovernmental providers, who between them have about 83 percent of the total number of institutional beds (ISTAT 1990). They consist of the IPAB institutions, which care for 43 percent of the residents, and a group of nonprofit, voluntary organizations that serve 41 percent of the institutionalized population. About 9 percent of the residents are in institutions operated for profit. At least 85–90 percent of the income of residential care institutions is derived from public sources, mainly local government. The institutional sector is the only one in which rehabilitation services are offered on a significant scale.

Five organizations were analyzed in the institutional care category of this study, as listed in Table 2.3. The average number of paid staff is 338, augmented by forty-five volunteers. The oldest organization is Sacra Famiglia, founded in 1896. Except for one organization, the Istituto dei Ciechi, all are motivated by religious ideals of charity and were founded by priests. They are examples of a larger movement in which traditional Catholic relief agencies have maintained their ties with the church while developing more modern organizational structures.

The growth of the Don Gnocchi center, which doubled its staff and its budget between 1981 and 1992, provides a good example of this type of evolution. This institution was founded in Milan at the beginning of the 1960s to serve boys affected by polio, and to provide health care in a residential setting. The introduction of the polio vaccine reduced the number of polio cases, and the center began opening its doors to other types of handicaps, starting with birth defects. This new mission required many new services such as surgery, day care, and home assistance. It also required new cadres of professionals, including nurses and social workers. This growth in services has been accompanied by the establishment of centers for the study of multiple sclerosis and orthopedic injuries, physiotherapy training programs, basic research, and public education.

In addition to the process of goal succession similar to the Polio Foundation in the United States, Don Gnocchi exemplifies two seemingly contrary trends common to institutional care organizations. One is a move toward high technology, greater medical specialization, and the centralized administration this requires. The other is the attempt by centers to decentralize their programs and integrate them into their clients' communities. These efforts have resulted in a partial move away from the large, isolated, traditional institutional homes, and toward an integration of institutional care and community-based rehabilitation. In contrast to community care agencies, these organizations have lost most of their political drive and reform fervor in favor of a commitment to a high degree of professionalism.

In 1984, the total budget of Don Gnocchi was about 11 billion lire, of which 82 percent came from public sources. In 1988, the budget reached 18 billion lire with about the same proportion from public agencies. Nearly 90 percent of its income comes from statutory bodies in Lombardy where it has been designated as a Highly Specialized Regional Center for Health Services since 1976. Don Gnocchi also has contracts with the Municipality of Milan for two day care centers and for a residential home.

Don Gnocchi's pyramid-like governing structure is headed by a board of directors that meets monthly. It consists of only four persons not professionally engaged in the organization, and the board president is a priest. With one exception, board membership has remained constant since 1980. Under the board are three executive directors for the administrative, social, and health services who in turn supervise the heads of the individual programs. Don Gnocchi, with several departments each devoted to a specific rehabilitation service, has many of the organizational characteristics of a hospital.

The Don Gnocchi staff is unionized and governed by a collective bargaining agreement modeled on the one used in the public health sector. There have been recent conflicts between physiotherapists and nurses and the administration regarding salaries and labor organization. In this respect, large, complex residential centers like Don Gnocchi have much in common with other similar public and private institutions.

Advocacy Agencies

The advocacy agencies selected for this study include five Milan-based organizations that promote the interests of people with specific handicaps. All of them are part of a national association. Many such organizations depend on volunteers, though the degree of volunteer involvement varies greatly. The average number of paid employees is three, with fourteen volunteers.

The oldest of the advocacy organizations are for the deaf and the blind; one was founded in the middle of the nineteenth century, and others were established during the 1920s and 1930s. The work of these agencies is bolstered by particularly favorable legislative treatment, in contrast to the other types of voluntary organizations, which are only now being recognized in law. Because of their favored political status, these former para-governmental associations became private organizations in 1977, although they always had a high degree of autonomy.

ANMIC (Agency for the Physically Handicapped and Invalids) was founded in 1954 in Rome and the 6,000-member Milan branch was founded in the 1960s. It is staffed by eight paid persons and about ten volunteers and focuses primarily on counseling activities and some rehabilitation services as well. ANMIC's budget has been fairly stable, and there is little turnover in governing roles. The president of the Milan branch, a member of Parliament, has been in office for the past twelve years.

In contrast to the large, well-established agencies like ANMIC are far smaller, more informal volunteer-based groups such as AISM (Association for Multiple Sclerosis). AISM has only one paid staff member, about twenty-five volunteers, and 1,800 members in Milan. It provides counseling, leisure-time activities, and home assistance. Its budget was 12 million lire in 1984, and 98 million lire in 1988. It receives no funds from public bodies. There are at least twenty membership organizations of this type in Milan.

Sheltered Workshops

The four sheltered workshops included in this study consist exclusively of cooperatives, the oldest of which was founded in 1978. They have an average of eighteen paid staff and two volunteers each. They provide vocational training and job placement for their disabled clients, with a staff–client ratio of one to one. All four began as voluntary agencies and are strongly rooted in their respective communities. Many of their founders have come from political or union backgrounds. One organization, for example, was set up by former employees of a mental hospital in Milan, to serve the noninstitutionalized mentally ill. Launched in 1983, it now has a budget of 670 million lire, employs thirty-five persons (five part-time), half of whom are handicapped, and uses no volunteers. It focuses on gardening activities carried out under contract with rural municipalities.

Internal Organizational Changes

This section summarizes the major findings regarding the changes in the structures of the organizations, their governance, and interorganizational relationships.

Structural developments

Three types of structural changes were found: (1) diversification of activities accompanied by increased professionalization; (2) increased specialization of services, particularly those related to health; and (3) decentralization of local service units through the proliferation of local branches.

Beginning in the 1980s, many nonprofit organizations underwent a period of expansion: as noted earlier, Don Gnocchi nearly doubled in staff since 1981; ANFFAS had 32 staff in 1982, 108 in 1989; Sacra Famiglia had 815 in 1984 and 980 in 1989. Changes in organizational structures accompanied these rapid increases in their size, but, at the same time, the use of volunteers has decreased in recent years. Only eleven of the twenty organizations now use volunteers, and they play a leading role in only three agencies—AISM, UILDM, and Polisportiva Milano. As the number of paid staff increased, the role of volunteers was limited to serving mainly as assistants to the professionals, and volunteers became less essential in their own right.

At least ten of the twenty agencies underwent significant bureaucratization as they expanded—ten had personnel manuals, and five hired a management consultant to recommend ways of dealing with structural problems. This trend was not found among the advocacy organizations at all, and in the residential care sector only ANFFAS and AIAS exhibited these structural changes. On the whole, however, all but the advocacy associations are now complex organizations that little resemble their origins as traditional "charitable associations."

For example, Sacra Famiglia, a highly centralized organization, has been managed for five years by a president who is also a priest, a five-member board of directors consisting of persons not professionally involved in the organization, and an executive committee of six, plus the heads of the departments. The board of directors has remained the same, but its role has devolved to ratifying the decisions of the executive committee. There is an administrative department for each of the three sections of the organization—administrative, health, and social—and a new unit was constituted to coordinate activities among them.

The sheltered workshops, by contrast, have adopted relatively nonbureaucratic modes of organization. The Cooperativa Lotta Contro l'Emarginazione, for example, was founded by a priest who is still the chief executive. The executive committee consists of the original four members plus three others. There are now three committees—training, job placement, and relations with public bodies. While maintaining organizational stability, it has expanded significantly. From 150 worker–members in 1983 and an executive committee of four people, it now has more than 200 members. Two new apartment houses for the handicapped were founded in 1986–1987, and a leisure-time activity program was also initiated.

Professionalization and increased autonomy are the other major trends among these organizations. Almost all of them, especially those providing residential care, now conduct their own staff training programs, which have been thoroughly incorporated into their ongoing activities. Some have even started their own professional schools, such as Nostra Famiglia's school for therapists and social workers, and Sacra Familglia's school for professional nurses and health/social workers. Sacra Famiglia also publishes a journal of research conducted by its professional staff members.

Governance

The twenty organizations exhibited a wide range of governing structures. Cooperatives must have, by law, an assembly of members responsible for most administrative decisions, while policymaking is vested in a small board of directors. Eight of the twenty organizations are affiliated with a national body, and these local branches vary between informal structures dominated by a few members, and more traditionally structured associations where power is often concentrated in the president of the local branch. Typically, these affiliated organizations have an annual meeting of their general assembly. They also have a board of directors that is represented at their regional- and national-level governing bodies as well. Local branches are usually quite independent of the parent national organization. This is partly because many local leaders have regional or national authority as well. The national administration usually focuses on long-range planning, strategic decisions, and nonlocal programs such as conferences and training activities.

There is an increasing tendency for boards of directors simply to ratify Executive Committee decisions, particularly in large, hierarchical organizations such as Sacra Famiglia, where most of the board members come from outside the organization. The opposite condition is found in the sheltered workshop cooperatives, where the boards have great influence in setting policy.

Based on the assumption that staff members' familiarity with day-to-day operations raises the quality of the board's decisions, board members are often staff members too, in sharp contrast to the practice in Britain and the United States, where this is proscribed. In the sheltered workshops, all board members are in fact key staff members. In residential care, however, board members are never part of the staff. Community care and advocacy agencies have a combination of staff and nonstaff board members, with major participation by the handicapped and their parents.

Boards of directors average seven members, meet six to ten times a year, and have a high rate of turnover. Presidents of the organizations we studied stayed in office for an average of seven years and as long as thirteen years. In only four cases were there formal limits to the length of time a person can serve on the board.

Only eleven of the twenty organizations had Executive Committees distinct from the board. The Executive Committees are generally composed of professionals employed by the organization. The average membership is nine, with a minimum of three and a maximum of fifteen members. Only three of the eleven Executive Committees had women members.

The participation of handicapped people in governing bodies is found mainly in organizations that are affiliated with national associations. On average, they constitute half the board membership of such agencies. In the workshops where employment of the disabled is a major goal, clients are a major part of the administrative staff. Disabled clients also constitute between 40 percent and 90 percent of the membership of the advocacy groups where they are prominently represented in the governing bodies. They are a much smaller part of the community care associations, ranging from 10 percent to 20 percent. The disabled do not participate at all in the governance or membership of the institutional care organizations.

Interorganizational Relations

There is growing competition for public funding among advocacy organizations, but in spite of this, the exchange of information and collaboration between these membership organizations has grown rapidly in recent years and matches the high level of cooperation exhibited by the agencies offering direct services. A national conference promoted by ANFFAS in December 1989 was supported by organizations such as Sacra Famiglia, which would formerly have seen itself in a different class from ANFFAS. Another consortium, "Dopo di noi . . . ," involves both community and residential care organizations on a pragmatic basis.

With a membership of more than thirty-five organizations, the Milan-based LEDHA (the League for the Rights of the Disabled) is probably the best-known national umbrella organization for the handicapped. It carries out advocacy activities, along with a free legal counseling service. It successfully promoted a regional law on architectural barriers, and it also formed a coalition with other social service agencies that influenced the legislation to encourage the employment of disabled people.

These new coalitions have increased the political power of voluntary associations (Ranci 1992). Because of their concentration of influence, they can often gain support for their proposals from local authorities who would not accede to the demands of an organization acting alone. This newfound power was proven at a 1990 conference in Milan in which local authorities, bending to the combined pressure of an alliance of voluntary organizations, agreed to the establishment of new residential homes for the disabled.

The increase in interorganizational communication is due largely to a lessening of ideological and religious conflicts, for while these differences still exist, they are less pronounced than in the past.

Funding and Income

Thirteen of the twenty organizations analyzed in this study have contracts with government bodies. These contracts typically stipulate the obligations of the voluntary agencies regarding types of services to be provided, work plans, guarantees of continuity of service, and some provision for in-service training. Accountability requirements are usually restricted to periodic reports about the activities funded. Payment is generally calculated on a fixed per capita daily charge, and funds are released following a review of quarterly or yearly reports. Contract negotiations are conducted by local civil servants, with the final decisions reserved for the relevant local politicians.

Projects are selected for contracting by two separate criteria—pragmatism and "clientelism." An example of pragmatism is the innovative service of apartments for the handicapped, which are managed by private nonprofit agencies and funded by the municipality. This is mainly because public agencies find it difficult and expensive to operate such homes directly due to their need for twenty-four-hour staffing. In Milan there are now four such *comunità,* where three to five disabled people live with resident social workers and educators.

Political clientelism is illustrated by the way contract funds are distributed for home assistance to the handicapped in Milan. According to one public official, decisions regarding which cooperatives would be funded for the expansion of these services were designed to conform to the political orientations represented by the cooperatives competing for contracts. This is not unusual because partisan political criteria are used in virtually all decision making, particularly in allocating public funds.

Table 2.4

Average Organizational 1988 Income (in U.S. Dollars)

	Community care	Institutional care	Advocacy	Sheltered workshops	Mean
From government	$797,997	$13,097,770	$11,732	$239,400	$3,419,757
From clients	5,126	243,933	1,578	122,135	88,221
From private contributions	36,872	1,254,609	15,475	7,133	312,625
From commercial activities	6,075	496,045	10,304	8,137	122,593
No. of organizations	6	5	5	4	—

Table 2.5

Average Percentage of Sources of 1988 Income of Twenty VNPOs in Milan

	Community care	Institutional care	Advocacy	Sheltered workshops
Government	94	87	30	63
Clients	1	2	4	32
Private contributions	4	8	40	2
Commercial activities	1	3	26	3
No. of organizations	6	5	5	4

Dependence on public funding varies by budget size and organizational structure. The larger the agency, the more important public funding. In the eight largest agencies, government funding in 1988 was 86 percent, while in the other twelve it averaged only 36 percent. Smaller agencies rely more on donations, membership fees, and commercial activities. On average, public sources account for 87 percent of the study agencies' budgets (see Tables 2.4 and 2.5).

Public sources cover 94 percent of total income in the community care sector, but only 30 percent in the advocacy area, which relies more on private contributions from both the general public and members. The sheltered workshops sub-sector depends primarily on revenue from sale of its products and services. Table 2.6 displays inflation-adjusted income between 1984 and 1988.

Income from commercial activities has decreased since 1984, while in just

Table 2.6

Percentage of Variation in Real Income of Twenty VNPOs in Milan, 1984–1988

	Community care	Institutional care	Advocacy	Sheltered workshops	Mean
From government	+71.6	+35.3	+162.0	+98.0	+40.1
From clients	—	+165.0	+194.3	+27.6	+99.3
From private contributions	−58.3	+67.8	+14.8	—	+49.2
From commercial activities	−70.5	−65.6	+61.1	+392.1	−64.8
No. of organizations	6	5	5	4	—

four years public sources have grown by 40 percent. Private donations increased by 49 percent and income from clients nearly doubled. Most of the increase in client income derived from charges for services, particularly health services. In spite of the major increases, these charges remain at very low, "politically acceptable" levels.

Organizational Autonomy

An important finding of this study is that financial dependence does not mean organizational dependence, even in those cases where public funding accounts for a high proportion of the total income. Local organizations enjoy great autonomy, and no contract has ever been canceled. On the other hand, this does not mean that there is an absence of concern about the uncertainty of future funding, cash flow delays, and other typical problems associated with contracting.

Rarely do funding agencies assume a "watchdog" role in the sense suggested by DeHoog (1984). Indeed, several respondents expressed the wish for more involvement of the public agencies in their work! The Italian local government culture is, however, dominated by the idea of a minimal, formal fulfillment of functions ("I do my duty and you do yours"), and therefore, it is difficult to initiate meaningful monitoring and evaluation. This applies not only to delegated services, but also to the capacity of government to monitor the efficiency of its own activities. As a result, there is a facade of formal control confined to conventional activities such as analysis of annual reports prepared by the agencies under contract. In the few instances when public agencies do engage in active monitoring, it is limited to the managing of single cases, and not organizational performance.

The degree of agency autonomy varies according to the length of the funding relationship. The longer the history of funding, the less likely is it to be terminated and the greater the autonomy enjoyed by the recipient agency. Paradoxically, the closer the links between funder and recipient, the more dependent the funder becomes on the work of the recipient organization. This is particularly true among institutional care organizations, since they have the closest ties to local government.

Conclusions

The social services portion of the Italian third sector is undergoing a transformation toward more differentiated and professionalized organizational structures. Relationships with government are still at an early stage of development, but this study suggests that the future will see voluntary, nonprofit organizations assume greater importance in the social services delivery system, accompanied by further institutionalization of these relationships with government.

Although professionalization is a leading trend, there are many agencies, especially the advocacy organizations, that exhibit only a very moderate degree of professionalization while maintaining an element of informality. Although there is a strong trend toward more secular and pragmatic organization, the influence of the church has not been totally eclipsed. Indeed, priests or nuns are deeply involved in 61 percent of Italian social welfare organizations (Rossi and Colozzi 1985).

Professionalization, specialization, and departmentalization have contributed to these organizations becoming more complex and bureaucratic, although the smaller ones still maintain some of their more informal characteristics.

The case studies confirm the broader trends in voluntary-governmental cooperative relationships described earlier. Italian voluntary organizations depend heavily on public resources (87 percent of total cohort revenue), yet state controls are minimal and voluntary organizations are highly autonomous. The Italian style of privatization includes a preference for large organizations and the starting of new programs, rather than the transfer of programs from the public to the private sector.

Contracting out is, for local authorities, a necessity, not an ideological choice. Public agencies are pressured to expand and improve their services, but they lack the required resources and confront other constraints. The answer is frequently a process of incremental change made according to immediate need, but without a broad policy direction. A convergence of economic and political interests thus forms the basis of the Italian "contract state," which seems to be gradually evolving in an unplanned way.

3

The Netherlands:
Institutionalized Privatization

Introduction

In the Netherlands the general term used to denote the voluntary sector is *particulier initiatief,* or private initiative. The Dutch system differs from its counterparts in other countries in two principal ways. First, the functions of advocacy and service are rarely combined in one organization. Instead, advocacy is the province of diverse national organizations, typically small mutual-benefit associations staffed by member–volunteers and financed by donations, lottery income, and government subsidies. In contrast, services are provided by large, professionally managed local and regional service organizations, which are financed primarily by social and private insurance and, to a lesser extent, by fees from clients. The second noteworthy characteristic of the Dutch system is that the local and regional service organizations have a monopoly on the delivery of almost all social services, with the exception of health care.

In this chapter, we begin by describing these distinctive features of the Dutch pattern and their historical roots. To understand the changes that have been taking place in the Netherlands since the mid-1970s, we then turn to an analysis of data we collected from twenty-eight advocacy and service organizations, nineteen of which are concerned with the disabled. We conclude with a look into the future of the voluntary sector in the Netherlands and in the welfare state.

Two Types of Organizations:
Advocacy and Service Provision

In the Netherlands, unlike England and Norway, only rarely does a nonprofit organization undertake both advocacy functions and service functions. Instead, advocacy—which includes lobbying the legislature, promoting and sponsoring scientific research, and organizing rallies and demonstrations—is conducted by national mutual-benefit associations. These advocacy organizations are few in number and small in size. Some have local branches, but most operate only one

Table 3.1

Characteristics of Two Types of Voluntary Organizations in the Netherlands

	Advocacy	Service
Size	Small	Large
Membership	Yes	No
Local/regional/national	National; sometimes local branches	Local/regional
Manpower	Member–volunteers; some office staff for support	Professionals/managers/ office staff
Income	Fund-raising secondary: central government subsidies	Social and private insurance + some fees from clients or local government

national office, which is run by member–volunteers supported by a small full-time secretarial staff. If they engage in service delivery at all, it is usually to provide small-scale, supplementary, or pilot-project services for their own members or target group. (The only membership group in our survey to provide large-scale service delivery is the AVO association, which works on behalf of the disabled.) More typically, when an advocacy organization wants to see existing services expanded or new services established, it arranges for an existing or new service organization to fill the need.

Compared to the advocacy organizations, the service organizations are both more numerous and much larger in size and budget. Local or regional in scope, the service organizations are professionally managed agencies responsible to their boards of directors. They do not have members, and their use of volunteers tends to be minimal and restricted to marginal tasks (van Daal 1990). All social services and all services to the handicapped are provided by these local and regional service organizations. The service organizations' monopoly on service delivery extends to all fields except health care—where most doctors, dentists, and physiotherapists operate in private practice.

Table 3.1 summarizes the major structural differences between the advocacy and service organizations. Figures 3.1 and 3.2 illustrate the differences in budget and staff.

Two Systems for Service Delivery

Within the service-delivery sector, there are two wholly different systems of regulation, control, and financing. All basic personal services (health care, mental health, home help services) and residential and social care services for the handicapped are provided under a national insurance-based system. Community-oriented social and cultural services (including day care, libraries, and general

Figure 3.1. **Average Budget Size of Advocacy and Service Organizations in the Netherlands** (in DFL*)

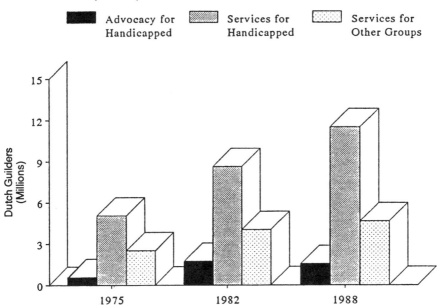

*DFL = Dutch guilders; one guilder is approximately U.S. $0.50.

social work) are financed and controlled by local governments. Let us look more closely at each system.

The basic personal services are organized through a nationally regulated, controlled, and financed system. The central government promulgates the policies and regulations, local service organizations design and implement the programs, and most of the financing is provided by social insurance. The premiums for this insurance are deducted directly from workers' paychecks. Private insurance is used only to cover primary health care (doctors' fees and hospital bills) for the elderly and for people whose earnings exceed a specified threshold (currently, about U.S. $30,000 a year). Day-to-day management of services is left to the health insurance organizations, but the national government regulates the cost of insurance premiums and requires both social and commercial insurers to provide certain levels of coverage. The national government also regulates hospital budgets, the incomes of family physicians and specialists, and the kinds of treatment and services that are available.

In all areas, the system stresses cost-effectiveness and accountability. For example:

• Services are divided into three echelons (general, specialized ambulatory, and institutional) and care is provided at the least expensive level that is appropriate.

Figure 3.2. **Average Number of Paid Staff in Advocacy and Service Organizations**

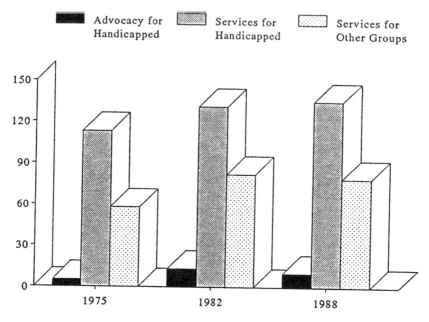

- Regional service areas are monitored for capacity, and service providers negotiate their annual budgets based on capacity and use (rather than fees for treatment).
- General multifunction service providers are promoted over specialized care providers.

Under a decentralization policy implemented in the early 1990s, the national government gives local governments block grants to spend as they see fit on community-oriented social and cultural services. Because this policy is relatively new, it is unclear how the municipal administration of these services will develop, especially in the four largest urban centers, which are experiencing budget deficits. Most municipalities have thus far tried to maintain services, though some are working to transfer the financing of services to the national insurance system.

Historical Origins

To understand why advocacy and service provision are handled by different organizations and how the service organizations attained their monopoly on service provision, we must look to Dutch history, to the unique interrelations among the people, organized religion, and the government. Above all, three sociopolitical traditions played crucial roles in the development of the Dutch pattern of service delivery: egalitarianism, the absence of a powerful central state, and religious pluralism.

According to Schama (1987), the Netherlands was the first European country to achieve some success in preventing the concentration of wealth and power among a hereditary elite. In the late sixteenth century, the Netherlands established itself as a republic with an egalitarian ideal; by contrast, in England, France, and other countries on the continent, wealth and power were concentrated in the royal house and among the nobility.

Having liberated themselves from the rule of the Spanish crown, the Dutch maintained reservations about establishing a strong centralized state. Until the end of the eighteenth century, the country was really a loose federation of towns and provinces. When the country moved toward creating a large central government, it was on the principle that the government was to support and follow developments in society, not to impose its will on the people.

By the turn of the nineteenth century, the Netherlands, no longer an officially Calvinistic (Dutch Reformed) country, had become a refuge for people who were being persecuted elsewhere for their religious beliefs and political ideas. This influx and the schisms among various Protestant churches created in the Netherlands a kaleidoscope of religions and sects. Despite the prevailing tolerance of religious pluralism, strict separations were maintained among different churches. In the belief that social and health problems had religious implications and could therefore be treated only by helpers of the same religion, each church created its own network of organizations to provide essential services and care for its members (James 1982). This system was known as *verzuiling,* based on the Dutch word for a pillar or column, *zuil,* and is usually referred to in English as "pillarization" (see Kramer 1981:19–24).

Within this sociopolitical landscape, the Dutch developed two key concepts by which, until recently, the voluntary sector was structured. Under the *subsidiarity* principle, government was to be subordinate to private initiative in the provision of social goods and services. Only if private initiative had clearly failed to meet a specific need could government intervene.

Pillarization, the second concept, held that a citizen's educational, social welfare, and health needs should be met by providers from the same religious background. Pillarization reached its height in the 1920s, at which time nearly all nongovernmental nonprofit organizations were organized along parallel denominational lines (Jolles 1988). At that time, the churches were responsible for financing these services (which, we must add, were far fewer and far less expensive than the services provided today). Because the churches, with the exception of the Catholic Church, had no centralized power structure, control over social services was in the hands of local parishes and congregations.

Subsidiarity and pillarization dovetailed neatly to create a system of neighborhood-based services provided by the private sector. This system tended to preclude government involvement in service delivery and to obviate the need for national programs. When there was a concern to undertake advocacy functions, new organizations were established, since the service organizations, nearly all of which were local, did not want to take on national campaigns that would distract them from servicing their clients.

Beginning in the 1930s, however, the demand for social services accelerated and neither the churches nor the nonreligious charities could afford to operate the needed programs. At this point the government became involved in financing, but not administering, social services. For primary health care, the mixed system of social health insurance and private insurance was introduced. The national and local governments offered subsidies for social and mental health services, including many services for the handicapped, while residential and home help services were funded through individual welfare benefits.

This transfer of financial responsibility from the private sector to the public sector was not based on any comprehensive master plan. It was accomplished gradually, over several decades, through a piecemeal process. By the 1960s, the funding from churches had dwindled to nominal dimensions, and the Dutch network of voluntary service organizations was almost wholly dependent on public moneys in the form of taxes and social insurance premiums. Nonetheless, pillarization and nominal church control of the service system appeared intact. And despite the fact that the public was paying the bills, the government, the churches, and the service organizations maintained the fiction of subsidiarity. The government, it was claimed, was simply following what was happening in the private voluntary sector.

The Disintegration of Subsidiarity and Pillarization

Toward the close of the 1960s it had become clear that pillarization was a lost cause. Secularization (*ontzuiling,* or "depillarization") was proceeding rapidly, and many churches and churchgoers had ceased to believe that clients and service providers needed to be of the same religious faith. Most of the social service and health care organizations abandoned their denominational ties, though some retained their original names, and they began serving clients of all faiths. Only a small minority of orthodox Protestant churches continued to operate organizations that served their members exclusively.

Adopting a professional approach or a client/consumer orientation, the service providers realigned themselves along rational organizational principles. As a result, many small specialized organizations merged into large general organizations bound by an ecumenical inspiration or without any religious orientation.

The collapse of pillarization coincided with unprecedented increases in the cost of providing social services. In the so-called Policy Bottlenecks Paper, Beugels and Peper, two senior consultants to the minister of social services, explained how fragmentation, duplication, and under- and overcapacity were needlessly driving up costs (CRM 1974; Kramer 1981:33–35). They urged the government to abandon any lingering allegiance to subsidiarity and to restructure and rationalize the service-delivery system.

The subsequent reforms retained the principle that services should be financed through social insurance and delivered by the voluntary sector. Debates over centralization versus local control resulted in a compromise. The central government took responsibility for the more expensive personal services, and local governments were given responsibility for the less expensive community-oriented services. For political reasons, however, general social work was placed under local control. Though many of those involved in forging the compromise regret this decision, several efforts to change it have proved unsuccessful.

Case Study of a Cohort of Dutch Voluntary Organizations

Following up on an earlier study of Dutch voluntary organizations that work on behalf of the handicapped (Kronjee 1976; Kramer 1981), we obtained data from nineteen organizations, of which eight are national advocacy groups and eleven are local service providers. In addition, we obtained data from nine service organizations that work with populations other than the handicapped. The three sub-samples are listed in Table 3.2. Here we describe the major changes that have taken place since the earlier study.

Budgets and Sources of Income

In recent years the Dutch service organizations have realized very little real growth in their budgets, about 4 percent annually, and there are indications that this rate is decreasing. In contrast, the comparable budgets in Britain have been increasing at about 12 percent a year, and in Norway at about 28 percent annually. The explanation is that much of the increase in those countries represents a privatization of service provision, the transfer of responsibility from government-operated services to funding voluntary nonprofit organizations in the hope of ultimately reducing costs. In the Netherlands, as we have seen, no move toward privatization is possible since services have always been provided by private initiative.

Since 1975, and especially since 1988, service organizations in the Netherlands have experienced dramatic shifts in the sources of their funding as shown in Figures 3.3 and 3.4. The comparatively high level of national government funding for service organizations that work with the handicapped reflects large allocations from the Ministry of Education to finance schools for disabled children. In all other cases, costs have been shifted from the national government to the social insurance system or, under decentralization, to local governments.

The financial picture for the advocacy organizations is rather troubling. The largest portion of their budgets, by far, comes from private donations, which dropped slightly between 1982 and 1988 and have remained roughly level since

text continues on page 77

Table 3.2

Income and Number of Staff of Three Types of Dutch Organizations, 1975–1988

Organization	Income in Dutch guilders × 1,000			Number of paid staff		
	1975	1982	1988	1975	1982	1988
I. Advocacy organizations for the handicapped						
ANIB, Association of the Disabled	505	559	656	14	20	14
AVO, Association for the Integration of the Handicapped	2,635	3,683	3,825	n.a.	30	27
BNMO, Association of Military War Victims	234	3,235	2,089	2	28	19
BOSK, Association for Brain Damaged Children	223	251	411	3	4	4
GON, Dutch Organization of the Handicapped	117	133	120	2	2	2
Multiple Sclerosis Organization	158	989	730	1	1	4
Association for the Blind and Visually Impaired	454	588	673	6	10	10
Muscular Diseases Association	141	610	727	4	6	10
II. Service organizations for the handicapped						
Amman, Education for the Deaf, Rotterdam	7,900	8,751	10,262	200	200	220
Amstelrade, Sheltered Housing for the Physically Handicapped, Amstelveen	5,000	5,538	6,495	110	110	110
AVO-werkplaats, Sheltered Workshop, The Hague	4,608	5,738	5,498	25	19	19
BNMO Centrum, Social Care for Veterans	n.a.	n.a.	3,277	n.a.	n.a.	45
EFFATHA, Residential Care and Education for the Deaf, Voorburg	4,100	9,729	15,100	n.a.	275	300
Tytyl Centrum, Day Care, Treatment and Education for Multiple Handicapped Children, The Hague	2,281	2,815	3,668	82	82	82
Hartekamp, Day Care and Residential Care for the Mentally Handicapped, Haarlem	16,185	18,594	22,551	330	366	431

SMDG, Social Work Services for the Mentally Handicapped and Their Parents	558	506	751	17	11	12
Ellemare, Day Care, Treatment and Education for Multiple Handicapped Children	800	738	876	20	20	19
Christofoor, Residential Care and Social Work Services for the Mentally Handicapped and Their Parents	3,482	3,790	5,154	n.a.	100	100
Van der Woudenstichting, Day Care and Residential Care for the Mentally Handicapped, Delft	5,563	7,174	8,517	119	130	150
III. Service organizations for other groups						
Centrum Buitenlanders, Social Services for Migrant Workers, Alphen a/d Rijn	832	1,160	619	16	16	8
Dienstencentra Bejaarden, Coordinated Services for the Elderly, Haarlem	1,285	1,241	1,700	n.a.	21	18
FIOM, Social Services for Problems Related to Pregnancy, Motherhood, and Adoption, The Hague	140	488	299	3	15	6
Catholic Home Help Services, Dordrecht	2,215	3,068	3,523	75	150	150
Home Help and Social Services, Brielle	3,561	4,599	7,006	160	229	237
Social Services, Breda	n.a.	3,241	2,441	n.a.	70	65
Community Organization, The Hague	3,654	3,234	3,113	22	56	55
RIAGG, Community Mental Health Clinic, Haarlem	5,833	6,173	5,802	77	82	80
COK, Day Care Centers for Children, Leiden	n.a.	n.a.	2,598	—	—	100

* To correct for inflation, all amounts have been converted to 1975 guilders.

Figure 3.3. **Organizational Income from Public Sources for Services for the Handicapped** (in DFL*)

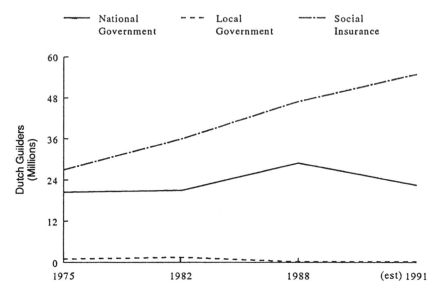

*DFL = Dutch guilders; one guilder is approximately U.S. $0.50.

Figure 3.4. **Income from Public Sources of Organizations Serving Non-Handicapped** (in DFL*)

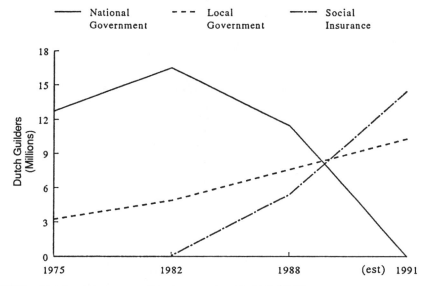

*DFL = Dutch guilders; one guilder is approximately U.S. $0.50.

Figure 3.5. **Income Sources of Advocacy Organizations** (in DFL*)

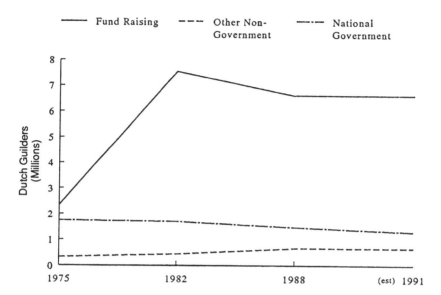

*DFL = Dutch guilders; one guilder is approximately U.S. $0.50.

then (see Figure 3.5). National government funding, already quite modest, has also declined, and this trend is expected to continue as the government pursues its policy of reducing subsidies. Although high interest rates in the 1980s boosted the value of the organizations' income from stock and real property as in England, these gains did not offset the downturn in annual income.

Structural Changes

The government's policy of repealing regulations that were thought to constrain innovation and initiative among service providers led to the abolition of various formal regulatory structures. At the same time, the spiraling costs of services, the growing demand for services, and the inefficiency of the network of nearly autonomous service providers prompted the government to undertake efforts to modernize the system by imposing more strict, uniform regulations in the personal services sector. Local governments also began to implement their powers to regulate community-oriented services.

Even as deregulation spawned a countertrend of reregulation, the move toward centralization, which began after pillarization collapsed, has also been met with trends toward decentralization. At first, particularly in rural areas, formerly pillarized service organizations merged into larger units. (Six of the service organizations in our sample were the result of such mergers.) The next trend was to concentrate services—for example, community mental health services—into one large multifunctional unit. But then the government restructured services, and some organizations reconstituted themselves to conform to the new categories. For example, when the government defined ambulatory services and residential services for the mentally handicapped as two distinct categories, the affected social work organizations split in two.

Splits or spin-offs also occur when advocacy organizations decide to provide services; for example, the BNMO service center for disabled veterans operates independently of the BNMO association, which restricts itself to advocacy work on behalf of disabled veterans. Finally, in the larger cities, service organizations have responded to the local governments' preference for decentralizing services at the neighborhood level.

All these developments have caused some major restructuring. A noteworthy example is the reshuffling of ambulatory mental health services. In 1965, a typical Dutch city of 100,000 inhabitants would have had as many as five different service systems: aftercare for adults recently discharged from psychiatric hospitals, aftercare for recently discharged youths, child guidance, marriage counseling, and psychotherapy. Each service was provided by each of three or four religious groups, which meant that as many as twenty organizations, each with one or two professional staff members, were providing ambulatory mental health care. By 1980 this system had been replaced by one organization that provided all services for the 250,000 residents of the city, a neighboring city, and the surrounding countryside.

A second example concerns two organizations in our sample—SMDG and Christofoor—which provide a wide range of institutional educational services for mentally handicapped children and their parents. When pillarization ended, these organizations lost their religious character and merged with compatible local organizations that had been established by other churches. Under echelonization, these two organizations' former tasks of providing residential care and sheltered housing were reassigned to other organizations, and under regionalization their service areas were changed. Today they operate as near-monopolies in their newer, though smaller, service areas.

Governance

In the Netherlands all voluntary organizations and other private nonprofit organizations are governed by boards that have between five and twenty-five members. The advocacy organizations (which are constituted as associations) elect their boards at a general membership meeting. The boards of the service organizations (which are constituted as agencies that do not have members) are selected either by the board itself or by outside civic or religious organizations.

Nonetheless, six of the advocacy organizations in our sample have adopted the policy of drawing at least some of their board members from outside the organization's membership rolls. Their motive for doing so is to improve management and policymaking by installing expert, or quality, boards.

A similar trend is found among the service organizations, with quality boards gradually replacing boards recruited from patrician families (so-called *regenten* boards). Experiments with representative boards, which first became popular in the 1960s and 1970s, have been mixed. Although community, staff, and client representation enhance an organization's relations with these constituencies, most service organizations report that the representative boards suffer from indecisiveness.

Typically, the boards address major issues in a broad, strategic manner, leaving daily operations to the organizations' professional management. Focusing on the mission and survival of their organizations, boards discuss such topics as the organization's relations with members, clients, and major social institutions (government, political parties, churches); the organization's tasks, structure, and staffing needs; and financial affairs, including subsidies, fund-raising, and accountability. The trend toward smaller boards has led to the gradual disappearance of the so-called daily board, or Executive Committee, although many organizations appoint board committees to work on specific tasks or policy issues.

Membership

As noted earlier, only the advocacy organizations have members. Among the advocacy organizations in our sample, membership increased by about 23 percent between 1975 and 1982 but then decreased by about 5 percent between 1982 and 1988. Our data also suggest that the more specialized advocacy organizations (e.g., multiple sclerosis and muscular dystrophy) are gaining members, while the more broadly chartered advocacy organizations are less successful in attracting new members.

Among these members, only a small fraction are active as volunteers. ("Always the same small group of people," one board member sighed.) In the local branches, volunteers perform all of an organization's tasks. But at the national headquarters, many of the tasks have become too complicated and demanding to be assigned to lay volunteers. Instead, these duties are handled by volunteer professionals (many of whom began as volunteers and then acquired the necessary professional skills). In several organizations, professionals who were living on disability pensions performed professional services as volunteers.

Professionalization is also marginalizing the volunteer forces in some service organizations where volunteers are asked to provide transportation and perform maintenance chores, minor repairs, and gardening. Other service organizations, particularly those that serve the frail elderly, rely on volunteers to provide direct service to the clients. One organization serving blind people, however, banned volunteers from providing direct services because service provision required too much professional skill. Overall, the trend is toward working with fewer volunteers, although trainees and interns are used in large numbers. For the moment, unemployed human services professionals constitute a special class of volunteers. This practice, however, is frowned upon by many who fear that it will tempt government and insurance organizations to replace paid staff with volunteers.

Several service organizations complained that it has become more difficult to recruit volunteers. Some cited the movement of women into the paid work force and the ever-increasing competition among organizations needing volunteers; others blamed the difficulty on society's materialistic ethos. Yet two organizations said that the general increase in leisure time had facilitated efforts to recruit volunteers.

In general, the lay volunteers come from the upper lower class and the lower middle class. Their level of education is most often in the low to medium range, although two organizations that train and educate their volunteers reported higher levels. The majority of volunteers in organizations serving the elderly were over sixty-five; in other organizations, most volunteers were between the ages of thirty and forty.

Paid Staff

As noted earlier, the advocacy organizations have only small paid staffs. For the organizations in our sample, changes in staff size tended to mirror changes in annual budgets and membership. Staffing at the advocacy organizations whose missions were broader tended to grow between 1975 and 1982 but then to level off or contract between 1982 and 1988 (see Table 3.2). Just as the more specialized advocacy organizations tended to be more successful than the more general advocacy groups in attracting members, so too the former outpaced the latter in staffing increases. The staffing decline for the BNMO, which specializes in helping disabled veterans, reflects the spin-off of the BNMO center. A truer picture of the BNMO's growth results from combining the size of the two staffs.

Among the service organizations, staffs tended to increase between 1975 and 1982 and then to level off between 1982 and 1988. Over the entire period, however, staff sizes did not increase as fast as budgets did. Our data indicate that the explanation is not that service organizations were allocating a larger portion of their budgets for other items but that they were hiring better-qualified, and therefore more highly paid, personnel. Organizations serving the handicapped also faced considerable increases in the cost of equipment and residential facilities. The decrease in staff at the AVO sheltered workshop resulted from tighter budget controls, and the decrease at SMDG in staff serving the mentally handicapped was the outcome of the major reshuffling mentioned earlier.

Noteworthy as well is the increase between 1975 and 1982 in staffing at organizations providing home help services, the demand for which grew at a fast pace throughout the nation. After 1982, the government's austere cost-control policy, however, curtailed growth in this sector.

Regarding the composition of their staffs, all organizations reported an increase in professionalization: either a greater proportion of their staffs were professionals, or training and qualifications requirements had been raised. In the larger service organizations, management had also become more professionalized. The old policy of promoting professionals within the organization into managerial positions was gradually yielding to a policy of hiring professional managers from outside the organization.

Administrative Climate

The service organizations all reported that their manner of operations as well as the character of relations between staff and supervisors were becoming increasingly democratic. This development reflects general trends in Dutch society as well as recent legislative requirements that compel larger organizations to establish organization councils. These councils, composed of staff and labor union representatives, must be informed of major policy developments, and their approval is needed for appointments to the board and for certain policy decisions that affect personnel.

A majority of organizations reported the introduction of modern management techniques, such as the clearer definition of the organization's structure, lines of communications, and position-by-position mandates and tasks. One result of these efforts has been the discarding of hierarchical decision-making structures and the adoption of the management team (general manager, unit managers, and heads of support departments) as the principal decision-making body. Many organizations also implemented a more sharply differentiated distinction between professional and managerial tasks.

A majority of organizations also mentioned efforts to decentralize day-to-day operations, giving executive departments more managerial independence and the freedom to develop operations policies within the organization's overall policy framework. It was not possible, however, to discern how much of this move toward a decentralized management style was real and how much was mere lip service. Many organizations observed that an informal climate and a loosening of rules and formalities led only to anarchy, unclear responsibilities, and the need to involve everyone in every minor decision. These organizations subsequently tended to reimpose new regulations and structures designed to reduce confusion and increase efficiency.

Power and Control

After pillarization diminished, control of the service organizations by the clergy yielded to professional domination. More recently, professional control is becoming subordinate to control by management and by outside forces, including the funders (Schnabel 1988).

The national advocacy organizations have remained more independent, although the government exerts its influence through its policies on subsidies. For example, the government can decide to subsidize only one organization for each mission or category of clients. By means of such regulations, various advocacy organizations representing the parents of disabled children were merged into one organization.

Changes in Programs and Services

Only a few organizations have suspended programs, most often because government-imposed restructuring transferred these services to other organizations.

Among those special-interest advocacy organizations whose budgets and staff increased (e.g., multiple sclerosis and muscular dystrophy groups), programs and services were also expanded and diversified. The BNMO association (for disabled veterans), the BOSK (for brain-damaged children and their parents), and the Association for the Blind also undertook new projects and tasks.

In addition to lobbying, various advocacy groups engaged in such activities as:

- providing information about their work to their clients, the general public, and students in the helping professions;
- adding new individual treatment and services (for example, distributing communication equipment to the visually impaired);
- organizing mutual-aid and self-help networks;
- establishing employment services for clients;
- inaugurating coordination centers for all efforts related to their mission.

Within the service organizations, consolidation of programs was a common theme. All the organizations were working to reinforce, enlarge, and differentiate their programs, and some were reconcentrating their efforts on their core programs.

Among the changes in basic philosophy, treatment approach, and methods, the most notable developments were:

- more flexible and less hierarchical procedures in the larger institutions;
- a shift from institutional-scale care toward care that approximated a family situation;
- the opening up of institutions through exchanges with local communities and through the removal of guarded gates and fences;
- the disappearance of religion as an important factor, with the exception of a few still-pillarized institutions;
- more special service approaches for certain groups of socially underprivileged clients;

- a reduction in polarizing approaches to community organization and an increase in efforts to mobilize all parties behind a cause;
- the abolition of classical psychoanalytic orientations and the adoption of treatment methods that focus on a patient's current situation, rather than on historical life events;
- an increased use of group work in treating veterans.

Interorganizational Relations

Advocacy organizations are always involved in some competition for funds and public support, however mild. In recent years this competition has become more intense, especially for the more general advocacy organizations.

The service organizations also reported increasing competition, but with a few exceptions, it appeared rather mild. Service organizations cited competition between the more general organizations and the more specific ones; between organizations that offer similar services (such as mental health clinics, psychiatric wards, and personal social work services); and between nonprofit and commercial day care centers. Because of the enormous shortage of day care centers, however, such competition is barely noticeable. Calls for the commercialization of services, however, could in the future prompt fierce competition throughout the social service sector.

All the organizations emphasized the importance of strong interorganizational relations, and each communicates with others in its environment in order to promote its own interests, to exert influence on behalf of members and clients, and to disseminate knowledge and information. Many service organizations belong to national umbrella groups that represent members in discussions with funders and other parties. Most service organizations also participate in local networks that promote the coordination of service provision.

Relationships with Government and
Social Insurance Organizations

The majority of advocacy organizations described their relations with government as antagonistic. In response to funding cutbacks, the organizations believed that they must remain extremely vigilant to ensure that the interests of their members do not suffer. Despite their watchdog posture, these advocacy organizations have developed friendly relations with the high-placed civil servants and politicians whom they seek to influence.

Relations between the service organizations and the government are becoming ever more ambivalent. While government financing and regulation have injected stability, coordination, and quality and accessibility standards into the system, the growing influence and intervention of government have provoked complaints and fears. The service organizations claim that the central government and the social insurance organizations are staffed by "stingy bureaucrats who have no sense of what is happening in the street." Local governments, the organizations complain, are unpredictable and are motivated by politics rather than by a strong grasp of human needs. Local politicians, they add, are more interested in devising quick fixes that they can point to during the next election than they are in deliberating on sound long-term public policy.

None of the service organizations was pleased with the financing system that had been introduced by the social insurance organizations and the national government and which was quickly copied by the municipalities. Their most frequent complaint was that the system would be too rigid to respond to real problems, too complicated to implement, and too inefficient, likely to produce both waste and shortages in services.

Recent Legislation

The welfare reform bill passed in 1986 was a so-called frame law, one that offered a system and procedures that were to be specified through later regulations regarding the level and quality of services. The government, however, failed to enact the specific regulations, and the bill remains an empty shell. In contrast, the social insurance for "Extraordinary Medical Expenses" (AWBZ) and the legislation authorizing the echelonization and regionalization of services have become very influential.

More recently, several laws have been enacted to require employers to take specific measures to increase the quality of the work force. One such measure requires employers to hire a certain percentage of disabled workers. Although both AVO organizations are pleased by the opportunities this legislation offers to disabled people, they fear that part of their work may be taken over by employers. Furthermore, they worry that they may lose their best disabled workers to other employers.

In other legislative matters, the legal acknowledgment and protection of the profession of psychotherapist gave an enormous boost to the community mental health clinics. The legalizing of abortion in the late 1970s, however, caused such a dramatic drop in the number of unmarried mothers that the FIOM, which provides services related to pregnancy, motherhood, and adoption, almost went out of business.

The Future of the Dutch Voluntary Nonprofit Sector

The fate of *particulier initiatief* depends largely on the outcome of the current intense debate over the so-called Plan Simons, a master plan proposed by, and named after, the Secretary of Health. The plan would give the insurance system greater freedom in running service delivery provided that the system met four criteria: low cost, solidarity (which means that richer citizens pay more for services than poorer citizens), universal access, and high quality. Under the plan, the government would limit its role to monitoring—to ensure that the criteria were being met—and to promoting and supporting research and innovation.

The first experiment in deregulating the insurance organizations, however, led to a dramatic rise (from 10 percent to 20 percent) in premiums for nearly all citizens and deficits for the insurers themselves. Needless to say, these results have slowed further implementation of the new plan.

Despite the current uncertainty, the advocacy organizations are likely to remain much like small membership associations. They will have greater difficulty, however, in meeting government criteria such as efficiency and accountability for subsidies and grants.

Under government demands to rationalize services, the service organizations that offer personal services financed by the insurance system may find themselves developing into service contractors, although their basic loyalty to clients and society will continue to distinguish them from profit-making organizations. These organizations are likely to be large, professionally staffed and managed, and financed principally by health insurance and social insurance. Such para-commercial organizations might well merge into national organizations, much on the British model.

The service organizations that offer community-oriented social and cultural services financed by local government might develop more or less in the same way, as contractors offering services to various municipalities. Already, some organizations of this type exist in the countryside and in suburban areas. In the big cities, however, the ruling neighborhood councils prefer to maintain close control over services. Within the cities, then, small voluntary organizations, not unlike those in the pillarized era, may persist.

Finally, it can be predicted that the demand for social services in the Netherlands will continue to increase faster than the availability of professional care. The aging of the population, medical advances in life-sustaining technology, and the ongoing AIDS epidemic all contribute to the need for more services. Most likely, a larger share of services will have to be provided by volunteers, a practice that is considerably underutilized in the Netherlands today.

Conclusions: Voluntary Organizations in the Welfare State

The welfare state is in crisis in many countries, including the Netherlands: it costs too much; it is inefficient; it is uncontrollable; services are of uneven or poor quality; there is too much bureaucracy. Given these complaints, some have argued that the cure for the welfare state lies with voluntary organizations, which are thought to be less bureaucratic, more flexible, more efficient, and more responsive to their clientele.

The Dutch example, however, casts doubt on the voluntary sector as a cure-all for the ailing welfare state. Despite the voluntary sector's near monopoly on service provision in the Netherlands, the nation is by some measures no better off than its neighbors. Indeed, the voluntary sector is so much a part of the Dutch welfare state that many of the problems inherent in state provision now pervade the voluntary sector. Though the organizations are chartered as independent private voluntary groups, they function as semigovernmental professional service providers. This is not to say that the voluntary sector has no solutions to offer in response to the problems of social service provision in the welfare state; rather, that nonprofit private initiative is not a panacea.

If we look at how services are provided in the Western welfare states, we see that each country has a mixed system containing some or all of the following elements: (1) government, (2) a network of professionals in private practice financed by government or a publicly regulated insurance system, (3) voluntary organizations financed in the same manner, (4) profit-making organizations financed in the same manner, and (5) informal networks of relatives, friends, and neighbors, sometimes partly paid by government or insurance. In the Netherlands, the third and second categories predominate in the health care system, supplemented by the fifth category. Up to now, this has been the preferred compromise and it has functioned relatively well in providing generally high standards of care for everyone. In the future, some aspects of the fourth category are likely to be added to the mix. Also, a number of control measures will be enacted to give government the means to intervene when private initiative fails to function adequately.

But what works in the Netherlands will not necessarily work in other countries, each of which has to arrive at a consensus on its values and priorities. Any decisions to shift responsibilities to the private nonprofit sector must be based on an analysis of a nation's particular situation, not on an unconditional belief in the virtues of voluntary organizations. For although voluntary organizations appear at first to offer a cost-effective, high-quality alternative to government inefficiency and bureaucracy, the larger the voluntary sector becomes, the more it is prone to suffer from the same problems that plague government provision of services. A laissez-faire approach seems doomed to fail: a large-scale private nonprofit social service system requires social controls.

A different approach has been recommended by Dutch and European neoconservatives, who claim that the problems of the welfare state can best be addressed by reliance on free-market mechanisms (Pierson 1991). If for-profit organizations were allowed a larger role in service provision, the neoconservatives argue, the ensuing competition would result in better service quality and lower costs. This thesis has yet to be tested, but it is significant that at present the best-functioning systems are found in countries where there is strong public involvement in care, either on the Scandinavian or the Dutch model. How would the welfare of citizens be ensured when the tendency of private corporations is to maximize profits at the expense of all other interests? Clearly, small-scale experiments need to be conducted and carefully evaluated to discover under what conditions specific services could be improved through commercial competition. One cannot simply proceed from the untested assumption that health care and social care can be effectively designed, marketed, and delivered in the same way as dishwasher detergents or personal computers.

4

Norway: Integrated Dependency

Introduction

As is typical in the Nordic welfare states, voluntary organizations have generally received little attention in Norway. Because the founding fathers of the Norwegian welfare state did not create an ideological space for voluntarism, as William Beveridge did in England, the role of voluntary organizations was almost totally neglected in political planning. In the years following World War II, public welfare provision was regarded as a victory over individual charity and the need for voluntary organization. Behind the expansion of public welfare, one can trace convictions about the necessity of rejecting conceptions of the "deserving poor" and individual guilt related to poverty, illness, and handicaps. There was no reason for a public policy toward a sector that would shrink in response to the expansion of the welfare state.

Also, among researchers the interest in volunteerism and voluntary services was almost nonexistent until the mid-1980s. The third sector concept was not introduced in the welfare debate until the late 1980s, when the welfare state was perceived as becoming a welfare society (Kuhnle and Selle 1992a). In contrast to other European countries, the Norwegian Left have never been advocates of the third or voluntary sector. Neither have the emerging self-help groups been perceived as different from the older voluntary organizations, as they have in the UK, Germany, and the United States. In spite of this political and ideological negligence, voluntary organizations as welfare providers have played an important historical role in the development of the welfare state.

The Historical Roots of Voluntarism

The first voluntary associations in Norway were founded around 1840. Two large temperance movements with local affiliates, originating in the 1820s, were gradually transformed to national organizations with more than 350 local affiliates in 1855, and almost 40,000 members (Raaum 1988). In the 1850s, a religious revival resulted in several new missionary organizations, and more than twenty others were established, nine of them after the turn of the century.

Organizations for the disabled also trace their roots back to the 1850s. The first school for the deaf and mute was established in 1848, and the first association for the blind in 1858. These first associations were organized in local communities mainly by persons who were not themselves handicapped (Onarheim 1990:77; Kuhnle and Selle 1992b). In 1865, the first consumer cooperatives were founded in Oslo, and by 1872, 276 consumer cooperatives were active.

Three sets of conditions can explain the appearance of this first generation of voluntary associations: (1) ideas imported from other European countries that influenced the temperance, missionary, and philanthropic organizations; (2) political changes beginning with the reform of the law in 1837 resulting in extensive autonomy for municipalities and more local political activity; (3) changes in the infrastructure of communication, with more newspapers and periodicals that stimulated debate and the formation of associations.

In the years after 1880, voluntary associations experienced a new period of growth. Between 1890 and 1900, the Norwegian Temperance Association *(Det Norske Totalavholdsselskap)* had a tenfold growth of members. In 1905, the total number of members of temperance organizations was estimated to consist of almost 10 percent of the population (Fuglum 1984).

Several large national philanthropic associations were also founded during this period. The Norwegian Medical Care Association for Women *(Norske Kvinners Sanitetsforening)* was founded in 1896, with the education of nurses for the army as its original function. In the years after World War I, several nursing schools were established by this association in the larger cities. After 1899, health work combating tuberculosis became the prime function. In the years after World War II, when tuberculosis almost disappeared, the association made infant welfare its primary task, and in 1970, the association operated 270 infant welfare clinics throughout Norway.

In contrast to the many movement-initiated voluntary organizations, the foundation of the National Association against Tuberculosis (1910) was initiated by the Association of Medical Practitioners. Established as an umbrella organization, the intention was to engage local voluntary associations in preventive health work (Erichsen 1960). In 1911, 117 associations and almost half of all local councils were registered as members. In 1954, the organization changed its purpose to preventive work and research for elderly people.

Between 1880 and 1940, national voluntary associations were engaged in all kinds of health and social work, mainly through institutions. Missionary organizations established a structure of educational institutions for youth, deacons and deaconesses, missionaries, teachers, and health personnel. In addition, sanatoria, rest homes, homes for the aged, hospitals, institutions for the mentally retarded, and work schools for the blind and visually impaired were established all over the country.

In Norway, more than two-thirds of the population of over four million are members of at least one organization. There has been a small downward trend for participation in humanitarian/social and religious organizations compared with the increase in sports and recreational associations, as well as in the organizations for the disabled and self-help groups. While the number of members in the largest voluntary associations decreased by 37 percent from 1974 to 1982, the number of full-time paid staff increased by about 56 percent (Kolberg 1984).

Relations between Public Authorities and Voluntary Associations

Public policy concerning organizations varies according to the sub-sector. Cultural, athletic, youth, and political organizations have mainly been funded since the 1970s through block grants. The amount of support has depended on their purpose, number of members, and democratic structure. The dominant political view has been that these organizations should be left alone; they should not be regarded as instruments of public policy, and public transfers should not be used to regulate their activities in any specific direction.

In the health and social services sub-sector, however, it has been more legitimate to regulate programs and services of the organizations. These institutions have been almost totally financed through public sources, and a comprehensive system of rules and regulations influences their performances. Public transfers to such institutions amounted to about NOK 2.8 billion in 1988, an amount approximately two times higher than state transfers for all other voluntary purposes (Dulsrud 1988).

It is difficult, however, to trace a clear policy behind the public use of private institutions, and the incremental increase in the funds that they have received from the government in the postwar period. During this period, the actual fiscal transfers were not political issues. However, after 1985, questions of privatization, including both the market and the voluntary sector, have increasingly been put on the political agenda. In 1984, questions of governmental approval of private, profit-making hospitals generated a strong political debate. In 1988, the first governmental report on voluntary organizations was published (Raaum 1988:17). In 1990, the nonsocialist government coalition adopted one proposal from this report, opening the door for a limited tax deduction for donations to national voluntary organizations (Gjems-Onstad 1990).

There has been a contrast in Norway between the ideological neglect of the voluntary sector and its actual performance in the welfare state. There is also no single explanation for the growth of voluntary services during the greatest expansion of the social-democratic welfare state. A possible reason may be that ideological resistance against voluntary solutions was strong on the national political level, while local politicians and bureaucrats have regarded the advantages of local initiatives and solutions more pragmatically.

Voluntary Services

The number of voluntary service providers has been considerable in selected fields. In 1989, 25 percent of all homes for elderly people were administered by private owners, and 70 percent of these were owned by voluntary associations. In day care centers for elderly people, voluntary organizations have been a dominating force. From 1968 to 1988, the number of centers increased from 50 to 265, and in 1988 about 50 percent of these were owned by voluntary associations.

In 1985, approximately 15,000 man-labor years were worked in "private" institutions (or about 15 percent of the public effort in the health and social sector). "Private" here includes institutions owned by voluntary organizations and a very small share of private owners, that is, 0.8 percent of all man-labor years (NOU 1988:17, 120).

Public Policies toward Voluntary Welfare Services

In the past, Norwegian governments never tried to formulate an explicit policy toward the welfare-providing voluntary organizations. Before 1940, a division of labor was evident between the municipality of Oslo and voluntary welfare providers, which were responsible for all homes for the aged, while nursing homes were the responsibility of the municipality.

In 1985 the Norwegian government provided about NOK 4.6 billion to voluntary and third sector organizations and their services, of which 60 percent was received by institutions in the health and social services. Funds were allocated according to three different main principles:

1. For *basic organizational support* in the form of block grants, mainly to cultural, youth, and sports organizations. Representing about 18 percent of the total, this support is given on the basis of the main goals of the organization, and with no specific obligations in return.
2. For specific *project support;* about 38 percent of the total funds were allocated for support of a project, mainly to voluntary organizations engaged in humanitarian and international work.
3. For *institutional care,* given by many third sector institutions, which constituted 44 percent of the total transferred to voluntary organizations in 1985.

The second and third types of fiscal transfers can be characterized as support for *services* initiated or managed by third sector organizations. Sometimes this is based on a contract that regulates the conditions for the public support. In some cases, such contracts are vague, with few conditions specified, giving a high degree of freedom to the voluntary organization. More often, the support is conditioned by some form of budget control whereby any surplus funds must be returned to the government at the end of the year. For the institutional services, various laws specify operating conditions such as the working hours, professional competence of the staff, room standards, living conditions, and so on.

Between 1985 and 1989, there was a considerable increase in the total state support to voluntary services. Altogether, transfers increased by 40.7 percent, or approximately NOK 800 million. Block grants increased by 50.6 percent, project support by 36.8 percent, and institutional support by 40 percent (NOU 1990:4, 16). In this period, voluntary organizations also experienced an increase in incomes from lotteries and games by 140 percent, or NOK 229 million (NOU 1990:4, 33).

A New Trend?

Beginning in the late 1980s, Scandinavian governments paid more attention to voluntary organizations. The first general presentation of the third sector in Norway appeared in a governmental committee report in 1988 describing the traditional, national organizations, but with most of the newer self-help and local groups omitted. Political statements from both the Labor and the non-Socialist parties in recent years have signaled a more positive attitude toward the voluntary sector. For example, in their political program for 1990–1993, the Labor government referred to voluntary organizations for the first time in a chapter entitled "The Contribution of Users and Organizations to the Solution of Common Tasks" (Grindheim and Selle 1990). In addition, in 1990 the government launched a separate program to establish and support ninety-five volunteer centers with NOK 30 million for a period of two years. This program can be seen as the first step in the formulation of a general policy toward the voluntary sector.

Development of the Voluntary Organizations
of the Disabled

Since the first decades of the nineteenth century, care for the disabled has been a divided responsibility with a mixture of primarily church sponsorship, and limited public support through poor laws and private philanthropy. As in most other European countries, the sensorial handicaps were first recognized and supported by the state. These same groups (the visually impaired, hard of hearing, and deaf) were also the first groups of disabled to found their own organizations in the last part of the nineteenth and at the beginning of the twentieth centuries. In 1921, parents of the mentally handicapped organized their own association.

This first generation of associations was locally initiated, and after some years they established national organizations. After the Second World War the trend changed: a national body was the first unit, and local affiliates were gradually established for people suffering from common diseases such as tuberculosis, diabetes, rheumatism, asthma, and psoriasis. Beginning in the late sixties, organizations serving smaller numbers of people affected by disabilities such as Parkinson's disease, osteogenesis imperfecta, and others were founded. The greatest growth in health and social service organizations, as well as in membership organizations of the disabled themselves, took place between 1966 and 1983 when thirty new member organizations were founded (Onarheim 1990:74).

There is a general trend away from broad, inclusive associations toward single-disease organizations, based on narrower diagnostic criteria, and composed mainly of the disabled themselves and their relatives. While people without disabilities can be members, the purpose of the first organizations was to enable the members to speak for themselves and to create a social network among themselves.

Although many large national organizations like the Red Cross, religious groups, housewives associations, and civic clubs have also established services for them, disabled persons have claimed their right to welfare state benefits and to be independent of volunteers and voluntary services. Gradually, the organizations of the disabled have emphasized their role as interest mediators and pressure groups at the expense of their provision of social services. This development, together with the generally strong position of welfare state services and benefits in the postwar period, is probably the main reason in Norway for the lack of "mixed" organizations—combining services and advocacy—which are found in other countries.

In Norway there are approximately fifty nationwide associations of the disabled, the majority of which are administered by volunteers, with no paid staff, and a relatively small number of members. Only twenty organizations have more than 1,000 members. Forty-one of these organizations are members of the Norwegian Federation of Handicap Organizations *(Funksjonshemmedes Fellesorganisasjon,* FFO), an umbrella organization for political pressure and interorganizational collaboration.

The organizations of the disabled have a total of more than 200,000 members. Six associations have more than 10,000 members, and five of these consist of members with heart-and-lung diseases, diabetes, asthma and allergic reactions, rheumatism, and psoriasis. The Norwegian Association of the Disabled, which organizes a heterogeneous group of physically disabled, also belongs in this group. During the 1980s, all of these organizations experienced a substantial increase in their size, and five of them more than doubled their membership. Only a few associations reported difficulties in recruiting new members, usually because of a stigma attached to a disease such as psoriasis.

The analysis that follows is based on information collected from a cohort of seventeen organizations of the disabled, all with 1,000 members or more.[1] Eight of these also operate a variety of hospitals, clinics, schools, and residential and other facilities in the community. There were three main sources of data: (1) interviews, using the same schedule as the other three countries, with the top administrator of the organization; in three of the large organizations, leaders of the labor union representing the employees were also interviewed; (2) documents provided by the national organizations and their local divisions such as annual reports and financial statements from 1982–1988; (3) background information obtained from informal discussions with staff and board members, newspaper and journal articles, and historical and other studies. The findings are summarized by: finances, administration, structure, governance, program, and interorganizational relations.

Fiscal Trends

The Norwegian voluntary organizations, like their counterparts in other countries, obtain their income from many different sources. Analysis of the financial accounts of seventeen national organizations showed the following six major sources of income:

- *Commercial income*, which includes all types of sales of products and publications;
- *Government income*, which includes all fiscal transfers from local or central governmental sources in the form of payments for care and other services to clients or patients, and block grants or earmarked funds for specific projects or programs;
- *Contributions*, including gifts, transfers from local organizations, general fund-raising income, and other donations from private sources;
- *Lotteries*, which includes income from the sale of tickets for lotteries conducted by the organization;
- *Fees*, for membership;
- *Rents/investments,* which includes income from interest, rents, and capital investments.
- *Other* is a residual category for unidentified income sources and income that does not fit into the above categories.

These six income sources can be reduced to three categories designated as state, market, and internal income sources. The *state* category includes government transfers; *market* encompasses lotteries, commercial activities, and rents/investments; while *internal* sources includes contributions and membership fees. These categories can be used to show major shifts in the sources of revenue of these voluntary organizations from 1982 to 1988, corrected for a rise in the consumer price index from 100 to 146. The relative importance of the different income sources for the cohort in 1982 and 1988 is shown in Figure 4.1.

For all organizations in 1982, government and internal income sources (contributions and membership fees) constitute approximately 86 percent of their total income, while income from market sources was 15 percent. Government grants and internal sources each contributed almost equal shares: government, the largest single source, was almost 42 percent, while funds from members, contributors, and internal fund-raising activities constituted approximately 44 percent of their income.

However, when divided by size of income into large and small organizations—using NOK 5 million income in 1988—this overall picture changes as shown in Figure 4.2.

In 1982, the income structure of the nine large organizations differed in several ways from the overall pattern as shown in Figure 4.1. They earned a slightly larger share (6 percent) of their income from government sources because of earmarked transfers for certain programs such as library services for the

Figure 4.1. **Income Sources of Seventeen Norwegian Organizations, 1982 and 1988** (average percentage)

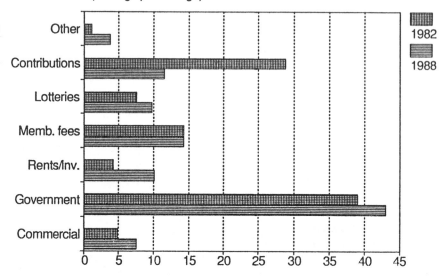

Figure 4.2. **Average Percentage of 1982 Income Sources by Organizational Size**

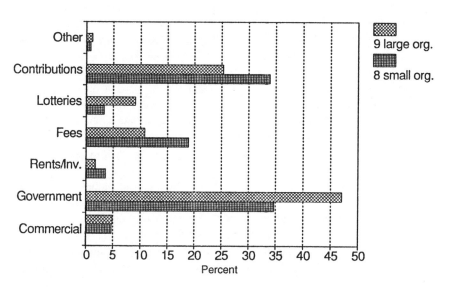

blind and partially sighted, and adult education. The large organizations also received a smaller share of their incomes from internal sources than the average (25.3 vs. 29.4 percent), while the market share was almost the same.

For the smaller organizations that may not have many service programs, block grants are the most common form of income. Also the small organizations showed an income structure that differed from the overall picture. These organizations received 53 percent of their incomes from internal sources and approximately one-third from government transfers. They were more dependent on internal sources than the large ones by 9 percentage points.

Thus, in 1982, internal sources and government transfers were the main income sources for all the organizations. Small organizations were more dependent upon members and supporters, while the major programs of the large organizations were mainly supported by governmental funds. For all organizations, *market incomes* (lotteries, commercial activities, and rents/fees) played a minor role—about 15 percent of the total income for all organizations, and with only small differences between the two groups.

Total income in 1988 for the cohort divided by size is shown in Figure 4.3.

While the share of government transfers is more or less the same as in 1982 for all organizations, the importance of internal sources dramatically decreased, from 44 percent in 1982 to 25 percent in 1988. During this period, market sources increased its share, from 14 percent in 1982 to 29 percent in 1988. Thus, organizational growth was supported by an increase in market sources and not from government transfers.

Again, organizational size is related to different trends. In the large organizations, the share of market incomes more than doubled: from 15.7 percent in 1982 to 39 percent in 1988. The share of state transfers decreased by approximately 9 percent (from 47 to 38 percent), and the share of internal sources decreased by 25 percent, from 36 percent to approximately 10 percent in 1988.

In the small organizations, the importance of market incomes was more or less unchanged: they increased their dependence on the state by 12 percentage points (from 35 to 47 percent) in 1988, and the importance of internal sources was reduced by 18 percent to 34.6 percent.

To summarize: The importance of market incomes (that is, incomes from sales, investments, and rents) increased dramatically between 1982 and 1988, while the government share was more or less the same, and the importance of internal sources decreased. This overall change is, however, essentially different when split into small and large organizations. The "market orientation" is found exclusively in the large organizations where half the income came from market sources in 1988. The small organizations increased the share of their income from state sources to almost half of the total amount.[2]

However, these data do not tell us anything about the changes in total amounts from the different sources. The increase in percent from 1982 to 1988 for all organizations is shown in Figure 4.4.

Figure 4.3. **Average Percentage of 1988 Income Sources by Organizational Size**

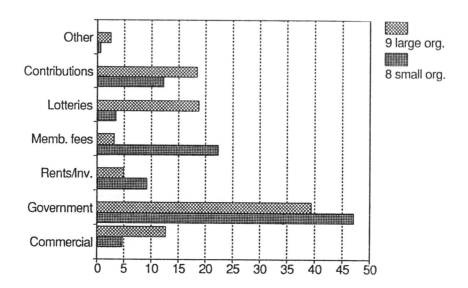

Figure 4.4. **Percentage of Change in Income Sources, 1982–1988**

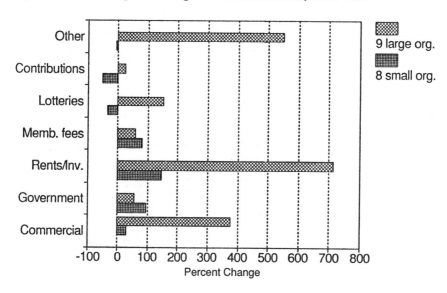

In large organizations, income from commercial sources increased by approximately 360 percent. Transfers from government increased by 54 percent, while lotteries increased by almost 150 percent. Again, the small organizations show a different development. Their revenue from lotteries and contributions showed a real decrease. Government transfers increased by approximately 90 percent, while rents/investments increased by about 140 percent.

Figure 4.4 also confirms that the large organizations have expanded mainly by means of market incomes. Incomes from rents/investments have increased by more than 700 percent, commercial activities by approximately 380 percent, while lottery incomes have increased by approximately 150 percent. Government transfer contributions show a real decrease of about 55 percent.

Figure 4.4 shows that the expansion of activities in these organizations has occurred by means of two different revenue sources: mainly through increased market incomes for large organizations, and through government transfers for small organizations.

Seven out of the eighteen organizations also reported some reductions in their income from central government, while five received some increases. It is significant that all organizations stated that there were no disadvantages in receiving funds from central or local authorities. This unambiguous attitude probably has two main reasons: Even when governmental grants are earmarked for specific purposes, the public authorities rarely make any attempt to control the use of the funds. Although many voluntary services are regulated through general laws and specific regulations, these means are not perceived as "mechanisms of control." Also, several organizations regard public support as a more stable source of income than lotteries and gifts. These positive attitudes may also be the result of the lack of political controversy about such governmental transfers.

Administration

In the organizations studied, all but two of the secretariats are run by paid staff. The substitution of volunteers by paid staff has been a general trend during the last fifteen years, and there is no reason to believe that this pattern has been reversed. All but two of the organizations have expanded their secretariats during the last decade, and three major associations have more than doubled their number of employees.

The secretariats differ greatly in numbers of employees. Three organizations each have between 65 and 118 employees in the national administration. Six organizations have from 9 to 15 employees, and 11 have from 1 person on part-time to 5 employees. Of the 41 members of the Norwegian Federation of Handicap Organizations (FFO), 22 associations have either no paid staff or very few. In only 4 organizations are there staff members who are disabled.

The administrative leader of the secretariat is called the general secretary or "daily leader," the latter term being used in the smaller organizations; the elected leader of the board is the chairman. This function is mostly the same within all the organizations, but differs between the associations of disabled and the largest humanitarian organizations, where the elected leader is usually called the president. Within the cohort of organizations, ten of the general secretaries have been in leading positions for more than seven years, some of them since the founding of the organization.

The shift from voluntary help to paid staff has had significant consequences for the structure of the secretariat, whereby it has become more professionalized and departmentalized. Use of volunteers in the secretariat is almost nonexistent; virtually all personnel are paid, and they have an educational background relevant for the job. Most of the secretariats, particularly those with five or more employees, have staff members with university degrees. In the Association of Heart and Lung Diseases and the Association of the Disabled, about one-third of the employees have a degree from a university or advanced college. At the same time, most of the staff have to be "generalists," and their jobs are broadly and loosely defined.

The three largest organizations, each with more than sixty-five employees in the secretariat, all have been structured into departments for fund-raising, education, housing, social policy, and information. Within each department there is a hierarchical structure of authority and a division of labor. Viewed from the outside, this departmentalization presents an image of professional and bureaucratized enterprise. The representatives of the unions stated that the administrators of the different departments often were reduced to "professional assistants" who had been delegated the responsibility of implementing the plans of the general secretary, but with few opportunities to use their own competence. The employees often regarded the operational goals of their organization as too abstract, and the administrative methods ineffective. Despite the departmentalization and a more professional staff, the administrative leader was often perceived as seeking to control the details, and thereby undermining the authority of the heads of the departments.

All the organizations had written statements about their governing bodies, organizational structure, and the purposes of the organizations. The bylaws and other prescriptive documents describe the formal organizational structure and emphasize the official goals of the organization. On the level of services, most of the organizations have a low degree of formalization, except for those providing various forms of residential care where there has been a trend to regulate nongovernmental institutions that are financed by the national government.

Only six organizations had formalized pay scales and a written manual of personnel policies. Even in these organizations, neglect of the manual by the administration was rather common. Documents from the unions revealed that disagreements between the administrative leaders and the employees' representatives frequently referred to ignorance of written statements, lack of training programs for the employees, and inadequate personnel policies in general. In the majority of organizations without union representatives and with no staff representatives on the board, the general secretary was the official spokesman of both the board and the staff. His task was to try to reconcile different views and interests. In referring to his double role, one general secretary stated: "The members of the board are not familiar with the role of the employer." Most of the general secretaries interviewed acknowledged that their personnel policy had severe deficiencies. "Personnel policy has not been given much attention," was one common statement. Another general secretary said, "I don't know if it is correct to call what we practice here a personnel policy."

All the organizations had local affiliates in the counties (provinces) or in the municipalities, which are said to be "rather autonomous." The transfer of funds from the central to the local level of the organization is in most cases very limited. The affiliates have their own budgets, mainly based on membership fees, local lotteries, and limited support from local authorities. In most organizations, the local, self-governing affiliates have a high degree of autonomy regarding the right to use their own funds in the development of service programs. In some organizations, however, local affiliates had to transfer a portion of their income to the national level, thereby reducing their own resources. For example, when the Association of Heart and Lung Disease was building its own clinic for open heart surgery, the local affiliates were told that larger projects in the local community should first be approved by central administration.

In the largest organizations, paid staff at the county level mediated between the local and central levels of the organization, but this linkage was missing in the smaller organizations that had only volunteers. Generally speaking, the relations between the central and local levels in these organizations were quite loose, but not particularly problematic.

Structural Changes

During the last decade, the organizations studied have emphasized the role of their local affiliates as political pressure groups. Perhaps the main reason for this is the general change in the financial relations between state and municipalities that took place in Norway in the early 1980s. This reform has made it possible to allocate block grants for different sectors of the municipality. One intention of this decentralization was to obtain greater flexibility in the distribution of local resources in accordance with local needs.

For organizations of the disabled, this reform had enormous consequences. While previously they could exert pressure on one or a few government departments, they now had to promote the interests of their members in more than 400 municipalities. This change also affected the role of their umbrella organization, FFO, which was established to influence the central authorities. As a result, many organizations with few members at the national level are today more or less invisible in the municipalities. The trend toward single-disease organizations is now counterbalanced by another pattern of more cooperation between organizations at the local level in order to be strong enough to be heard by local authorities. So far, only a few national organizations have succeeded in developing an effective local organizational network; only four organizations have more than 200 local affiliates and only eight have county affiliates in every, or almost every, county.

In spite of the decentralization of public administration, it is still within the central secretariats of the organizations that there has been growth during the last decade in number of employees and tasks undertaken. Locally, both client services and pressure-group activities are rather limited. The social function of the local affiliates, including peer group support, is still one of their most significant aspects. In the future, it is expected that there will be more activities directed toward local politicians in an effort to improve the conditions of the disabled in the community.

It is, however, in the county and local affiliates where volunteers do ordinary administrative and organizational work. Seven organizations have paid staff in their county offices, but only three have employees in all counties. In local municipality-based units, paid staff is very rare. There is usually a big gap between the availability of paid staff and the growth of local affiliates.

To maintain local activities, most of the local affiliates depend on volunteers, who are difficult to recruit, but who are needed to deliver the rather limited local social services to clients. In addition, many members of these organizations have disabilities that sap their energy and this weakens the stability of the local associations. All of the informants stated that if the county and local branches were to develop their services, paid staff would be a necessity.

While data about local participation is limited, the annual reports from county and local affiliates reveal that their major activities mainly involve:

- attending board meetings and preparing for meetings of members;
- arranging open meetings attended by medical staff and/or politicians;
- planning and participating in seminars and courses offered by the county office or the secretariat;
- providing information services to newcomers among both the members and the client group (hospital and home visits);
- providing general information about the organization in the community;
- fund-raising.

Governance

In addition to the national level, all associations are active on the county and/or municipal level, with more or less autonomous affiliates. If the organizations have affiliates only on the county level, this is either due to limited numbers of clients or because the organization is newly established. In most organizations, the county level exercises no formal authority over local branches. Local affiliates have their own general assemblies in the form of annual meetings.

The governing structure on the national level is, however, quite complex and includes the following components:

All national organizations hold an annual meeting or a General Assembly, which meets every second or third year. In either case, it is a delegate body, usually elected by the county or local affiliates, and it has final authority on all policy matters, bylaws, and financial affairs. In between the meetings of the General Assembly, an elected Committee of Representatives meets several times in the course of the year to prepare the budget and to implement the decisions of the larger body. In addition, a board of directors of the national organization is elected by the General Assembly, often with members from different regions of the country. The board has executive authority, financial responsibility, and can adopt certain types of policies.

Large organizations may also have a small Working or Administrative Committee consisting of the chairman of the board, the general secretary, and the head of the administrative staff. They meet every month, before the board meeting or at the request of the administrative leader/chairman. Their principal function is to prepare the agenda for the board meetings and to implement certain decisions. In reality, these small committees have sufficient authority to exercise most of the executive power of the national organization.

The top administrators are called either general secretaries (GS) or just "daily leaders." The different terms reflect the size of the organizations and their formal authority. All but two of the organizations use the term "GS." In the larger organizations, the GS have often held their positions for many years, and they tend to be the dominant influence on policy, having usually been appointed from within the organization. In only one major organization is there a requirement that the general secretary and the administrative leadership be recruited from the client group alone.

The general secretaries perceived themselves as having a very strong influence on policymaking by their boards and committees, but they did not regard this as problematic. Only in some of the smallest and most recently established organizations were the "daily leaders" clearly subordinated to the board. While there may be disagreements among the levels of an organization, there are, according to the majority of the general secretaries, few differences between the administration and the board. The GS and the deputy leader of the administration meet with all of the formal governing bodies, but without the right to vote.

In general, the national boards are rather small, consisting of 5 to 13 representatives, with the majority having between 5 and 7 members on the board. Women constitute 41 percent of the representatives. In all but two organizations, the handicapped themselves have between 80 and 100 percent of the places on the board. In only two organizations are the disabled a minority, but the others are either parents, spouses, or other close relatives. Professional medical staff or other professional groups are represented on only a few association boards.

Institutions belonging to these national organizations often have their own boards where professionals are frequently represented. The chairmen are normally recruited from the central organization, often being the general secretary, the deputy secretary, or the chairman of the associations. The average age of the board representatives is estimated to be lower than the average age of the rank-and-file members, and they come from the different regions of the country. The frequency of board meetings varies greatly; only seven organizations have regular monthly meetings of their boards. Only a few organizations have made any important change in their governance structure, mainly in reducing its size in an effort to be more efficient and to reduce expenses.

Social Service Programs

Eight of the national organizations of the disabled operate various types of institutions that are almost completely financed by governmental funds. These include hospitals, clinics, schools, guide-dog schools, and residential homes for the handicapped; in some fields, voluntary organizations are the sole providers. About 50 percent of the hospitals and recreation centers for persons with cerebral palsy are owned by the Association of Cerebral Palsy, while most of the other organizations operate only one facility for their patients. Historically, the traditional humanitarian organizations together with some of the organizations of the handicapped have dominated the field of residential care for the physically handicapped. The Norwegian Association of the Disabled still owns a few residential homes, but these are destined to be taken over by public authorities.

A few organizations, such as the associations for Heart and Lung Disease, the Hard of Hearing, and the Deaf also operate educational programs and schools that are financed by the state through the Law on Private Schools. With the exception of the Association of the Disabled, none of the other organizations wants the public authorities to take over the formal responsibility for their institutions. One typical response was: "As long as we own the institutions ourselves, we know that the service still exists."

The voluntary organizations have developed only a very limited program of services in the local community, usually some type of a day center that serves mainly a social purpose for the elderly. Also, some visiting services are offered both to private homes and to hospitals. Most local organizations also sponsor special activities such as holiday trips and recreational activities.

Figure 4.5 is based on a study of activities of local affiliates of organizations of the disabled in the city of Bergen and shows the percentage of total expenditures for different purposes such as transportation, excursions, public information about various diseases, and medical assistance.

The organizations also sponsor two forms of advocacy—one that seeks to influence the policies and practices of the public authorities, and another that helps individuals find their way through the governmental bureaucracies. The latter type of advocacy includes the collection and dissemination of information

Figure 4.5. **Types of Expenditures of Twenty-four Organizations of the Disabled in Bergen, 1984**

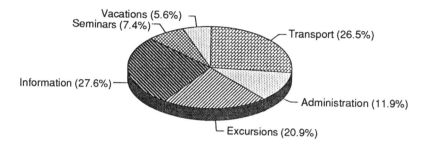

on resources, technical assistance, and advice. While everyone regards these functions as very important, the quantity and quality of advocacy is difficult to ascertain, and it may be that the individual members may benefit more from their participation in the activities of the organization.

A few of the organizations also sponsor sheltered workshops, which in Norway are organized as private limited companies. Only the Association of the Blind is an important shareholder, owning 50 percent of the shares of a sheltered workshop for the blind. Two-thirds of the costs of these facilities are paid by the central government, but the facilities themselves are operated by the municipalities.

Interorganizational Relations

The Federation of Handicap Organizations (FFO) is an umbrella organization of the organizations of the disabled in Norway, and is comparable to the "peak" associations in the Netherlands. FFO traces its roots back to the year 1950 when five organizations representing disabled persons in Norway joined to form the National Committee of Organizations Representing the Occupationally Disadvantaged. This initial cooperation evolved into more permanent meetings with a secretariat circulating among the member organizations. In 1974 the organization changed its name to FFO, and in 1975 it established a permanent secretariat. Since 1980, the number of member organizations has more than doubled.

Today, FFO is a coalition of more than forty interest groups on the national level for the disabled and their relatives. Resolutions passed by FFO organs are, however, not binding on the individual member organizations. FFO's primary goal is to promote social equality for the disabled, and to establish its right to be recognized as the legitimate representative of the disabled. FFO also offers its member organizations technical assistance in organizational development, including their contacts with media and local and national authorities, and it tries to help member organizations coordinate their activities.

FFO also initiates research to document the life conditions of the disabled, and in 1983, it launched a separate research program, financed by the central government, to produce data that could be used by its member organizations for their own advocacy efforts for the disabled.

FFO requires that each of its member organizations be founded on democratic principles, providing members with equal opportunities to influence the decisions of the organization. FFO also functions as a forum for debate among its more than forty member organizations.

The governance bodies of FFO are similar to those of other national organizations described earlier: the annual general meeting, the representative committee and the working committee, and a permanent secretariat. There is a general meeting every other year, with each member organization entitled to three representatives, and a working committee of seven, assisted by a staff of twelve employees, based in Oslo. As an umbrella organization, FFO's finances depend upon membership fees, state support, and direct contributions from individuals and other organizations. Unlike its member organizations, FFO is not allowed to sponsor lotteries and other money-raising activities. During the last ten to fifteen years, government funds have been the principal support for FFO general operations and special projects. In 1979 the general support from the government amounted to approximately NOK 700,000 or 91 percent of its total income. By 1988, this support had increased to NOK 2.2 million, which represented only 52 percent of the total income. Although general support almost tripled in this period (in nominal kroner), it was the earmarked support that had the largest increase. In 1988, FFO received a total of NOK 3.8 million in block grants, of which NOK 1.6 million were distributed to member organizations.

As part of a response to the decentralization of some governmental functions, FFO established sixty local and six provincial (county) affiliates, which seek to develop more cooperation between the member organizations and the municipal and state authorities. Cooperation between the organizations and public authorities is most often informal, but important formal bodies include the government-appointed advisory councils for the elderly and the disabled: the National Council for the Elderly and the National Council for the Disabled (*Eldrerådet og Råd for Funksjonshemmede*), both of which have a secretariat with a board consisting of representatives from central government and the voluntary organizations.

The FFO and the National Council for the Elderly are by agreement entitled to meet with the social minister and/or ministers from other relevant departments before the annual regulation of pensions. The purpose is to give pensioners and disabled persons an opportunity to influence decisions regarding regulation of pensions and other matters of special interest to them. Another coordinating unit is a large body of thirty-eight organizations called the Coordinating Board for Health Education (*Samarbeidsrådet for Helseopplysning*).

A large component of the interorganizational network is informal and therefore difficult to map. For example, some of the largest organizations have a
network to discuss their relationship to the "new voluntarism," which is being
considered in government circles. Since member organizations of the FFO are
highly specialized in their focus on specific client groups, the sharing of goals is
more ideological than operational. Similarly, the service-providing role of the
organizations is either very modest, or directed toward specific client groups.
Consequently, the coordinating role of FFO is of necessity quite limited in a
context where there seems to be relatively little interdependence among its member organizations. Although cooperation is limited, FFO member organizations
seem to experience a feeling of belonging to part of a larger structure. At the
same time, there is considerable competition among the organizations' lotteries,
as each strives to expand its share of a market that includes the government.

Conclusions

While voluntary organizations have historically been integrated into what has
become the Norwegian welfare state, relatively little attention was given to their
role until the 1980s. Probably influenced by similar developments in Western
Europe, all of the political parties made favorable statements about the special
contributions that nongovernmental organizations could make to the society.
These organizations are still not perceived as part of a sector, even as an intermediary one, partly because they lack the necessary infrastructure to exert any
significant influence on broad social policy. This is not the case in particular
sub-sectors, such as in services for the disabled where there is considerable
governmental support and recognition of both their service provision and advocacy functions.

In contrast to other countries such as Britain, where the government increasingly views voluntary organizations as partners for contracting out public services, in Norway this idea has not been favorably regarded, partly because it is
viewed as inconsistent with the responsibilities of a social democratic state. The
small number of voluntary agencies interested in and capable of functioning as
contractors, as well as the opposition of some unions, are also factors.

The Norwegian answer to the idea of privatization has been the launching of
several programs to modernize the public sector through more decentralization,
introducing some principles of marketing in governmental agencies, and improving the quality of public administration by recruiting leadership from outside.
Another approach has been the adoption of a three-year program to establish and
evaluate ninety-five volunteer centers throughout the country, with about one-
third each divided among municipalities, churches, and voluntary organizations.
Their purposes are not only to mobilize volunteers, but also to act as clearing-
houses and to coordinate client-centered activities in the community.

This is perhaps the first sign of an explicit policy by the social democratic regime to strengthen some forms of voluntarism. This action, however, poses a fundamental question: can the values of the market and of voluntarism be reconciled with the basic ideals of the Norwegian welfare state? Seemingly, there are conflicts between: the policy of using taxes for redistribution purposes by the state and the encouragement of charitable giving; the ideals of justice, equity, and assistance as a right, and the discretionary character of services by voluntary agencies; the science-based knowledge of welfare state professionals and the experience-based knowledge of many community and self-help groups; and the presumed value-neutrality of public services and the value-based programs of voluntary associations. The future character of the Norwegian and other welfare states will be influenced by the ways in which these issues are resolved.

Notes

1. The sample does not include several large national organizations that provide services for the disabled at the local level, such as humanitarian organizations like the Red Cross, the Norwegian National Health Organization, the Women's Public Health Association, the Norwegian People's Relief Association *(Norges Røde Kors, Nasjonalforeningen for Folkehelsen, Norske Kvinners Sanitetsforening,* and *Norsk Folkehjelp),* and others. These organizations pioneered institutional-based care, and they still own many institutions for mental retardation, cerebral palsy, and rheumatism. Local branches of these organizations also provide some visiting services, transportation, and day care centers. These more generic organizations differ from the cohort in this study because service to the disabled is not their main purpose, nor do they have an advocacy function.

2. Some of these changes are related to the establishment of three new state lotteries after 1986. Several organizations complained that these lotteries took away their customers and they demanded a share of the lottery incomes of the state. In 1987, the government compensated this estimated loss of incomes by a grant of NOK 3 million. The issue of losses was also considered by a public committee, which concluded that while the lotteries of the organizations had increased their earnings by 140 percent, it was mainly the smaller organizations that benefited. The larger ones suffered from increased advertising and distributional costs, and a decrease in net incomes (NOU 1990:4). This trend was not, however, reflected in our sample.

Part II

Comparative Analyses of Third Sector Voluntary Organizations

5

Cross-National Sectoral Patterns

Introduction

Based on the preceding four national case studies, in this chapter we begin the first of a series of comparative analyses, starting on the societal or national level of the third sector and, in Chapters 6–8, focusing on the four cohorts of voluntary organizations in England, Italy, the Netherlands, and Norway.

The third sector has taken various forms in different national settings, reflecting different cultural traditions, legal structures, and political histories (Gidron, Kramer, and Salamon 1992:12–16; McCarthy, Hodgkinson, and Sumariwalla, 1992:6–20).[1] In this chapter, we seek to account for the *differences* in the character and role of the third sector and its relationships to government in the four countries, as well the *similarities*, for example, in the rapid growth of interest in the third sector, the increased number of organizations, and their greater reliance on income from government.

After noting the variations in the degree of awareness of the voluntary sector and in the impact of the "welfare state crisis" in these countries, we shall compare some of the leading characteristics, patterns, and trends in their third sectors. The similarities and differences in the national status and role of voluntary organizations, and the public-private welfare mix is then analyzed as an outcome of predisposing, historic church–state relationships as manifested in the extent of religious pluralism and a decentralized structure of political power, which, in turn, have influenced the civic culture and role of philanthropy. Also discussed are the influence of ideologies such as subsidiarity and welfare pluralism on the policy environment of voluntary organizations in Europe, as well as sociopolitical trends such as modernization, secularization, and the election of conservative governments in the 1980s.

Identification of the Third Sector

We begin with a macro, cross-national perspective which also serves as the context for the micro or interorganizational level in Chapters 6–8. We have noted the development of four distinct patterns: institutionalized privatization (the Netherlands), statutory alternative (England), unplanned contract state (Italy), and integrated dependency (Norway) in the evolution of a group of nongovernmental organizations whose perception as a "sector" varies from country to country.[2] For example, mostly in England, and much less even in the Netherlands, is there some *explicit* recognition of an entity—the voluntary sector—whose constituent organizations have historically had a special legal and constitutional status and which are the subject of social policy. While *verzuiling*, or "pillarization," based on sectarian religion, provided the historical legitimation for the distinctive and institutionalized role of *particulier initiatief* in the Netherlands, there is relatively little discussion of it as a "third" sector; rather, it is considered part of the "collective sector," so central is it to the state and society.

In contrast, any awareness of the existence of a voluntary sector as more than a rhetorical abstraction in Italy and Norway is a very recent phenomenon. While there was a rapid growth in the number of secular, voluntary associations in Italy during a period of extraordinary social ferment during the late 1970s, this has not led to public recognition of the existence of a third sector (Perlmutter 1991), although it is noteworthy that the first law providing for some tax deductions for contributions to voluntary organizations was adopted in Italy in 1991. While not regarded as an important public policy issue, *volontariato* and organizations described as *non per profitto* were the subject of some scholarly research and debate in the 1980s.

Similarly in Norway, official recognition of the existence of a voluntary sector did not occur until 1988, when the first public committee issued its report. There were, however, some earlier references to voluntary organizations in the long-range plans of the government prepared during the 1970s (Kuhnle and Selle 1992b). Historically, an important role was played by voluntary associations toward the end of the nineteenth century in laying the groundwork for the Norwegian welfare state through their pioneering of services and in their persistent support for state intervention in dealing with social problems. There has been some concern that the growing attention to and use of voluntary organizations in Scandinavia might further weaken the sense of collective responsibility as the foundation of welfare states, which have become more selective and segmented since the 1970s (Pierson 1991). These differences in the length of time that the sector concept has been part of the public domain in these countries has affected the public debate—to the extent that there is one—about the role of voluntary organizations.[3]

Despite the paucity of comparable sectoral data, we propose to account for the similarities and differences in the historical development of these voluntary organizations in the personal social services, and in their current patterns and trends. For example, what explains the earlier, more extensive development, and greater importance of voluntary organizations in England and the Netherlands compared to Italy and Norway? Why are the p.i.'s the primary providers of public services in the Netherlands, whereas their counterparts in the other countries mainly supplement the basic governmental programs in the countries? (The question of what difference this makes will be considered in Chapter 10.)

Before we compare the cross-national trends in the third sector, we start with what many believe to be a precipitating factor in the "rediscovery" of the third sector and its diverse effects in the four countries.

Impact of the "Crisis of the Welfare State"

The concept of a "crisis of the welfare state" is generally acknowledged to have originated with the changes in most Western economies in the mid-1970s following the quadrupling of oil prices. The action of OPEC precipitated an era of "stagflation," of high rates of unemployment, inflation, and ever-rising taxes. In many countries, as part of a backlash, the spiraling expenditures of the welfare state were blamed for the state of the economy, and governments were perceived as overloaded, overregulating, and overbureaucratized (Hirschman 1991). These views contributed to a crisis of legitimacy of the welfare state and a search to reduce the role of government in the lives of citizens (Mishra 1984). Among the policies adopted to varying degrees by the conservative governments that came to power in the industrialized democracies of the late 1970s were privatization of state-owned and operated enterprises, and a greater utilization of nongovernmental organizations, often by contracting, as means for reducing the role of the state in the economy and the society. In addition, the social services were criticized in England and the Netherlands because they were regarded as controlled by professionals operating out of large, impersonal bureaucracies unresponsive to the needs and interests of ordinary people (Gladstone 1979).

The case of the Netherlands is unique in this respect because the p.i.'s, rather than the government, were defined as the problem. In contrast to other countries such as England, where voluntary organizations were seen as a means of curtailing the welfare state, in the Netherlands they constituted its essential components as the *primary* delivery system for public services, comparable to the Local Authority Social Service Departments in Britain, and not as a supplementary system as in most other countries. Consequently, they were regarded as responsible for the high costs and inefficiencies such as duplication and fragmentation, bureaucratization, and professionalism of the welfare state.

There was less of a backlash against the welfare state in Norway and Italy, perhaps because there was a blunting of the impact of the oil shock in both countries: Norway had the revenues from its North Sea oil venture, and Italy avoided any significant retrenchment in its governmental expenditures by continuing throughout the 1980s to add to its public debt, which ultimately exceeded its GNP (Ascoli 1992).[4]

While the growth rate of public expenditures may have been slowed in these countries, relatively few voluntary organizations suffered from the type of drastic cutbacks in their governmental funding that occurred in the United States. On the contrary, most organizations obtained increased support, except for those in the Netherlands where government budgets were more tightly controlled. Only in England could it be said that the opposition to the welfare state had some influence on the increased recognition and support of the voluntary sector. Indirectly and perhaps unintentionally, the enlarged use of voluntary organizations served as a means of extending the legitimacy of the welfare state when it was under attack (Sosin 1990).

Comparative National Trends in the Third Sector

Despite the four countries' different starting points and pathways, there was a convergence of three major trends in these four countries and most of the other industrialized democracies in Europe and North America:

1. a rapid increase in the number and type of voluntary organizations;
2. the widespread belief, particularly among conservative political groups and other supporters of privatization, that the third sector should be utilized by government as a more economical provider of public services;
3. an underlying cluster of institutional changes generally described as modernization.

Increase in Voluntary Organizations

The worldwide expansion in the number of nongovernmental organizations of all types during the last twenty-five years has been described as a cross-national "administrative mega-trend" (Hood and Schuppert 1988:93). Hood and Schuppert refer mainly to the widespread establishment of quangos (quasi-nongovernmental organizations) and other para-governmental organizations as substitutes for classic governmental bureaucracies in performing public functions, but one could also include the unprecedented explosion of peer self-help groups and community-based organizations with advocacy and/or social service functions. This was paralleled by social movements for greater citizen participation or "co-determination" in the formation and implementation of public policy and for greater decentralization of governmental functions. Some evidence of this organizational growth is found in our data—and in virtually every community survey undertaken since the 1970s—which found that the majority of voluntary organizations were established since the 1960s (Salamon 1987; Hatch 1980). It is significant that this development occurred at the same time that the welfare state was expanding, and was reflected in the increasing interdependency between the two sectors since the 1960s (Wuthnow 1991).

An important source of the growth in the number of voluntary organizations of all types in Europe and North America, even in countries that did not experience the welfare state crisis, seems to be related to the anti-establishment, populist, and other social movements of the 1960s, which produced a mobilization of students, consumers, the disabled, the poor, the elderly, feminists, homosexuals, "Greens," and ethnic and other minority groups opposed to the prevailing social policies of their governments. The formation of some of these voluntary associations was, paradoxically, facilitated by the increasing availability of public funds from welfare states whose expenditures were reaching a peak before their downturn in the mid-1970s. Representing diverse constituencies that sought a greater measure of self-determination or empowerment, many of these organizations shared an ideology that opposed government bureaucracies, and they sought a greater measure of equity in the distribution of the state's resources (Wolch 1990, 107–11).

The political and organizational climate in Europe was probably also influenced by the dramatic developments occurring in the United States with its War on Poverty, the civil rights movement, and later, the protests and demonstrations against in the war in Vietnam. Voluntary citizen action, increasingly called "advocacy," became popular even in countries that did not have a civic culture comparable to the United States and England, such as France, Italy, Germany, and Spain. This process was facilitated and nourished by various forms of international communication such as TV and newspapers, which spread the ideas that animated voluntary organizations.

As far as it can be determined, the growth rate of voluntary organizations increased more in England and Italy in the 1970s than in Norway and the Netherlands. In the latter, there were a large number of mergers among many of the denominational social service agencies that were required as a condition of continued governmental funding. This resulted in an increased number of large organizations whose size was a political advantage in their participation in the corporatist structure of the Netherlands.

Along with the growth in their number and size, the income received by the third sector organizations also increased as a result of additional support from government, particularly for those voluntary agencies providing public services. Those organizations that stressed advocacy and had minimal social service programs tended to fare less well. In England, for example, statutory fees and grants were the fastest growing source of revenue in the third sector, rising from one-third in 1975 to two-thirds in 1987, and they were the major factor in an aggregate increase of 200 percent in real income. Behind this statistic is a tenfold increase in grants from the Department of Health and Social Security (Knapp and Saxon-Harrold 1989). As will be seen in the next chapter, this increased reliance on governmental funds was reflected in the fiscal experience of the four cohorts of agencies in our study; for example, in Italy there was a 40 percent growth in governmental income in the eight largest organizations in the sample.

In these as in other countries, the necessity for reducing governmental expenditures was associated with the renewed interest in the voluntary sector: this seemed to be the "real" reason—if there was a primary cause—with the ideology of voluntarism providing the "good" reason for the renewed interest. While the growth rate of public spending on social welfare started to decline in the mid-

1970s, voluntary organizations had prospered in varying degrees during the expansion of the welfare state in the preceding decade, and they continued to increase in number and size even under the more restrictive economic conditions of the 1980s. In England and the Netherlands, for example, nonprofit organizations (NPOs) flourished under both Labour and then under Conservative governments. Contrary to widespread belief, few of the organizations in our sample were affected by any retrenchment in governmental spending (Brown 1988:3–28).

Compared to the other countries studied, the scope and importance of the voluntary sector in England expanded the most during the 1980s, perhaps because more was expected of it by the Thatcher government. Much of this added attention was expressed in the political rhetoric of the Thatcher regime, which reinterpreted the nineteenth century laissez-faire ideology in its efforts to extend the market values of choice and entrepreneurial competition to the social services, at the same time stressing the values of individual and family responsibility and charity. While there was substantial real growth in funds and in functions for many voluntary social service organizations in England, one of the unintended and less noticed consequences was the potential bifurcation of the sector based on size, structure, and the capability for delivering public services. The large national agencies able to obtain government grants and contracts may constitute one sub-sector, and the smaller, locality-based organizations, including most of those serving minority groups, could become even more disadvantaged (Taylor 1992).

In both Italy and Norway, the role of the third sector entered into public discussion for the first time in the 1980s, and it is likely that there will be more attention given to the future possibilities of "indirect public administration," a term used to refer to the process of governmental funding of voluntary organizations in Denmark, Finland, and Germany. A significant beginning was also made in Italy and Norway toward the development of a data base consisting of the number and income of voluntary organizations. In the Netherlands, a major restructuring of voluntary organizations occurred, reducing the number of organizations and resulting in somewhat less fragmentation and duplication on both the national and local levels. There is also a more secure and predictable basis for financing most of the personal social services, largely because of their inclusion in the social insurance program. On the whole, these measures should serve to strengthen the sector at least on the national level, although decentralization has led to more competition and uncertainty for many community-based organizations in both the Netherlands and Norway. In the Netherlands, the disproportionate reduction in municipal governmental income has seriously disadvantaged certain types of service-providing organizations.

Third Sector as Economical Provider

In addition to the proliferation of voluntary organizations, there was a related phenomenon found in many countries. Whether the process is called "imitative diffusion" (Hood and Schuppert 1988:96) or "societal learning," the third sector has been increasingly regarded throughout North America and Europe as an alternative if not a substitute for government in the provision of public services, or more polemically, as "a corrective to the abuses of the welfare state." Again, the Netherlands is an exception in reverse because government was not perceived as an alternative to the p.i.'s. Yet in the Netherlands and England—in addition to the United States—groups on the Right as well as the Left also urged a more active involvement of the informal sector of family, friends, and neighbors instead of reliance on overloaded, bureaucratically provided social services (Wolfe 1989:180–84).[5] This social goal, with its assumption of a Golden Age in the past when there was less dependence on the state (before the advent of the "providential" view of government) was embodied in the Dutch ideal of the "caring society," which it sought to achieve in the mid-1980s along with the "no-nonsense society" that emphasized efficiency.[6] Similar ideas about the virtues of voluntarism even penetrated the Scandinavian welfare states, expressed as a "longing for the small society in the larger society." This occurred in a country where societal responsibility, as promoted by a long succession of Social Democratic governments, seemingly had wide public acceptance. Nevertheless, there was growing dissatisfaction with the costs of its welfare state, and Sweden elected its first Conservative-dominated government in 1991, ending the forty-four-year rule of the Social Democratic Party.

While echoes of these themes were also heard in Italy, the emergence of *volontariato* in the late 1980s was limited to a few cities mainly in the North where there were more attempts to develop partnerships with government. Similarly, there was little support in Norway for voluntarism as a substitute for government; rather, the establishment for the first time of ninety-five local volunteer centers in 1991 was regarded as a means of supplementing existing state-operated programs. Also, voluntary agencies have been closely integrated into the social welfare system for many years, and it is recognized that local organizations do not have sufficient resources of their own to carry any additional responsibilities. In general, there was no evidence in any of the countries to support the wishful thinking that the voluntary sector has the financial resources to replace governmental responsibility for the social services (Salamon 1987; Johnson 1989). A failure to make the critical distinction between financial provision and service production often continued to confuse the issue. There are, in fact, eight possible divisions among these two functions between government and nongovernmental organizations as shown in Table 5.1.

Yet why did this belief persist? Perhaps because the political climate in these countries reflected the rise and domination of conservative parties in the coalition governments of the 1980s, a condition epitomized in the Thatcher regime in England. Many of these governments were also committed to privatization through the public sale of state-owned enterprises, so it is not surprising that the voluntary sector was also regarded as an economical way of reducing the

Table 5.1

Models of Government–Third Sector Relationships

	Model			
Function	Government dominant	Dual	Collaborative	Third sector dominant
Finance	Government	Government/ third sector	Government	Third sector
Provision	Government	Government/ third sector	Third sector	Third sector

Source: Gidron, Kramer, and Salamon 1992:18. Reprinted courtesy of Jossey-Bass Publishers.

government's role in the production of the social services. Policies ostensibly based on this ideology, however, were not noticeably effective in reducing the overall costs of government, which continued to increase; rather, they resulted in more fiscal and administrative interaction between the two sectors, and in the development of new working relationships between them that altered the public-private mix.

Modernization

The third common social trend affecting the third sector in these four countries consists of a series of institutional changes usually associated with the concept of modernization on the organizational and societal levels. This would include tendencies toward greater formalization, bureaucratization, and professionalization; toward more rationalization and restructuring of organizations, emphasizing greater efficiency and effectiveness; and toward the increasing secularization of functions originally under religious auspices. Naturally, these trends, which comprise their shared context, were more evident in certain countries. For example, all aspects of modernization were more pronounced in England and the Netherlands. Secularization was, however, more significant in Italy and the Netherlands, where it led to a more extensive development of nonsectarian services and the growth of civil society. In England, there were also notable expansions in organizational size, program diversity, complexity, and the spreading commercialization of fund-raising—processes that paralleled the government's interest in introducing the principles of competitive marketing into the voluntary sector.

Only in the Netherlands and England was there emphasis on improving organizational efficiency and professionalizing management, trends that emerged in the 1970s. Also, in none of the other three countries was there any restructuring of the national agencies comparable to those instigated by the Dutch government. In England in the 1980s, the Thatcher government sought to promote an "enterprise culture" that would also spread to the voluntary sector, which had much in common with the Dutch slogan of "no-nonsense" governance. Some observers of the voluntary sector in England and the United States were disturbed by these trends and interpreted them as a loss of distinctive identity as these ostensibly voluntary organizations became more like governmental agencies or for-profit enterprises (Lipsky and Smith 1989; DiMaggio and Anheier 1990).

The four countries were each affected by similar trends toward modernization, but because of their unique histories, they evolved different public-private mixes, such as statutory alternative (England); institutionalized privatization (the Netherlands); unplanned contract state (Italy); and integrated dependency (Norway). We turn now to the historical origins of these different national patterns of the relationship between the third sector and government.

Historical Development of the Third Sector

Comparison of the contrasting roles of voluntary organizations in these four countries is a reminder of the critical influence of church–state relations in shaping national patterns of the third sector. This is seen with great clarity, particularly in Italy and the Netherlands. Prior to the 1970s, indeed for centuries, the church filled much of the "participative space" in Italy—as well as in France—that was occupied by voluntary organizations in other European countries such as Germany and Scandinavia. Historically, church institutions were, in effect, the first sector in Italian society, and to the extent that there was any awareness of a third sector of nongovernmental, nonprofit, and nonpartisan organizations in the post–World War II years, it was dominated by church-related organizations. Relatively few nonchurch-sponsored associations developed as long as the church was able to keep the primary loyalty of its members. But church power weakened as secularist trends, particularly in the turbulent 1960s, seemed to provide a more encouraging environment for the development of the civil society and its voluntary organizations. The latter were constrained, however, by the firm hold that political parties have on all aspects of Italian public life: "Parties usurp space that in other advanced industrialized countries is held by bureaucracies and by local grass-roots organizations" (Perlmutter 1991:157).

A similar secularist trend was found in the Netherlands at about the same time: *ontzuiling* ("depillarization") gradually eroded the religious sectarian sponsorship of most p.i.'s in the social services starting in the 1960s, and later made it easier for the government to press for mergers among denominational agencies with the same function.

Thus, in both Italy and the Netherlands, the historical relationship between church and state is the key to understanding the special character and role of a third sector of voluntary organizations, rather than one or another of the theories of "institutional failure" of government, the market, or the voluntary sector itself.

The other major predisposing element—the extent of diffused political power—will be considered subsequently.

The Netherlands provides strong evidence to support the hypothesis, first posed by James (1982), that voluntary organizations are more likely to flourish in societies where there is no state church, that is, where no single religious group dominates, and there is religious and cultural pluralism. Under these circumstances, groups compete for members by providing social services such as hospitals and schools for their members, and these institutions also serve as a means of group identification. This close, historical association between pluralism and voluntarism helps explain the highly developed third sectors in England the United States, and the Netherlands. In the Netherlands, a nineteenth-century compromise based on the principle of subsidiarity, originally negotiated by the Catholics and the leading Protestant denominations for the field of education, was eventually adopted for the provision of virtually all other public goods and services with the result that the Netherlands is perhaps the most "privatized" country in the Western world because virtually all of the public services have traditionally been provided by nongovernmental organizations. Because of the pragmatic belief in "live and let live" in the midst of religious diversity—in sharp contrast to Northern Ireland and most other countries—the Netherlands developed a religious-political structure of denominational compartmentalization known as "segmented integration" or "vertical pluralism." In a decentralized unitary state, pillarization served a conflict-avoidance function and was a means for the diffusion of future conflict (Aquina 1992). These characteristics are, however, no longer appropriate in describing Dutch society since the late 1960s, when secularist trends weakened the power of the various *zuilen* over their adherents, and over the departments of central government (Idenberg 1985). The proliferation of voluntary organizations in the Netherlands during the postwar years thus contrasts with the pattern not only in Italy but also in Norway, where religious homogeneity, albeit of a different type, has prevailed.

There is additional similarity among these countries in the nineteenth-century origins of the pioneering role of religious sponsorship of social services, which predated governmental programs that typically were either nonexistent or inadequate. Particularistic social services, first established by and for the members of a religious denomination, were subsequently adopted and universalized, beginning with the takeoff period of the welfare state in the 1950s. The public-private mix of social welfare services changed over time as governments assumed more responsibility for financing, but utilized existing voluntary organizations, sectarian and nonsectarian, for service provision. Clearly, the growth of the welfare state was not at the expense of voluntary organizations, as some have claimed; rather, both grew at the same time. As noted earlier, the spectacular growth of the welfare state coincided with the expansion of the voluntary sector: the process was not a zero-sum, nor was it either/or, but rather both/and. Governments not only funded voluntary organizations, but even established new ones as a way of implementing their public responsibilities. Even in Norway, as the social democratic welfare state expanded, there was a parallel growth in the number and income of voluntary organizations.

This historical approach is somewhat at variance with theories of "institutional choice," which suggest a rational and deterministic decision-making process. Obviously, societies do not "choose" particular patterns of social allocation (Gassler 1990:96); the respective roles of the public and private sectors evolve over a long period of time and are influenced by sociocultural factors such as religion, the political economy, and the legal system of a country. These are expressed in the form of ideologies pertaining to the role of the state, and in the civic culture of a nation, that is, its norms regarding voluntarism and citizen participation. The civic culture of England has long sanctioned voluntary associations and a partnership between social service agencies and government. Similar collaborative relationships have been favorably regarded in Italy, although the extensive use of contracts with voluntary agencies seems to be more a pragmatic expedient by government and little influenced by ideology. In Norway, there is evidence that there has been a long-standing partnership between government and voluntary organizations, although it may not have always been recognized as such.

Similarly, the perspective being proposed here suggests that ascribing the development of nonprofit organizations to the "failure" of government or the market is also inadequate; historically, there is more evidence to support the belief that government intervened when voluntary organizations failed to meet the needs of the times.

Religious Homogeneity

It is necessary to qualify some of the generalizations about the relationships between organized religion and voluntary associations. While Norway is predominately (96 percent) Lutheran, religious homogeneity by itself is not decisive: it makes a difference whether the dominant religion is Catholic or Protestant, and as we shall see, whether political power is decentralized. This helps explain the close association between religious pluralism and voluntarism in the United States, England, and the Netherlands.[7]

While England nominally has an established church—the Anglican Church of England and the Church of Scotland—the church's state functions are largely symbolic and ceremonial; there are no major restrictions on other religious denominations, and the Anglican Church itself has little political advantage over other institutions (Beckford 1991:52–58). Indeed, attitude surveys show England to be the most secular of European states, with the lowest proportion of church membership and participation; only Hungary has a lower percentage of citizens (less than 20 percent) who attend a church once a month (Jowell, Witherspoon, and Brook 1989). Similarly, in Norway, the existence of a state church, which is

Lutheran, has not prevented the extensive development of voluntary associations, to which over two-thirds of the population belong, in a highly secular society. Not only is there a tradition of collaboration between government and voluntary organizations in Norway; the latter were in the forefront in pressing for greater state responsibility.

Political Factors and the Third Sector

In addition to religious pluralism as an element that can help explain national differences in the character and role of the third sector and its relationship to government, the power structure of the state is another major influence, particularly the degree to which governmental powers are decentralized. As Anheier (1992:54) concluded in his analysis of the third sector in Germany: "For comparative purposes, the relationship with the State is perhaps the most important factor in understanding the nonprofit sector cross-nationally. The 'State,' however, is a shorthand for both the regulatory regime and the institutional arrangements." In England, for example, the state is conceived as composed of individuals, while in the consociational Netherlands, the corporatist state operates through intermediary bodies, many of which were originally based on socio-religious groupings.

There is considerable evidence that religious-cultural homogeneity and a strong central government are not conducive to the development of a strong third sector, perhaps because it has the potential of becoming an alternative center of power and opposition to the hegemony of the dominant religious and political establishments. This phenomenon is evident in the way in which totalitarian regimes monopolize all forms of citizen associations, permitting only those sponsored by the state. As mediating organizations between the market and the state, voluntary organizations can be "crowded out" by government *or* by a monolithic state church that preempts the available organizational space. This may also explain the comparatively late, slow, and underdeveloped state of the third sector in Italy, France, Spain, Austria, and the Scandinavian countries.

The converse hypothesis can account for the early emergence of voluntary organizations and their diffusion in England and the Netherlands, as well as the United States; namely, the interaction between a political regime where power is decentralized and there is religious pluralism is an environment conducive to the organization of a variety of educational-cultural and social service organizations.[8] Belgium, a largely Catholic country, would also appear to be an anomaly because of its extensive array of voluntary organizations, but its decentralized political power structure might account for this. For example, since the end of World War II, despite the continuity of the rule of the Christian Democratic Party, Italy has had a conspicuously weak central government, with great variability within, and a high degree of autonomy between each level of government (Freddi 1980). With tax collection centralized but evaded by large sections of the population, local governments have been severely constrained in administering the social services delegated to them (Mingione 1988); hence, they have had strong incentives to make extensive use of voluntary organizations to deliver public services whenever possible. Structural, geographic, and historical factors in Italy have resulted in serious weaknesses in both the civil society and the national government that, in a context of pervasive politicization and corruption, militate against the development of a strong voluntary sector (Perlmutter 1991).

The Dutch distrust of a strong, centralized state which might be dominated by one of the religious blocs also led to a weak national government, empowered mainly to defend the country and to allocate most of its tax revenues to nongovernmental organizations originally divided along denominational lines. Norway, on the other hand, is a "state-friendly" society in which there is a historical blurring between state and society, and government is not regarded as an evil—as it is by many in the United States—but as a necessity. Norwegian voluntary organizations, half of which have been established since the 1960s, have not usually been viewed as mediating or buffering organizations between the individual and the state as in the other three countries (Grindheim and Selle 1990).

On the other hand, generalizations about the influence of centralized political authority also need to be qualified: the trend in the 1980s toward more centralization of state power in England occurred at the same time that there was more recognition and financial support of the voluntary sector, a policy related to the Tory strategy of reducing the spending and taxing powers of local governments (Wolch 1990). In the Netherlands, where the central government has exerted more control over its third sector since the end of the 1980s than at any other time in its history, there was at the same time a counter-trend of decentralizing other fiscal functions. Formerly regarded as a "prisoner" of the p.i.'s and the "Fifth Power" (the large national "dome" organizations), a cabinet minister was able to take advantage of the mounting constraints on public spending and the weakened political power of the *zuilen* to act decisively. As a result, the Dutch government finally succeeded in delegating funding of some of the community-oriented social services to the municipalities, transferring the financing of most of the other services for the disabled to social insurance, and restructuring most of the national organizations through mergers and withdrawal of support. This unprecedented assertion of ministerial authority was the culmination of a struggle for power since the 1970s in which the p.i.'s were periodically charged with lack of efficiency, coordination, and accountability in delivering their state-subsidized social services. While there seem to be some administrative improvements, the financial constraints on the government have inevitably resulted in some reductions in service provision and a slowing of the rate of establishing new organizations.

Because of these different histories and structures, there is considerable variability in the distance of the third sector from central government: in the Netherlands, the p.i.'s would probably complain that they are too close, but in Italy they are very far removed from the authority of Rome, as are most other social institutional systems. The tradition of an "arm's length" relationship in England between the state and nongovernmental organizations has served the sector well in providing access to resources, opportunities for some influence and collaboration, and a relatively high degree of independence. There is some likelihood that England could move more closely to the Dutch model, and for many organizations this would represent a worst-case scenario because of the likely constraints on equity, entitlements, and access (Kamerman and Kahn 1989; Johnson 1989; Taylor 1992), a topic to be considered further in Chapter 10. This is much less of a problem in Norway where, because of its small size, homogeneous population, and continuity of the Social Democrats' political rule, voluntary organizations have generally been integrated into the state systems, evidently with little loss of autonomy.

Ideologies and Models

Underlying these historical and structural developments affecting the third sector are different ideologies and models concerning the role of the state and voluntary organizations—for example, the extent to which they are perceived as *adversaries* or as *partners*, and whether the service role of the voluntary sector is an alternative to or substitute for government, a supplement, or complement. Posing the relationship between government and the third sector in either/or terms is, however, more characteristic of the political debate in the United States than in Europe, with the exception of England in the 1980s during the Thatcher regime. The belief that there is an inherent conflict between these two sets of institutions does not seem to accord with the historical development of the welfare state in most countries (Salamon 1987). Yet, relationships between government and voluntary organizations have traditionally been conceived of either in dualistic or holistic terms, as shown in Table 5.2.

As part of its failure to distinguish between the fiscal and the service-delivery functions of government, the conflict paradigm overlooks the ways in which voluntary organizations have helped government to build and maintain comprehensive social welfare systems by providing alternate mechanisms for the provision of public services (Gidron, Kramer, and Salamon 1992:27) Indeed, voluntary associations in Norway and England, and church-related organizations in the Netherlands and Italy were often pioneers in pressing for expansion of the social welfare functions of government; in the 1980s, their increased utilization by government helped sustain the welfare state when its legitimacy was seriously weakened. Finally, the trend in most countries is for increased collaboration, not competition, between the third sector and government. This suggests that future working models of these institutional relationships should be based on a continuum rather than a dichotomy; on the notion of a mixed economy, characterized by interpenetration in the areas of policy development and financing. The use of

Table 5.2

Two Models of Governmental-Voluntary Relationships

Dualism	Holism
Competition	Collaboration
Conflict	Partnership
Subsidiarity	Pluralism/mix
Ideological	Pragmatic
Market	Planning and coordination
Residual philosophy of social welfare	Institutional philosophy of social welfare

a collaboration paradigm must at the same time also confront issues relating to the preservation of organizational identity, autonomy, and accountability in the third sector. These and other aspects will be considered in Chapter 10.

Underlying the public-private mix in the Netherlands and in England are two ideologies that deserve special mention: subsidiarity and welfare pluralism, which both have their roots in the classical theories of the state developed by Hobbes, Burke, and Mill. Because the principles of subsidiarity have become so institutionalized, the arrangement in which government finances all public services provided by the p.i.'s is rarely discussed any more in the Netherlands. Reliance on the p.i.'s is now less a matter of ideology and more a Dutch tradition: "this is how we do things in the Netherlands." It would be more correct to refer to the present pattern in the Netherlands as "neosubsidiarity," in contrast to the original nineteenth-century form, if the term were not often used to describe self-help and mutual-aid groups. Traditionally, government and the church-sponsored charities were quite separate. Government was, in a sense, more dependent because it could only intervene when the religious groups failed to act. As a result, most of the time government functioned in a supplementary role. At present, the p.i.'s are totally dependent on the government, which regulates their performance and sets the standard of payment. Under these conditions, one could describe much of the third sector in the Netherlands as a "quasi state," particularly for those organizations that have no connection with a constituency and where it is largely a matter of convenience for the government to utilize the legal form of a p.i. Consequently, many of the p.i.'s that are mainly service providers, in contrast to those voluntary associations that are mainly advocates for their members, are better understood as quangos (quasi-nongovernmental organizations).

While subsidiarity may appear to have much in common with the residual philosophy of social welfare advocated by the Thatcher government during the 1980s, the Dutch welfare state has more in common with the solidaristic and egalitarian aspects of the Scandinavian social democratic model (Therborn 1989; Esping-Andersen 1990), despite its lack of ideological space for voluntary organizations. In contrasting the United States, a "reluctant welfare state," with the Netherlands, one of the top spenders, Mishra (1991:112–13) has observed that "decentralization, pluralism and non-state forms of service delivery and administration nevertheless coexist with a high level of public expenditures and collective responsibility for maintaining a national minimum standard."

The basic principle of subsidiarity, that the state should encourage the work of voluntary organizations and the informal social systems, is an ideology now shared by both the Right and the Left in Europe and North America. Both favor a weak state, but in different domains: the Right is for law and order and economic freedom—for example, a weak state and a strong market was the goal of the Thatcher regime, according to Gamble (1988); the Left opposes bureaucratic intervention by the state and supports citizen advocacy and co-production of public services.

Not only has subsidiarity been revived as a guide to social policy in the 1990s by conservative politicians in response to an era of retrenchment in public spending, but it has been adopted as the basic organizing principle of the European Community (Spicker 1991). In this international context, it refers to the maintenance of the sovereignty of the individual nation-states whose powers may not be assumed by the EC without their consent. Because a lower, rather than a higher hierarchical level is favored—that is, voluntary auspices are preferred to governmental—the EC is subsidiary to the individual member countries and restricted to those tasks that are delegated to it. The Catholic presence in some European states also contributes to the legitimacy and influence of the philosophy of subsidiarity in the Benelux countries, Germany, and Austria. Curiously, in Italy, where until recently the church preempted the role of the dominant non-governmental institution, subsidiarity does not seem to have been as important as in the Netherlands, or in Germany where it has been institutionalized since the nineteenth century (Anheier 1992).

The other leading social policy, welfare pluralism, is identified with England, where partnership is the dominant model for governmental-voluntary relationships. Welfare pluralism has been proposed as a means of having the best of both worlds, the statutory and the voluntary, with the former "off-loading" many services onto the latter (Brenton 1985:54–74). This policy has been advocated on the assumption that public financing of voluntary social services delivery would be more efficient, responsive, and democratic, a notion not far from Salamon's "third party government," which is a form of compensatory complementarity. The "contract state" toward which the British social services may be moving thus bears considerable resemblance to the Dutch model, although there is much more diversity of income sources in England, in sharp contrast with the total dependence of the Dutch agencies on a single governmental source. Nevertheless, in both countries, extensive reliance on nongovernmental providers of public services raises issues of equity and accountability that remain unresolved.

International Comparisons: Toward a Typology

Among the four countries, then, there are varying patterns of relationships between government and the third sector, ranging from the Netherlands, where there is the sharpest division between public financing and service delivery by p.i.'s, to the others, where there is a mixed economy in which the governmental system is the dominant one, particularly in Norway, in both funding and production of public services. Thus the countries can be arrayed as shown below with respect to the dominance of the government and the type of welfare state:

the Netherlands	Italy	England	Norway
	conservative	liberal	social democracy
subsidiarity		partnership	state domination

Only in England—and the United States—do private contributions still play an important role in financing services also supported by government, although as a proportion of third sector income, this role is declining in relation to the growth of public funding. While changes in the British and Italian tax laws to encourage individual and corporate contributions indicate recognition of the importance of the third sector, they are not expected to have a significant effect on its revenue.

The four countries thus represent different types of welfare states, with Norway being the most universalistic and Italy the most particularist; the Netherlands is closer to Norway, and England not far behind. Nevertheless, there does not seem to be any consistent association between the type of welfare state, no matter on what basis it is classified, and a particular pattern in governmental-voluntary relationships. In these, as in other advanced industrial democracies, the growth and increasing recognition of the third sector was one of the responses to the declining legitimacy of the welfare state, fueled by the economic stagnation of the 1970s. Particularly in corporatist and consociational democracies, the existence of VNPOs also enabled the state to delegate sensitive, controversial, or unwanted public tasks to them, strengthening them as an interest group, as part of a process of "quangocratization" (Hood 1991). In the Netherlands, historically, this process "provided the institutional infrastructure to segmented and potential antagonistic publics" (DiMaggio and Anheier 1990:152). In Germany, corporatism and subsidiarity led to the formation of welfare cartels and supply oligarchies in the social services by nongovernmental organizations that are formidable power centers in contrast to their counterparts in the Netherlands.

Other differences are more deeply rooted. For example, Anheier (1990:375–78) identifies two types of societies: those based on the common law such as the English-speaking United States, UK, Canada, and Australia; and those rooted in the Roman or civil law in Europe such as Italy, France, Germany, and Austria. The former are largely Protestant, and the latter, with the exception of Germany, predominantly Catholic. The Netherlands and the Scandinavian countries are not included in this scheme and would be considered mixed types. In the common law countries, voluntary organizations are more competitive and oriented toward the market, while in the European civil law countries whose civic culture places less emphasis on voluntarism and citizen participation, they are more state-oriented. Historically, voluntarism and pluralism have been associated with each other, and this accounts for the highly developed third sectors in England, the Netherlands, and, of course, the United States. In the Anglo-Saxon countries, the state, when it is not perceived pejoratively, is the Great Enabler, funding but not necessarily delivering public goods, and promoting "third party government" through the use of nongovernmental organizations as service providers. Most of the European civil law countries are also more corporatist in their integration of nongovernmental organizations in public decision making and as a form of "indirect public administration." While identifying a group of variables deserving of further study, this classification obscures the contrasting roles of the third sector in France and Germany—it is a formidable power center in Germany—and it does not take into account the significance of decentralized political power.

Table 5.3 summarizes the distinguishing features of the four countries on nine dimensions, showing the association of the type of political regime, extent of centralization, religion, welfare state, and corporatism with the role of the third sector, philanthropy, dominant ideology, and trend in the public-private mix.

Conclusions

In each country, policy issues relating to decentralization, relationships among health, education, and social care, and privatization affect third sector organizations in widely different ways. This occurs not only because of their distinctive national characteristics but also because these issues are perceived differently by organizations in different fields of service or "industries," and by organizations that differ widely because of their size, level of operations (national or local), scope, emphasis on services or advocacy, degree of professionalization and bureaucratization, and so forth. The multiple and sometimes conflicting interests of the third sector are thus an expression of its inherent diversity. All of these factors affect the relationship with government, and they suggest the limitations of generalizations about the sector as an entity.

In this first set of comparisons on the national/sectoral level, we found that there were significant variations among the four countries in: (1) the degree of awareness or recognition of the voluntary sector *qua* sector; (2) the perception of its role as an alternative to government in the provision of public services; (3) their response to the "welfare state crisis."

These differences were the result of the historical interaction of church and state—that is, to the extent that there was a tradition of religious and political pluralism, the voluntary sector was more identifiable and visible. Norway and

Table 5.3

Distinguishing Features of Four Countries on Nine Dimensions

	England	The Netherlands	Italy	Norway
Major trend	statutory alternative	institutionalized privatization	unplanned contract state	integrated dependency
Sector role	supplement/complement	primary	supplement	complement
Dominant ideology	welfare pluralism	neosubsidiarity	pragmatic expedient	sociodemocratic
Private philanthropy	significant	minor	minor	minor
Religion	heterogeneous (Protestant)	heterogeneous (mixed)	homogeneous (Catholic)	homogeneous (Protestant)
Political regime	two-party parliamentary (conservative)	consociational	Christian-Democratic coalition	Social Democratic/Labor Party coalition
Welfare state	neo-universalistic	egalitarian solidaristic	particularistic, clientistic	comprehensive, Scandinavian model
Corporatist	no	quasi-state	yes	yes
Centralization	strong	weak	weak	strong

the Netherlands represent the ends on a public-private continuum of service provision, with government domination at one end and the p.i.'s at the other.

In both Norway and Italy, a modest recognition of the existence of a third sector occurred only in the decade of the 1980s, in contrast to the historic supplementary and complementary relationships between governmental and voluntary organizations in England and the primacy of the p.i.'s in the Netherlands.

These predisposing factors—religious and political pluralism—also account for the different status of voluntary organizations in law and public policy, and in the particular national pattern of their relationship to government. The character, scope, and role of the voluntary sector was also influenced by the prevailing civic culture and welfare ideology.

Despite their different historical, religious, and sociopolitical backgrounds, however, there was a convergence in all four countries of trends such as the following: (1) an increase in the number and type of voluntary organizations and their greater reliance on public funds; (2) greater attention given to their serving as an alternative to government; (3) growth in the spread of formalization, bureaucratization, professionalization, and another indication of modernization, secularization.[9]

Among the factors accounting for the expansion of the third sector were the growth in various forms of citizen action in the 1960s in Europe and the United States, the trend toward decentralization of governmental operations, and the increased availability of public funds before the onset of the backlash against the welfare state. During this period, diffusion of the idea of voluntary organizations as an alternative to government was associated with the election of conservative governments that pledged to overcome the alleged excesses of the welfare state.

Notes

1. As noted in the introduction, generalizations comparing the third sector in these and other countries are of necessity limited by the lack of agreement concerning definitions and classifications, as well as the paucity of valid and reliable national data. For our purposes in this chapter, the third sector refers to a collection of organizations that have a formal, self-governing structure, are non–profit distributing, have some degree of voluntarism, and are expected to produce some public benefit. More specifically, most of the references are to the sub-sector consisting of the personal social services, which also constitutes the context for our study of VNPOs serving the disabled. For further details, see the introduction, pp. 10, 13–14.

2. While Peter Dobkin Hall has warned against reification—"The sector is merely an analytical construct, not an institutional reality" (1992:14)—if, however, it is perceived as real by its partisans as evident in peak associations such as the NCVO in England, then it has to be considered as more than an abstraction.

3. The lack of recognition of a third sector is also reflected in the absence of comparable, national statistical data regarding the number and income sources of voluntary organizations in Italy and, to a lesser extent, Norway; it also accounts for the differences in the quality and validity of our macro (national) as compared to our micro (organizational) data.

4. In contrast, the public indebtedness of the UK was only 44 percent of its GNP; in the Netherlands, it was 78.4 percent. Also, in Italy, the takeoff period in the growth of

voluntary organizations occurred earlier during the 1970s and, as we shall see, it had less to do with the welfare state than with the declining influence of the church and the spread of secularist trends in the society.

5. Some scholars have seen in this process the workings of a cycle of forty-year swings from public to private, e.g., Hirschman (1982) and Paci (1987).

6. The U.S. counterpart of this belief in the advantages of voluntarism over government was President Bush's program of "A Thousand Points of Light."

7. In Protestant countries like the United States, the UK, and those of Scandinavia, poverty relief was established early during the seventeenth through nineteenth centuries as a parish function that was eventually transferred to the state by the end of the nineteenth century. In Catholic countries such as Italy and Austria, it remained a charity under the control of the church and served as a deterrent to government intervention until well into the twentieth century. In the Netherlands, the principles of subsidiarity dominated the operation of the Poor Law until 1965, although government, rather than the churches, had long provided most of the funds for public assistance (Woolf 1986).

8. For an explanation of Switzerland as an exception to these generalizations, see Wagner (1992).

9. Note, however, the phenomenon of rather similar policy outcomes from widely different national origins. Kamerman and Kahn (1989), for example, found that virtually all European countries have comprehensive public responsibility for child day care, despite the differences in their politics, religion, demography, and economies. Hence, it is quite possible that there may be few regularities or systematic variations in the relations between government and the third sector. For example, there does not appear to be any consistent association between particular patterns of third sector relations to government—the public-private mix—and the typology of welfare states developed by Esping-Andersen (1990).

6

Organizational Income Trends

Introduction

Like other types of organizations, the policies and programs of VNPOs are strongly influenced by the sources of their income. Inevitably, voluntary organizations tend to concentrate on those tasks for which they can obtain funding, whether from the government or from other sources. Conversely, the amount and nature of government and private contributions to voluntary organizations reveal something about a society's attitudes and priorities regarding the services and functions these organizations perform. In particular, the extent of government financing is an indicator of how a society has chosen to approach the task of providing and paying for social services.

In this chapter we analyze changes in the size and sources of income for voluntary organizations in all four countries during the 1980s, using data from 1982 and 1988. (When data for these benchmark years were unavailable, we extrapolated data from neighboring years.) In addition, for the Netherlands and Britain, we present financial data from 1976 based on their inclusion in an earlier study (Kramer 1981; Kronjee 1976). All data have been corrected for inflation, using the inflation rate factor for each currency. Because the size of an organization's budget tends to correlate with such factors as level of government support, type of service functions, and degree of government regulation, we divided the total sample into large and small organizations; separate data sets are presented for each sub-sample.[1]

The comparative findings should be viewed in the context of economic conditions in Europe during this period. Despite the oil crisis of 1973 and rising rates of inflation, the 1970s was a prosperous decade. Never before had wealth been so high, nor so equally distributed. Yet unemployment rose, investments soured, and national governments faced enormous difficulties in balancing their budgets. Social insurance and other welfare state programs softened some of the distress, but by 1982, Europe had succumbed to a worldwide recession. By 1988, the European economies were again booming, but unemployment remained higher than it had been in the immediate postwar decades. Thus, even as businesses were posting record profits and private incomes were rising, governments be-

Figure 6.1. **Percentage of Increase in Organizational Income, 1976–1988**

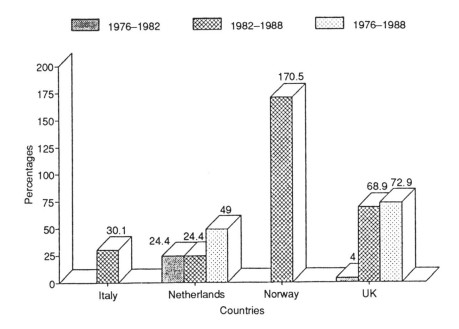

came poorer. The stubbornly high unemployment rates reduced the income tax base, increased the welfare rolls, and led to massive government deficits. Yet despite these budgetary problems, none of the four countries cut back its spending for social services and health care in any substantial way.

Trends in Growth of Income

Between 1982 and 1988, the budgets of voluntary organizations in all four countries grew—moderately in Italy and the Netherlands, considerably in Britain, and spectacularly in Norway, as shown in Figure 6.1.

To understand this wide diversity in rates of growth, we must recall that the Italian and Dutch VNPOs both depend on their governments for a large portion of their incomes. Thus, even a small rate of increase, expressed in percentage terms, represents a huge infusion of new funds. That the income of Dutch voluntary organizations increased at all during this period, when the national government was desperately seeking to enact cost-control measures, is rather surprising.

In contrast, the voluntary sector in Norway is relatively small, serving as a supplement to extensive government programs. In such a situation, double- and triple-digit percentage changes represent relatively small sums of money, easily transferred from the government sector to VNPOs. Furthermore, as we will see,

Figure 6.2. **Percentage of Increase in Income by Organizational Size**

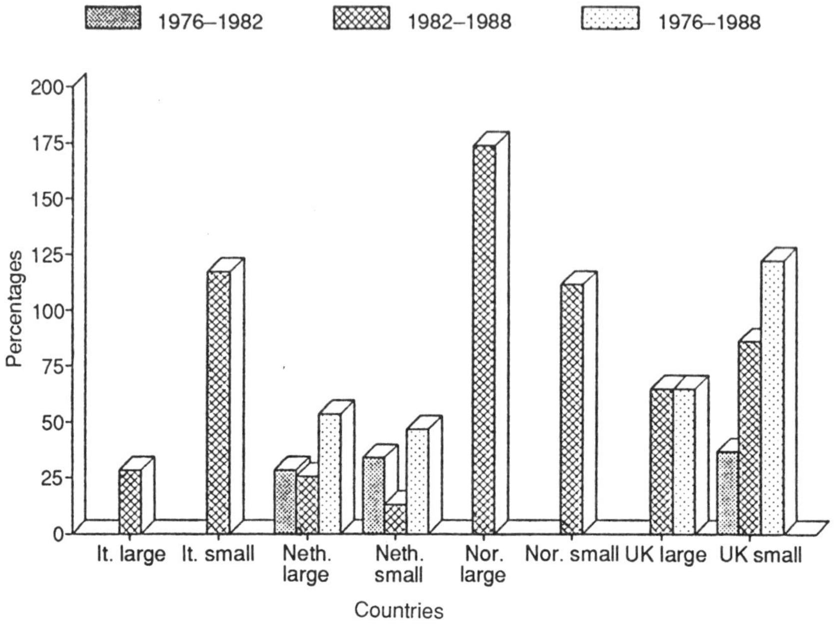

Norwegian voluntary organizations have been very successful in boosting their incomes from fund-raising campaigns, lotteries, and contributions from members.

The British situation is more complicated. During the 1970s the high rate of inflation leveled out the rather sharp nominal growth in the income of voluntary organizations. Between 1982 and 1988, however, the inflation rate fell by half, exerting a proportionately smaller leveling effect. Moreover, during the Thatcher years, the aversion to big government spurred various privatization efforts, whereby some social service funds that had been given to local authorities were reallocated to voluntary organizations. Public fiscal policy also caused an unforeseen expansion of residential care financed by social security from which the VNPOs benefited.

When overall income data is recalculated to determine differences between large and small organizations, as shown in Figure 6.2, several additional trends are evident. In Norway, the large organizations fared even better than the small ones. In Italy, by contrast, the small organizations far outpaced the large ones. Part of the explanation lies in the fact that several of the small organizations in the sample were very new organizations, and their income growth reflects a start-up spurt. Even a modest nominal increase in the income of a very small organization translates into an impressive percentage increase. Also, the rates of growth among small Italian organizations were extremely uneven. The income of most Italian organizations rose modestly (2 percent to 20 percent), but the income of some of the cooperatives rose by more than 200 percent.

In the Netherlands and in Britain, the small organizations were well established and therefore less likely to enjoy extraordinary growth. But whereas the 1980s was a generous time for small voluntary organizations in Britain, the decade was relatively unkind to the small Dutch organizations. Compared to the large locally based service providers, the small national advocacy groups were more deeply hurt by the Dutch government's efforts to hold down costs; indeed, by the early 1990s, many of the advocacy organizations saw their government subsidies severely curtailed or wholly discontinued. The small associations were also more seriously affected by the less generous mood among private donors.

Changes in Sources of Income

For the purpose of tracking changes in income sources, income was divided into three types: government and other public sources, fund-raising, and other. The first category includes all income from national, regional, and local government, including subsidies, grants, and payments for services rendered. Also included are the social insurance payments (deducted from paychecks) collected in the Netherlands.

The second category, fund-raising, includes all gifts, donations, and grants from private individuals, corporations, and foundations. In Britain, legacies are an important source of fund-raising income; in Norway, lotteries are a principal means of raising large sums of money for charitable purposes.

Under "other sources," we include fees from clients, paid directly or by insurance companies (except in the Netherlands); commercial activities such as sale of products made at sheltered workshops; and investment income. Only in Norway was this category of "other sources" of considerable importance.

In all four countries, voluntary organizations were heavily dependent on government and other public funding, and this dependency increased during the 1980s as shown in Figure 6.3. (In this and subsequent figures, income in the earliest year is set at 100 percent, and income in later years is expressed as a percentage of that baseline.)

In Italy and the Netherlands, nongovernment sources provide only a marginal contribution to the VNPOs. In Norway, however, the situation is quite different. Between 1982 and 1988, government funding more than doubled, but commercial activities and investment income grew even faster—which had the effect of reducing the government's percentage share as an income source.

Two details about Norwegian financing of the voluntary sector are noteworthy. First, Norway is the only one of the four countries in which fees for services are an important source of income. Second, it is the only country of the four in which income from commercial activities is increasing. As the manager of a sheltered workshop in the Netherlands explained, new automation tech-

Figure 6.3. **Income Sources of Organizations in the Four Countries, 1982–1988**

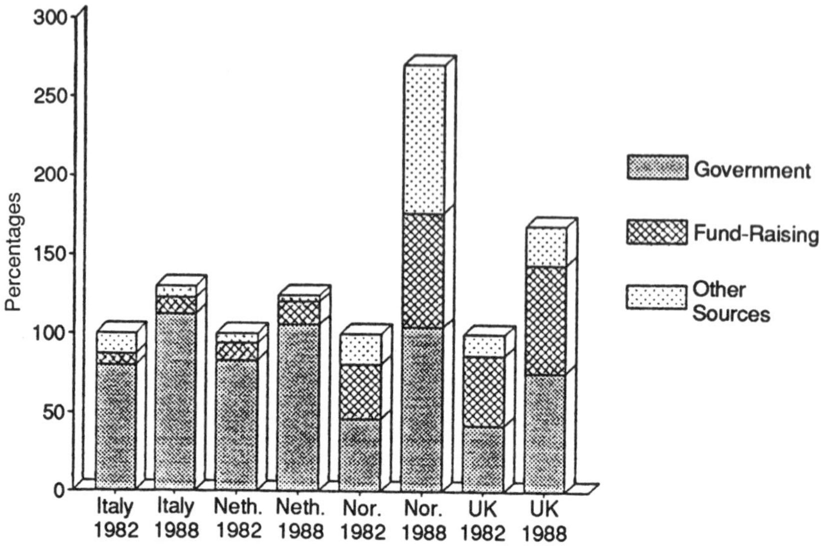

niques in manufacturing have made it more difficult to identify work that physically and developmentally disabled people can do at a competitive price, even if it is heavily subsidized by government.

For Britain and the Netherlands, we can also look at the longer-term trends as shown in Figure 6.4. In Britain, growth in the income of voluntary organizations stagnated between 1976 and 1982, with government assuming a proportionally larger share. During the 1980s, income from government sources continued to increase, but revenue from nongovernmental sources grew about as rapidly, producing a rather stable pattern. In the Netherlands, where reliance on government funding is far more pronounced, fund-raising has become a growing source of new money. The national government's efforts at frugality seems to have made the p.i.'s less reluctant to pursue sponsors in industry and private donations. During the 1980s, for example, televised fund-raising events became extremely popular.

When the changes in income sources for large and small organizations are analyzed, the trends for the large organizations, as might be expected, matched the overall trends depicted in Figures 6.3 and 6.4. For the small organizations, however, a different picture emerged, as revealed in Figure 6.5.

In Italy, the Netherlands, and Britain, the proportion of income that small organizations derived from government sources increased but did not rise to the

Figure 6.4. **Sources of Income of Organizations in the Netherlands and the UK, 1976–1988**

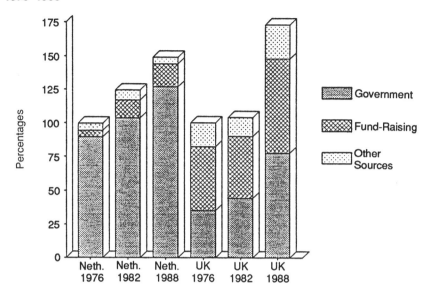

Figure 6.5. **Sources of Income of Small Organizations in the Four Countries, 1982–1988**

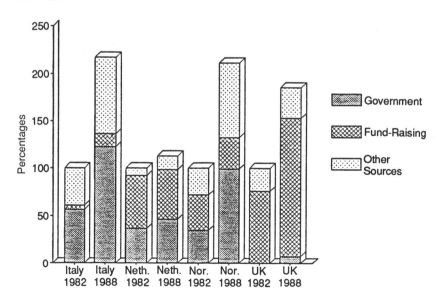

Figure 6.6. **Sources of Income of Small Organizations in the Netherlands and the UK, 1976–1988**

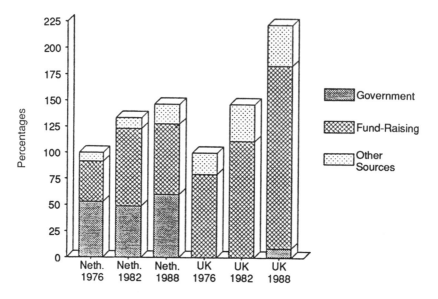

level enjoyed by large organizations. Thus, the small organizations in these countries had to rely on nongovernment sources for a substantial share of their income.

This pattern reflects the differences in the nature of the activities undertaken by large and small organizations in each country. In the Netherlands and Britain, the larger organizations provide services that are heavily funded by government, while the smaller organizations tend to be constituted as membership associations that focus more on advocacy. In Italy and Norway, however, both large and small organizations deliver government-funded services.

In turning to income from nongovernmental sources, fund-raising is very important for small organizations in the Netherlands and Britain. In Norway, small organizations are less dependent on fund-raising than large organizations, reflecting in part the dominance of the large organizations in reaping benefits from the Norwegian lottery system. But small organizations in Norway, unlike those in the three other countries, are becoming more dependent on contributions from members, especially for services members receive. Such contributions are of minor importance in Italy, the Netherlands, and Britain.

For small organizations in Italy, the principal component of the "other sources" category consists of income from commercial activities. Sheltered workshops in Britain also produce for the market.

The longer-term data for small organizations in Britain as shown in Figure 6.6

also reveal a sharp increase in income, but little change in the composition of the organizations' sources of income between 1976 and 1982.

Comparable data for the Netherlands illustrate the pattern of cuts in government financing between 1976 and 1982, followed by a modest recovery between 1982 and 1988. Since then, the total amount of government financing for small organizations has again declined.

Understanding the National Patterns

In all four countries, government has assumed responsibility for the provision of adequate social services, and for this purpose, it has allocated funds to voluntary organizations involved in service delivery. Today, most of these service organizations are quite large, and it is unclear whether and to what extent they are large because they received government funding, or whether they obtained government funding because of their size and capacity. The former seems to be more true of the Netherlands, and the latter true in the other countries. More specifically, in Italy and the Netherlands there seems to be a consensus that government is responsible for funding essential services, but that voluntary organizations are to administer and deliver those services. In both countries the involvement of nongovernmental organizations in service provision has a long history, for traditionally the churches sponsored and administered the social services needed in their communities.

This similarity between government–voluntary sector relations in Italy and in the Netherlands seems to contradict a theory proposed by James (1982) to explain the different functions of the voluntary sector in Sweden and the Netherlands. James asserted that in countries with a heterogeneous cultural heritage and a tradition of religious pluralism, private nonprofit (religious) organizations tend to assume responsibility for the provision of quasi-public goods; in countries that are relatively homogeneous in terms of culture and religion, government organizations tend to provide these goods. James's theory seems to hold for most of northwestern Europe, with the Netherlands and Germany conforming to the first type, and the Scandinavian countries and Britain conforming to the second. According to this theory, however, Italy, a Catholic country, should have developed a comprehensive government-run service system, as should have Belgium, which is also religiously homogeneous. That the Italians and the Belgians have not developed such a system suggests that James's formulation ignores a key variable: the presence or absence of a powerful, stable central government. Italy and Belgium, although they are old countries, are rather young states and are still quite decentralized as compared to Britain and the Scandinavian countries. The absence of a strong central state, as described in Chapter 5, may be as much of an explanatory factor as religious pluralism in the development of the Dutch and German patterns of service delivery.

The Italian and Dutch pattern of relying on government as the primary financier of services and voluntary organizations as the primary provider of services also reflects the rather weak philanthropic tradition in these countries. Rather than assuming that the wealthy will voluntarily contribute to organizations that benefit the needy, the Italians and the Dutch prefer to have the government use its taxing powers to redistribute income.

In Norway and Britain, by contrast, the government not only finances social services, it also provides them. Until recently, the Norwegians and the British considered it unnecessary and even undesirable to privatize service delivery. Private voluntary organizations, it was thought, had to remain wholly private and voluntary, which meant they should not receive government funding and were to provide only supplementary services. During the 1980s, this understanding was thoroughly up-ended in Britain by Margaret Thatcher's Conservative Party, which insisted on privatizing many governmental tasks whenever possible. Norway was not subject to such an ideological campaign, but in the last few years pragmatic officials have successfully argued that voluntary organizations are better suited than government to perform certain tasks.

Thus quite different paths seem to be leading these four countries to similar ends, with all of them gradually moving toward more government financing for voluntary organizations. Countermovements are under way as well, however. In Norway the government's nominal financial commitment to voluntary organizations is increasing, but the more rapid increase in other sources of income has made them less dependent on government funding. In the Netherlands, the government continues to support the large service organizations, but government funding for small advocacy organizations has all but evaporated.

Government Funding and Autonomy

One would assume that when a government funds voluntary organizations, it would insist on having a say in how those organizations are run. Overall, however, the voluntary organizations in the sample have retained a surprisingly high degree of autonomy. Yet those organizations primarily dependent on government for virtually all of their income may have lost some of their policymaking and operational independence. In the Netherlands, for example, the government has been partially successful in controlling the fast-growing costs of health and social care by budget controls, cost-efficiency, and quality-control measures. In Britain, when funding takes the form of a contract, the government specifies its requirements for service delivery in the writing of the contract and in decisions about whether to renew a contract.

Nevertheless, governments are generally not able to exert rigorous control over the voluntary organizations that they finance. First, the governments lack the means as well as the will and the capacity to do so. Second, many organizations obtain funding from several government sources, which gives them multiple opportunities to play off one against another. Third, the funding of voluntary organizations is often the outcome of a delicate political process in which strict controls are inadvisable. Finally, if one considers all the difficulties governments have in controlling their own agencies, it is not surprising that they cannot dictate point-by-point terms to voluntary organizations.

While every form of funding imposes some type of constraint on a VNPO, government funding has also been the key to the ability of most voluntary organizations to achieve and expand their missions. Increased government funding for the voluntary sector seems to be the next stage in the development of the modern welfare state.

Note

1. To create the sub-samples for the Italian and Norwegian organizations, we used the criterion of budget size. For the Dutch organizations, the sub-samples are similar, but not identical, to the distinction between large advocacy associations and small service organizations. For the British organizations, our criterion was percentage of income derived from government sources in 1987, which generally correlates with organization size. However, this criterion produced a few discrepancies: some of the smallest "large organizations" are actually slightly smaller than the largest "small organizations."

7

Structure, Governance, and Administration

Introduction

The purpose of this chapter is to compare trends in organizational behavior for the four cohorts, and to explain the observed patterns. Since we are concerned with change over time as well as differences between nations, we have a dual comparative approach: first, a somewhat static one, where structure, roles, and functions of the four organizational cohorts are compared; second, a more dynamic one, where change over time is the focus. Following a summary of the main organizational development trends and governance systems, explanations of the observed patterns are proposed.

Development trends are divided in four sub-categories: (1) *Organizational structure,* analyzed by means of changes in staff (in administrative as well as service units), members, and budgets. (2) *Formalization,* which refers to the degree to which organizational work norms are made explicit as routines. (3) The dimension of *reorganization,* that is, changes in the number of departments, routines and the relation between them and the governing bodies. (4) *National structure,* which encompasses relations between central and local bodies, changes in the number of affiliates and their functions, mergers, and spin-offs.

The second main category, governance systems, includes three types of democratic influence channels: members; users, consumers, or clients; and staff. The third category, administrative systems, includes task specialization, departmentalization, and computerization of administrative functions.

The explanation of cross-national trends in organizational behavior presents several methodological problems. Voluntary organizations are not isolated units; they arise out of and develop in close connection with their surroundings. Hence the importance of societal, historical, and cultural conditions in the four countries as they influence organizations. But the development of voluntary associations is also affected by international trends in welfare state ideology, economy, and policy. Studying changes in time and across national borderlines provides a unique opportunity to connect national development trends to international ones. Several organizational changes can only be fully understood when their external sources are taken into consideration. This approach also makes it possible to relate trends in organizational development to the more general societal processes.

Studying voluntary associations also presents a problem of demarcation. Large associations are complex structures; some are highly centralized, while others are loosely coupled elements with a high degree of autonomy. For example, voluntary associations can organize some of their activities as for-profit firms, controlled by the parent organization. Or, service-providing agencies and institutions may be separated, with their own boards and accounts. Voluntary service-providing organizations may have a centralized or decentralized structure, with administrative tasks placed on the national, regional, or local level.

When comparing smaller parts of these structures, one may risk identifying differences as "real" when they are due to the fact that functions are carried out on different levels of the organization. Some associations may fulfill functions on the national level that elsewhere are carried out by the local affiliates or in separate national units. Unless these aspects are taken into consideration, it may be incorrect to conclude that administrative differences represent real differences in the voluntary efforts for handicapped groups.

Trends in Organizational Development

Size of Staff and Income

In all four countries, the size of the organizations' staff and income is related to their functions. Associations that primarily ogranize the interests of the handicapped, or coordinate self-help activities, are usually not large bureaucratic units. Typically, their staffs numbered fewer than five, and their incomes were modest. During the 1980s, most of them showed little growth, and their organizational structures were relatively stable.

In contrast, most of the social service–providing organizations experienced growth between 1975 and 1988. In the Netherlands and in Britain the strongest growth occurred in the early 1980s, whereas in Italy and Norway, the greatest growth in administrative and professional staff occurred some years later. In Italy, the staff size of the advocacy groups was stable in the 1980s, while the sheltered workshops, initiated in the early 1980s, were mainly managed by volunteers. The community care organizations and the large residential institutions had staff growth ranging between 100 and 400 percent.

Almost all the British agencies experienced a growth in staff in the period of 1976–1988. The overall number of staff in service provision increased by 61 percent to 11,240 in 1988. The eleven smallest organizations almost doubled their staffs, but these employees only comprised 2 percent of the total for the twenty organizations in the sample.

All of the headquarters staffs in England also grew between 1976 and 1988. In 1988, headquarters staff size varied from 120 to 160 for the four largest organizations, up to 80 for five organizations, and 40 or less for the eleven smallest. Some of the smaller organizations had an even larger increase of their staffs: 800 percent for one and 350 percent for another.

Most of the Norwegian organizations expanded their headquarters staff between 1982 and 1988. The eight largest organizations had a growth of 162 staff members, or an average of 88 percent. For the ten smallest organizations, the total growth was twenty-one staff members, or 179 percent. Only one organization stagnated, with the same size staff in 1988 as in 1982. At the same time, most of the services managed by the organizations expanded their staffs. In 1988, approximately 340 persons were engaged in the service programs of the three largest organizations.

The number of staff in the national headquarters of the Dutch p.i.'s increased between 1975 and 1980–82 by ninety-six individuals, or an average of 216 percent in seven out of the ten advocacy organizations. Between 1980–82 and 1988 the staff growth was more moderate, ranging from three to twenty staff members. For four organizations the staff number remained unchanged, while three experienced a reduction of staff, ranging from nine to three individuals, or 30 to 10 percent.

The Dutch service-providing agencies experienced a total growth between 1975 and 1980–82 of only thirty-eight staff persons, or three percent. Between 1980–82 and 1988 some expanded while others reduced their staff. Out of ten agencies, four grew, ranging from sixty-five people to one individual, or from 17 to 9 percent. Two agencies had the same number of staff both years, and one had a small decline.

Between 1980–82 and 1988, many organizations stagnated or reduced their staffs in response to the budgetary crisis in the Netherlands. Six out of nine went through a reduction, ranging from nine to two staff members, or 9 to 60 percent. Small organizations seem to have had the largest reductions; two agencies reduced their staff by 50 percent or more, and both of these had less than ten staff members after the reductions. Only one agency increased its staff in this period, by 3 percent, or eight individuals.

In all four countries, there was no clear relation between changes in the number of administrative staff and in that of service-providing professionals. Some organizations increased their staff number without any proportional growth of services, and a few decreased their staffs but maintained their level of services.

Formalization

Formalization here includes several trends: toward more hierarchical structures, a more explicit internal division of labor, more written communication between staff members, and less informal relations between employers and staff.

In Italy, many of the community care services were established during the 1980s, often without any clear organizational model. Their organizational structure has usually been loose, and relations among staff generally informal. This has resulted, however, in a high degree of heterogeneity among staff members. Although professional social workers are employed, the innovative and community-based character of the activities limits the possibilities for traditional bureaucratic formalization.

The residential care institutions in all four countries adopted new norms of efficiency in the 1980s. Particularly in Britain and the Netherlands, the institutional services went through a development that favored more "business-like" administration and managers, where decision-making processes were streamlined. There has been a trend toward increased specialization of services with a greater degree of formal competence in the staffs. These same trends were found in the advocacy organizations, although not as pronounced.

Almost all of the British organizations reviewed their administrative and organizational structure in the 1980s, and twelve implemented a reorganization plan with a new departmental structure in the national headquarters and more formalized rules for administrative tasks. The number of organizations with manuals for personnel practice increased from five in 1976 to thirteen in 1988, and ten agencies also had written manuals for their service programs. In thirteen organizations, computerized accounting and word-processing systems had been introduced, mainly after 1985. These processes of formalization were found in all the national headquarters, independent of size or tasks, although the agencies providing direct services became more formalized because they were larger and more complex.

In Norway, eleven out of eighteen national headquarters were staffed by five persons or less, with fewer possibilities of comprehensive formalization. In the three major organizations, each with more than sixty-five employees, differentiation occurred with separate departments for fund-raising, education, housing, social politics, and information. Within each of these departments, a formal pattern of authority and division of labor was established. Within this formalized differentiation, however, the general secretary was said to control departmental decisions as before. There was also a trend toward the employment of more professional staff in the national secretariats, and in service provision, but many staff members felt unable to use their skills in the headquarters.

Only six organizations had pay scales and written manuals for personnel policies. The development of personnel policies often created disagreements between staff members and the general secretaries, reflecting a confrontation between leadership expectations of "voluntary spirit," and professionals' interests in improving their working conditions. State-imposed mergers dominated the reform wave of the 1980s in the Netherlands, where almost all organizations became more formalized. As in Britain, many agencies reported that much had been done to clarify the mandates and tasks for different types of personnel, as well as for board members and volunteers. More differentiated services also created a need for more specialized staff competence. Authority relations between managers and staff were clarified, as were relations between top managers and department heads. Clarified authority lines and differentiation of tasks did not, however, result in more formalized decision structures. In general, there was a development from hierarchical decision structures toward a more democratic and collective climate, and some agencies reported a period of relative "anarchy" between these two periods. Later, as a result of mergers, governing structures again became more hierarchical.

There was also a trend in the Netherlands toward reducing formalized structures. One organization expressed a growing concern about rigidity as a consequence of increased bureaucratization and hired a management consultant in order to develop more efficient structures. In service production, several agencies reorganized their programs and went through a shift from institutional care toward family- or community-based care. As a consequence, institutional, bureaucratic procedures were replaced with more flexible ones.

It was clear that in all four countries the development toward a more bureaucratized structure presupposed a certain organizational size. For organizations with few employees, such as the sheltered workshop cooperatives in Italy, decentralized community services, and small membership organizations, the possibilities for increased formalization of administrative structures are limited. This does not necessarily mean that small organizations did not try to make themselves more efficient; rather, that it may have taken other forms.

Reorganizations

The Italian VNPOs did not undergo comprehensive organizational changes comparable to those in the other countries. Several of the residential care organizations were restructured into three functional areas—administrative, health, and social service departments—with a parallel differentiation of leadership and staff. In these structures, professional and technical personnel seemed to increase their influence at the expense of the members and other constituent groups.

In Britain the incremental growth in personnel and tasks in the 1970s and early 1980s most often took place without major changes in organizational structure. In the last part of the 1980s, several organizations experienced management problems, and in some, boards were not satisfied with the practice of the top management and crises resulted in major changes in the executive leadership. Fourteen of the twenty boards hired management consultants, and during the period of transition, the boards played a more active and intervening role than usual. New directors initiated comprehensive processes of restructuring the organizations: determining and formalizing goals, objectives, and priorities, restructuring headquarters, and establishing new departments and control systems.

These rather dramatic changes in structure during a relatively short period of time were also evident in new leadership and administrative styles in these organizations. Some of these changes, such as new titles for the executive such as manager, director, or chief executive officer, represented influences from the world of business and industry.

In Norway, there were no major reorganizations reported apart from the trend toward more differentiated and formalized administrative structures. The societal development toward decentralized and deinstitutionalized services, and increased political power for municipalities, did not affect the organizational structure of the organizations until the beginning of the 1990s.

In the Netherlands, the need for cooperation and more flexible structures was behind several reorganizations of services. These reforms were, however, less the result of internal processes than of budget-driven pressures from central government. The rapid pace of secularization or "depillarization" in the Netherlands made it difficult to maintain the religious justification for the highly differentiated structure of the p.i.'s. At the same time, the general trend toward deinstitutionalization and more open, interactive, and community-based services also affected the activities of voluntary service providers. Several large institutions were reorganized, opened up, and their interaction with the surrounding community increased. Others were closed down and replaced by community services. Several organizations with a differentiated pattern of service programs also went through a process of consolidation, concentrating their scarce resources in their core programs, that is, those most relevant to their major purpose.

In many ways, the four cohorts seem to confirm the impression of voluntary organizations as stable and conservative. While for-profit organizations regard permanent change as a tool in the search for higher efficiency, the internal reorganizations of VNPOs occurred most often when they were confronted with some kind of perceived crisis or threat. No VNPOs went through comprehensive reorganizations as a part of a continuous development process.

Relationships between National and Local Organizational Structures

In Italy, all of the advocacy groups and 50 percent of community care organizations were local affiliates of national organizations, while all the institutional care and sheltered workshop cooperatives were autonomous local organizations. Like the British organizations, the Italian local affiliates also had a high degree of autonomy, but some financial restrictions were imposed upon them. The national organization usually undertook planning and educational activities, arranged conferences and training activities, developed information and propaganda leaflets, and coordinated national responsibilities. Local affiliates were usually free to decide on local matters, but some financial restrictions were imposed upon them, and over half of their income was sent to their national affiliate. Similarly in Britain, relations between national organizations and their local affiliates were loose, with little central control over income and programs. This was also true for Norway, where the average number of local affiliates increased by almost one-fourth between 1982 and 1988. In the Netherlands, the local/national level distinction is more significantly related to two different kinds of functions; advocacy organizations are usually organized at the national level, with some local affiliates, while service provision is found almost invariably only at the local level.

A common structural property of the four cohorts can be summed up as follows: *The general perception of local units as hierarchically subordinated to national bodies does not always fit.* It seems more reasonable to regard national and local operations as *parallel activities,* loosely connected and partly coordinated, and striving for common goals, but not always with common means.

Governance Systems

In the Italian sheltered workshop cooperatives, a democratic decision structure was stressed, with all members participating in common decisions. The local community care organizations also had boards where handicapped persons or their relatives took part. In addition to a board, some of the larger local organizations also had coordinating committees that linked the service and membership units. The residential care institutions were usually hierarchically organized and managed by a small board of directors composed of professionals and usually representatives of the founders. Priests were a dominant group on these boards.

Although all the British VNPOs had the structure of a membership organization, they differed in their governance, ranging from formal representation of local units to self-selection by other board members. Historically, many of these organizations were established from the top down and had very little turnover of board members.

The Norwegian organizations also had a membership, but unlike their British counterparts, they all had the same organizational structure. The disabled and their relatives were the dominating membership group, constituting between 80 and 100 percent of the board members, and they had great influence in making policy for the organization.

In the Netherlands, the democratic structure of the organizations underwent important changes in the 1980s. Several organizations began appointing professionals and experts to the board, usually recruited among civil servants, business executives, or financial managers. This pattern, which greatly resembles the practice in the United States among VNPOs, partly replaced the historical trend of selecting *regenten,* members of the old patrician families. Other boards were based on corporatist principles whereby municipalities, community groups, or religious organizations appointed representatives to the board. In contrast to other boards of service-providing organizations in the United States or the UK, members could rely on government for virtually all their funding.

Which actors control the voluntary organizations in these four countries? Board members represented different groups such as donors, members, professionals, religious societies, and public authorities, and were therefore accountable to a variety of norms and expectations (Leat 1988). On a continuum with board members representing societal groups at one end and the state at the other, boards could be grouped according to their dominant actors. The Norwegian organizations and the Italian sheltered workshops were at one end because they were controlled mainly by the handicapped themselves and were influenced by ideologies of participation and codetermination. In the middle of the continuum were the boards of the British, Dutch, and Italian service agencies where the number of professionals was increasing in the 1980s, usually at the cost of religious or more traditional representatives. At the other end were the Dutch local service-providing agencies, where the influence of public and insurance authorities in the early 1990s was increasing, usually at the expense of professionals. Here, private control was vanishing, leaving few if any differences between public and private.

Administrative Systems

Most of the membership organizations in the samples had their strongest administrative growth between 1975 and 1980. In this period, the average number of staff personnel increased by more than 200 percent. As noted earlier, almost all the British organizations went through considerable administrative reforms, resulting in more formalization, specialization, and professionalization. Within administrative units, the executives' span of control generally was reduced, and an increasingly formal differentiation of departments, corresponding to a similar differentiation of tasks, took place. Computerizing of financial accounts was introduced, along with other more rationalized management procedures. Many of these changes can be traced back to the succession of a new generation of executives, and several organizations went from stagnation and crisis to new growth.

There were similar trends in Norway and the Netherlands, resulting in the modernization of the large organizations, along with the development of more democratic and collective decision making among the professional staff. For example, workers in treatment institutions obtained the right to establish their own councils in order to strengthen their influence on the policy of the institution.

In Britain and the Netherlands, there was a shift in the professional competence of managers. Previously, many managers had been from the helping professions, but later, specialized management training and experience were more valued. There was also an increase in internal management and leadership training of existing staff members, as well as a higher educational level.

There are several factors that can help explain these trends in the administration of VNPOs. One is related to an increase of tasks, which created a need for more differentiated administrative structures and clearer staff responsibilities. A second reason comes from crises in the organizations that could best be coped with by administrative reforms. A third factor is general growth in tasks and service production, which may have created a need for administrative differentiation. The new generation of managers can be seen as a separate explanation by their introducing the principles of modern administration into the organization. Reforming administrative structures on the basis of such principles may be regarded as importing an institutional "package" where the relation between the content of the package and the goals of the organization is rarely explicated (Meyer and Rowan 1983). As a last factor, there is the general "spirit of modernity," which is manifested in the impact of the environment on the organization.

In comparing the development of administrative systems within the four countries, it is clear that most of the administrative forms and reforms presuppose an organization of a certain size. Formalized administrative hierarchies, decision structures, and rules for codetermination of employees are difficult to implement where the number of staff is five or less. Hence, the close association between size as measured by the number of employees and administrative reforms, and the paucity of the latter among the small Italian, Norwegian, and Dutch organizations.

Interpretation of the Comparative Findings on Organizational Trends and Patterns

As mentioned earlier, our data provide the opportunity to study VNPOs along two axes by making static, cross-national comparisons and noting similarities and differences in the ways voluntary organizations act as welfare providers. While the four countries are all considered welfare states, they differ in the ways welfare tasks are organized, and in the political/ideological descriptions of the division of labor between the state and the third sector. We will next compare these welfare-providing roles of the third sector in the four nations, looking for similarities and differences and for explanations of the different roles.

Second, we will analyze the changes over time for the four cohorts. The period between 1975/1980 and 1988 marks a shift in the political and ideological perception of the welfare state in Europe. In the late 1970s, most nations in Western Europe experienced an increase of unemployment, combined with increasing inflation rates. This so-called stagflation created different kinds of legitimation crises in several European countries, and it weakened support for traditional welfare solutions. The election of Prime Minister Thatcher in Britain in 1979 and President Reagan in the United States in 1980 marked the ascendancy of neoconservative ideology about the division of labor among market, state, and third sector. The goal of the minimized state affected policies in most Western European countries, influencing political attitudes as well as practical solutions. Many of the changes in organizational behavior were a response to these international trends, as well as specific, national conditions. Comparative studies of voluntary organizations often overlook the impact of national culture and history as explanations of differences in the welfare-providing roles of the third sector. We shall review some of these basic differences in national perceptions and treatment of third sector organizations in the context of social change.

National Similarities and Differences in Organizational Function

Cross-nationally, the four cohorts present a heterogenous picture. They differ in size, with staffs ranging from one person doing part-time work (in Norway) to more than 3,000 staff members (in Britain). They differ in their incomes, which range from less than £10,000 to more than £15 million. They differ in public support, varying from less than 5 percent to more than 90 percent. There are differences in the ways in which the disabled were organized, and how the prime tasks of associations were perceived. In each country, the structure of organizations for the disabled was unique, containing national particularities. Organizations that were large in one country could be small or absent in others. In England, the British Polio Foundation was among the top twenty charities; in Norway all polio organizations went out of existence in the 1960s. In some countries, handicapped adults and children were in separate associations, and in other countries they were in the same organization. In the Netherlands, Britain, and Norway, associations organizing extensive and socially accepted handicaps tended to be large in their national context. Organizations for the blind, deaf, and physically handicapped were among the largest in all four countries. These handicaps are widespread, and this may be one explanation for large organizations. But size can also be a result of age; some organizations have accumulated capital, experience, and a good reputation for more than 100 years, and these factors are important preconditions for growth. Organizations for the blind and partially sighted, for the deaf, and for the physically handicapped are all among the first generation of voluntary associations. So, within a national context, size can partly be explained as a result of social acceptance, the number of handicapped, and the age of the organization.

Other similarities and differences in national structure, size, and functions can be related to the ways these organizations are connected to religion, culture, public policy, and social conditions. For example, service and advocacy functions were most often separated in all but the British agencies. In the Netherlands, this separation also reflected the division between nonmembership and membership organizations, national and local, and was rooted in the origins of the p.i.'s in the various *zuilen.* In Italy, the sheltered workshop cooperatives were regarded as a special category of voluntary associations, closer to the political ideas of solidarity and collectivity rather than traditional religious institutions.

In the Netherlands and Italy, religious affiliation has been one of the most important organizing principles for the structure of associations. In Italy, the Catholic Church has historically been powerful, centralized, and relatively autonomous. In the Netherlands, religious pluralism has prevailed for several hundred years, and in combination with strong state skepticism, local church societies created a plurality of institutions and services in support of the family, the handicapped, and other marginal groups. In both of these countries, the principle of subsidiarity legitimized the protection of religious services from state intervention.

In Norway, local congregations of the state church played an important role as welfare providers up to the 1940s. But in the postwar period, the church has generally accepted the normative standards of the state's welfare model, with few attempts to shelter its social service production from state penetration. In Britain, the importance of religion in the voluntary sector has gradually diminished, with relatively little conflict between church and state.

The development of services under religious auspices in the Netherlands and Norway illustrates what has been called philanthropic insufficiency: the inability of organizations to "generate resources on a scale that is both adequate enough and reliable enough to cope with the human service problems of an advanced industrial society" (Salamon 1987:111). In both countries, the amount of public financing of church-sponsored social services increased markedly from 1945, culminating in the abandonment of the subsidiarity principle in the 1970s in the Netherlands. In Norway, several service programs were gradually taken over by public authorities in the 1960s and 1970s as a result of insufficient church financing.

The role of the churches leads to the more general question of the social groups behind VNPOs. From where do voluntary associations recruit their members and obtain their social support? To what extent can the social base of organizations explain cross-national differences in structure and roles?

In Britain, for example, traditional voluntarism and charity work were socially anchored in ideologies of the aristocracy and later the upper classes of the industrial society. During the industrial revolution, organizations were founded on the distinction between the deserving and undeserving poor, and charity work and gifts were regarded as moral and religious duties. Much of the work of the voluntary associations was carried out by people from higher social strata and middle-class persons with church affiliations (Macadam 1934; Braithwaite 1938).

In the Netherlands, the merchant classes traditionally had a strong position in voluntary organizations, but the old patrician families have been succeeded by professionals and civil servants. In Norway, the absence of an aristocracy opened the way for the influence of the civil servants of the state, who played an important role as ideological leaders in the second generation of voluntary associations from about 1910. The ideology of these organizations was an *extension* of the role of the liberal state. Important public tasks, such as the prevention of disease, health information, services for the disabled, and health care work among children and the elderly were performed by these associations. After 1945, the first generation of membership and advocacy groups appeared, representing marginal groups who demanded nothing radically different, but rather "more of the same" from government.

Structural Differences

One of the most important distinctions among these VNPOs is one between those that serve the disabled and those whose members *are* disabled; this often

Table 7.1

Staff and Income of Organizations for the Deaf

Country	Name	Staff (1987–1988)	Total income (£000 1988)
Britain	Royal National Institute for the Deaf	530	2,292
	British Association for the Hard of Hearing	6	25
	National Deaf Children's Society	28	259
	Royal Association in Aid of Deaf People	69	261
The Netherlands	EFFATHA, Christelijk Instituut vor Doven	300	4,777
	Koninklijke Amman- stichting	30	3,246
Norway	Norwegian Association of the Deaf	12	183
	Norwegian Association of the Hard of Hearing	13	248

parallels the primary emphasis on either services or advocacy. Only among the British organizations is there more of a balance between these two functions in which all the national agencies providing services engage in some form of advocacy, and where many of those whose membership consists mainly of the disabled and their families also provide some direct services. The legitimation of advocacy by voluntary associations is an integral part of the civic culture of both the UK and the United States. A more corporatist version of this role is found in the Netherlands and Norway where, paradoxically, there may be as much, if not more, user participation than in the UK. All of the national organizations with local affiliates in the four countries have some type of a formal democratic structure, but the participation of the members, regardless of their status as disabled persons or as users, tends to be nominal in these countries as in most others.

As an illustration of the different structures of VNPOs, we can compare the eight organizations for the deaf in Britain, the Netherlands, and Norway (see Table 7.1). In Britain, four of the organizations in the cohort with more than 300 staff members serve the deaf. In the Netherlands, two organizations for the deaf were included, of which one is an advocacy association and one a service-providing agency. In Norway, there are two associations with similar purposes. Table 7.1 shows the large differences in the annual income of these organizations, with variations from £25,000 to almost £5 million. With the exception of Norway, this is not a representative picture of the voluntary organizations for the deaf in the other countries. In both Britain and the Netherlands, there are many other local voluntary services for the deaf, and in Britain there are many other national organizations. Nevertheless, the data illustrate some of the important national differences in the structure of VNPOs for or of the deaf.

One dimension is related to the *differentiation of tasks*. In Norway, several administrative functions of local service agencies and programs are integrated in only one or two national organizations, which also undertake advocacy. These national organizations are usually highly centralized, hierarchical bureaucracies that control most local activities. In contrast to this more or less monolithic structure, service and advocacy are assigned to separate organizations on the local and national levels in the Netherlands, where there is a more pluralistic pattern; this is also the case in Britain. Thus, many small units serve the same functions as one single organization in Norway, and because of their smaller size, they are less likely to be departmentalized or professionalized.

There is also symmetry between the decision levels of organizations and those of the public authorities. Organizations tend to concentrate their activities on those levels where important public decisions are made, particularly as it may affect their funding. They also adapt and usually follow in their structure and operations the often cyclical movement in government between centralization and decentralization.

The Sociopolitical Context of Organizational Trends

For voluntary service-providing organizations, the period between 1975 and 1990 was rich in changes. At the national level, political and administrative reforms, as well as new ways of perceiving social problems and solutions, influenced organizational structure and functions, albeit in somewhat different ways. Four changes occurred in most countries that significantly affected VNPOs: trends toward more decentralization in government; deinstitutionalization in the social services; codetermination in the social services; and a political context of greater support for anti-state ideologies and efficiency values.

"Back to the community" was a major sentiment in Europe behind the move to decentralize many governmental operations in the late 1970s and in the 1980s. It was fueled primarily by the fiscal crisis of the welfare states, but also by the reaction against the overly bureaucratized departments of central government. In Norway and the Netherlands, the use of block grants increased the political and financial power of municipalities. In the Netherlands, financial, administrative, and some program responsibilities were moved from the national government to municipalities. At the same time, laws and rules regulating service production were tightened, the more costly services were transferred to social insurance, and on the local level, services were organized into larger units through governmental pressures for mergers.

In Norway, social policy decisions in the larger cities were transferred from the level of municipality to the level of neighborhood in the late 1980s, thus creating another public decision-making level. Earlier in the decade, block grants to the municipalities had shifted the locus of funding for many voluntary agencies and had required adaptation to the existence of many new power centers. This pattern of local administration of nationally funded programs had, however, long been the policy in Italy. In both Norway and the Netherlands, decentralization, as a form of "load shedding," also served to reduce the political pressure on central government during a time of cuts in public spending.

In Britain, the Conservative Party's strategy to reduce the spending authority of local government and the power of the Labour Party resulted in an expansion of the role of voluntary agencies providing various forms of community care under contract with the Local Authority. Because of this and other developments, the national agencies assigned more staff to their growing number of affiliates.

Several other health and social policy changes occurred at about the same time as the process of governmental decentralization. Drawing on some of the experience of "open psychiatry" in Italy in the late 1970s, there was a trend toward deinstitutionalization in many countries, resulting in the closure of large, centralized institutions and renewed efforts to reintegrate the elderly, disabled, mentally retarded, and mentally ill into the community. This basic change of social policy required the adaptation of services for the disabled to their individual needs and to their everyday life in the community. In the Netherlands, deinstitutionalization proceeded apace in the 1980s, and community- and family-based treatment superseded the more rigid structures of institutional care. In Norway, a reform closed down most institutions for the disabled and elderly in 1988 and transferred them to community-based care. Parallel with this, the decentralization of many social policy decisions moved the political focus to the local level, where policies vary from one municipality to the next. The local affiliates of more than forty national organizations are small and fragmented, making it exceedingly difficult to coordinate their advocacy activities. A redefinition of the role of the FFO and its constituent national organizations is necessary, but difficult to achieve.

In Britain, deinstitutionalization policies had been underway since the 1960s, and some of the largest national agencies had gradually expanded their community-based programs. It was expected that implementation of the new community care programs of the Local Authorities would involve both the national agencies and their affiliates more extensively, possibly even leading to competition between them for contracts. In Italy and the Netherlands, the responses of VNPOs to deinstitutionalization have been somewhat slower, but the policy has added to their importance as organizations and has changed the modes and balance of service programs.

A third trend was the spread of the idea of codetermination—sometimes described as empowerment or user democracy—for clients, consumers, and workers. The core of this policy is that the clients of health and social services should have the opportunity to influence decisions concerning themselves through a democratic process. It is justified on the grounds of a commitment to democratic values, as well as the principle that codetermination should also increase the interest and motivation of clients, members, or workers, and replace their passive status with the active one of participants. In this way, codetermination can be regarded as an extension of the demands of many marginal and client groups of the 1970s.

In the early 1980s, there was also an increase in the demands from the staff members of VNPOs for a greater voice in the decision making of their organizations. Only in the Netherlands and Norway were various forms of codetermination established by public law in several fields in which VNPOs operate. In Britain and the Netherlands, the number of disabled persons on the boards has increased slightly, but in Italy, only the sheltered workshop cooperatives provide for a measure of codetermination.

Ideological Influences on Organizational Behavior

During the 1980s, all four nations went through a period of political transformation due to the increased influence of the conservative "minimum state" ideology—a response to the prevailing fiscal crisis. The core message was that an overloaded welfare state should be freed of many of its responsibilities, and the provision of public services should be transferred to the market, to nonprofit organizations, or to volunteers. The wish to reduce public functions, spending, and bureaucracy took different forms, based on the political history and structure in these countries. A focus on VNPOs as "agents of the state" because of their ability to deliver public services according to public standards was widespread. This was a traditional, institutionalized feature of the service-delivery system in the Netherlands, and was not unfamiliar in England and Norway. In Italy, however, it represented a relatively new idea.

In addition to this gradual shift toward the nonprofit properties of VNPOs, and their status as producers of common goods, the conservative ideologies, particularly in the Netherlands and Britain, also stressed the importance of *efficiency*. Perhaps some of this emphasis on cost-efficiency and productivity was a reaction to the democratization trends of the late 1970s. Extensive democracy is time-consuming and usually difficult to combine with the need for strategic or long-term planning. Also, decentralization and pluralism make it difficult to promote coordination and cooperation among service-producing units. Toward the end of the 1980s, the values of more local control and democratic influence were gradually superseded by the goal of greater cost-efficiency in service-providing agencies. This was most evident in the Netherlands, where government was able to promote mergers on both the national and local levels through its role as the primary source of funding. In England, the increasing use of the contract by Local Authorities was one of the most important channels for the promotion of efficiency standards.

It seems as if the nonprofit aspects of VNPOs are most strongly articulated in countries like the UK and the United States, where the idea of the contract state has the strongest foothold. In contrast, in Norway, the social democratic welfare values served as a shelter for the influence of conservative ideologies on VNPOs. There were no significant pressures for any form of privatization of welfare production, nor any increase in the use of contracts as an administrative tool in the regulation of existing services funded by the Norwegian government. The increased interest in VNPOs in the 1980s focused mainly on their voluntary properties, such as the ability to mobilize volunteers as nonpaid helpers or self-help participants. Also, in Italy, the increased interest in *volontariato* focused on VNPOs' ability to strengthen values of altruism, community, and neighborhood. In both of these countries, the use of the term "nonprofit," as applied to organizations or to a sector was very rare.

In the four countries studied here, the division between the nonprofit and the voluntary properties of the organizations included in the study also coincided with an explicit or implicit policy toward third sector associations. In Britain and the Netherlands, nonprofit associations are treated as a separate category, and separate government bodies decide on their charitable or nonprofit status (Weisbrod 1991). In both of these countries, there is historically a complex legal and institutional framework within which nonprofits are recognized, while this was missing in Norway and Italy. In Italy, this absence might be partly due to the existence of a national state with limited power, although this is also the case in the Netherlands. More relevant is the historical domination of the church, and the recency of the development of secular organizations. In Norway, the explanation is more the traditional ignoring attitude of the social democratic welfare state toward the voluntary sector.

It can be concluded that in Britain and the Netherlands, important impulses for change in the roles and structure of third sector organizations in the 1980s came from ideological and political changes occurring in Europe and North America. While Italy and Norway were also influenced by conservative ideas in the 1980s, these were less directly related to the emerging role of voluntary associations than to local developments and intraorganizational processes.

Dominant National Trends

Particularly noteworthy were the comprehensive structural changes and reorganizations that occurred among the British and the Dutch VNPOs in the 1980s, many of which were in the name of efficiency (Miller and Pruger 1990). The Dutch service agencies went through major changes in their fiscal resource system—from subsidies to social insurance—and with many government-induced mergers, such as combining thirty-three small, local day care centers into one large organization.

In Britain, there was a general growth in service production, increased interaction with statutory bodies, and substantial reliance on public funding. Many of the changes in administrative and management structures were a response to this growth in service production. Tensions between more comprehensive tasks and existing administrative and governance structures resulted in a period of turbulence in the organizations. Most often the boards initiated the process of restructuring the administration, usually with the help of external management consultants, a process that often resulted in administrative reorganizations and a shift of chief executive. Replacements of leaders could not be related to any one factor: some managers failed to avert a serious financial crisis; others were reaching the age of retirement. Still others were not perceived as dynamic enough to cope with the modern role of the organization. In general, new leaders can also be perceived as a way of meeting the challenges from public authorities.

During the 1980s, the idea that management of third sector organizations was qualitatively different from public administration and business management spread from the United States to Europe. This was part of the growing recognition of the importance of executive leadership in voluntary associations, among whose ranks a shift was evidently taking place. For example, a study from 1988 to 1990 by Patton and Hooker (1990) shows that 44 percent of the managers in voluntary associations had been employed in the private sector, while only 41 percent of the managers had been employed in the voluntary sector before they joined their present positions. In both the Netherlands and Britain, management ideas originating in the for-profit sector to increase effectiveness and efficiency were exported to the nonprofit sector.

Conclusions

We have seen that the VNPOs in the four countries have different historical roots, and that they differ in the ways they are integrated into the production of public services. They vary considerably in their organizational structures and in the ways they relate to the problems of the handicapped. Comparative analysis has shown how the structure and functions of these organizations have been influenced by national political, cultural, and historical conditions. Yet, just as there is probably more continuity than change in their recent development, so their similarities are more extensive than their differences. Taking these factors into consideration, the following are some generalizations that can be made.

1. *In all four countries, voluntary associations perform a mix of service and advocacy functions* that reflect distinctive historical, political, and cultural elements. In general, advocacy activities and more comprehensive and complex institutional services are organized at the national level, while most of the service provision is in the local community.
2. *Local affiliates of national organizations usually have a high degree of autonomy* and do not fit the picture of a hierarchical subordination to the national headquarters. Despite, or perhaps because of, this loosely coupled relationship, tensions and conflicts occur between the two levels of the organization.
3. *The board representation of interest groups differs greatly.* Professional health and social workers, the handicapped, usually in their role as member rather than user, public agencies, and religious organizations are among the groups that are most often represented on the board.
4. *There are symmetrical relations between the political structures and organizations for the disabled.* Historically, state antagonism or a weak state has laid

the ground for pluralism and local autonomy in the voluntary sector. For these purposes, Italy and the Netherlands represent the decentralized extreme, while Britain and Norway are examples of nations with a strong state and powerful national organizations. Voluntary organizations adapt to changes in the degree of governmental centralization, but there may be a lag and it can take some time before they adapt to new public decision structures.

5. *Service provision is usually disconnected from membership activities.* In Italy and the Netherlands, membership is usually connected to advocacy and interest group organizations, while service-providing units most often lack a membership base. In Britain, most of the national service-providing agencies are formally membership organizations, but the influence of rank-and-file individuals is marginal. In each country, a few service-providing agencies for the handicapped are controlled by their members, although the experience with this arrangement does not suggest its clear advantages.

6. *When priests leave, health and social professionals enter.* Church-sponsored social services are losing ground in countries such as Italy and the Netherlands where they formerly predominated. Factors responsible include secularization trends, the greater influence of professional treatment standards, and the increased dependence on public funds, which generally favor less particularistic standards of social service.

7. *Norms of efficiency are gradually penetrating voluntary service agencies.* The fiscal crisis of the European welfare states increased the pressure for more efficient voluntary service production, in the voluntary as well as in the public sector. Efficiency values were mediated by conservative political norms, prevailing management theory, and a trend toward modernization of third sector organizations. The strength of this penetration seems to vary with the degree of integration between public authorities and nonprofit service provision: when integration is strong, efficiency norms are more easily transferred to third sector organizations.

8. *There are advantages of large scale.* Large national organizations can more easily adapt to the various processes of modernization. Size is also a precondition for the advantages of specialization of tasks and functions, such as fund-raising. Small and local organizations with limited resources are more vulnerable to cuts in public spending, mergers, and reforms.

8

Interorganizational Relations: Collaboration, Competition, and Interdependencies

The interorganizational relations (IOR) of a voluntary nonprofit organization (VNPO) are the medium through which it obtains from the environment the various resources it needs for its various tasks. These resources are both tangible and intangible, and involve other organizations, both governmental and voluntary ones. VNPOs are highly dependent on the external environment, from which they obtain funds, clients, information, staff, and volunteers, as well as more abstract qualities such as legitimation, status, and various forms of power. Each VNPO is in daily contact with many other organizations, and its IORs greatly influence its fiscal, governance, management, and service-delivery systems. As Aldrich (1979:265) concluded: "The major factors that organizations must take into account are other organizations."

In this chapter we examine the leading patterns of IORs—collaboration, competition, and interdependence—both *within* the voluntary nonprofit sector and *between* VNPOs and government.

IORs among Voluntary Organizations: Cooperation for Service Delivery and Advocacy

VNPOs collaborated with other organizations on the national and local levels, both formally and informally, mainly to exchange information and other resources, but less often to influence public policy and practice. The former usually involved both voluntary and governmental organizations for the purposes of referrals, consultation, exchange of information and case coordination, planning, and, infrequently, joint operations of programs.

The increase in these forms of collaboration, particularly in England, seems to have been a response to the growing number of voluntary organizations and the complexity of their interrelationships with each other and with government, partly due to the more extensive responsibilities assumed by each in the personal social services. There was also a growing acceptance of the unique dual and complementary functions of direct services and advocacy, of "case and cause," whereby voluntary agencies, through various forms of citizen participation, also operate as mediating organizations between their clientele-constituencies and government. Because each country has its own political and public administrative culture and traditions, the forms of third sector citizenship are quite diverse.

Relatively more interorganizational exchanges of resources were reported in England, perhaps because of the preponderance of older, larger, and more complex multipurpose national organizations, in contrast to their counterparts in the other countries. Yet frequent and/or intensive collaboration among VNPOs still tends to be the exception rather than the rule (Butler and Wilson 1990). While interagency cooperation is widely praised and invariably included as part of the solution for most social problems, there is considerable inertia in the world of organizations; usually VNPOs, like other types of organizations, do not collaborate unless they perceive it as clearly in their interest to do so. For example, the three Dutch roof organizations only agreed to form a single national body when faced with a government decision that only one such organization would be funded. That this was not exceptional is suggested by the decision of sixteen Dutch organizations of lesbians and gays to merge into one organization under similar circumstances.

In recent years, with the exception of Italy, many of the voluntary agencies and organizations also cooperated with each other in forming new coalitions and/or participating in "umbrella" organizations that sought to influence government to improve the lives of all disabled persons, and not just the particular group they served. Though the emphases and strategies differed slightly from country to country, the goals of VNPO advocacy activities were: (1) to influence legislation or regulations; (2) to improve government service programs; (3) to secure government funds; and (4) to obtain special benefits for clientele.

These national organizations, known in the Netherlands as dome, roof, umbrella, or, in corporatist terms, peak associations, had an important representative and legitimating function. Though differing in their structure, status, and power, their role was to speak to government on behalf of the interests of the various types of disabled populations they represented and/or served. These umbrella organizations included both those that were primarily voluntary associations *of* the disabled and their supporters, and those that were primarily service providers *for* them, although the latter usually included some participation from the disabled themselves or their families. The political role of the umbrella organizations in Norway and the Netherlands was much more significant than their efforts at exchange of information, or planning and coordination. This was somewhat less the case in England, where the National Council for Voluntary Organisations (NCVO), a well-established body founded in 1919, performed many of the functions of a trade association for the voluntary sector.

Apart from contributing to the institutionalization of the voluntary sector (Powell and DiMaggio 1991), advocacy has become increasingly important as more voluntary agencies have been used to implement public policy. England, for example, has the oldest tradition of advocacy activities at the national level by individual agencies and their coalitions. Advocacy for people at risk, especially the disabled, has long been accepted and respected as an aspect of the country's pluralistic welfare state, even though some agencies' fear of loss of their charitable status may inhibit their participation. Both generic, intermediary bodies such as the NCVO, and newer, specialized federations like the Central Council for the Disabled, engage in frequent lobbying and have important consulting roles in Parliament and other government bodies. Reflecting a division of responsibility among national organizations in England concerned with income, housing, access, and mobility, a new coalition of over 250 organizations—the Disabled Benefits Consortium—recently emerged as a leading advocate of higher allowances for the 4.3 million disabled persons dependent solely on their social security payments.

The Dutch pattern and experience differ markedly from the British because of the reliance on a few selected peak or dome associations, completely financed and regularly consulted by government. There is very little advocacy by single agencies, except perhaps on the municipal level. The consociational and corporatist political culture in the Netherlands has long been characterized by a deep integration of public and private bodies (Aquina 1992; Therborn 1989). For example, the Council of the Handicapped in the Netherlands, a leading umbrella organization representing sixty organizations, is funded entirely by public resources and is an official adviser to the national government. It has no counterpart in England—there is some resemblance to the Norwegian FFO and the National Council for the Elderly—although many of the British national agencies receive small "core" grants for some of their administrative expenses from Whitehall.

Such public-private interaction is rare in Italy, which has very few national coalitions or umbrella organizations of VNPOs. Moreover, the dominant ideology within the Italian political culture ascribes responsibility for social welfare issues to the state; thus, VNPOs tend to focus on "cases," not "causes." Lobbying on public policy matters is also constrained by the political party system, which serves as the gatekeeper of demands on the state emerging from the civil society. Thus some small-scale improvements in the quality, quantity, and scope of local service delivery constitute the primary goal of the infrequent collaborative activities undertaken by Italian VNPOs.

In recent years, as described in Chapter 2, Italy has seen a proliferation of membership organizations, special interest groups, and self-help associations, usually chartered as single-issue (i.e., single-disability) groups that are circumscribed in structure and scope. While these self-imposed limits may restrict an organization's ability to provide services, they encourage particularistic forms of advocacy. These newer organizations have, however, far less political power than the older agencies in Italy such as those for the blind and the deaf.

Patterns of Advocacy

The strategies adopted by these umbrella "organizations of organizations" differ in the degree to which they are integrated into the prevailing policymaking structure—that is, the extent to which they are regularly involved in a consultation process with the government, versus whether they function more as a lobbying or pressure group. Their effectiveness in influencing legislation, regulations, and rates of payment also varies considerably from country to country, and is related to the status and power they have acquired over the years, as well as the policy structure within which they function.

Despite the older tradition of citizen advocacy in England, the umbrella organizations of the disabled in Norway and the Netherlands may be more closely integrated into the policy process in their respective countries. Representing virtually all the leading membership organizations of the disabled in their countries, the umbrella organizations in both Norway and the Netherlands are dependent on government for their operating budgets and are consulted regularly. However, they differ from each other in some important respects. The Norwegian FFO operates in a context where there is still little recognition of a third sector, and no official policy concerning voluntary organizations, partly because they have been closely embedded in the state system of service provision. The political role of the FFO also changed in the late 1980s because of the fiscal decentralization policy of making block grants to local governments. Lacking a sufficient number of local affiliates—there are over 450 units of local government in Norway—the FFO status on the national level has much less value in the new pattern of community decision making affecting the disabled.

In the Netherlands, the government is dependent on the sixty organizations represented in the new umbrella organization, a product of its forced merger of three national federated organizations. As long as the locus of decision making remains on the national level, the views of the Council of the Handicapped can be communicated effectively and its influence exerted. While some Dutch organizations serving a single disability such as multiple sclerosis or muscular dystrophy may also have a consultative role, only the largest national dome organizations are legitimated as authentic spokespersons for the disabled as a special class of disadvantaged citizens.

In Italy, where the third sector is beginning to be recognized, advocacy activities remain organization-related and mostly defensive; they are far less integrated into, or accepted by, the political regime. As noted earlier, Italy has no national umbrella organization; the League for the Rights of the Disabled (LEDHA), founded in 1978 and based in Milan, is almost national—but not quite. Italy reported a greater presence of more spontaneous, less institutionalized, more fragmented advocacy activities in the public policy arena.

Given this context, it is not surprising that the effectiveness of the VNPO coalitions and umbrella organizations varies considerably from country to country. In Italy, very little has been accomplished in terms of legislative and regulatory reform, and the infrequent policy changes that do occur seem unrelated to the VNPOs' cooperative efforts. These voluntary organizations were powerless to stem the erosion of many of the progressive reforms of the 1970s.

In England, at the other extreme, one large national agency alone cited thirty pieces of legislation with which it was involved during the 1980s. While the advocacy undertaken by the voluntary agencies in England has been quite successful in securing passage of major legislation on behalf of the disabled, the record of implementation is much less impressive. Crucial to the effectiveness of any of these coalitions is their ability to mediate ideological differences among their member organizations when, in fact, they have no authority over them. In the last few years, for example, the strength of the Norwegian FFO was weakened by the departure of one national member agency that did not feel sufficiently represented by the FFO's collective identity.

Organizational specialization has been identified as one of the factors inhibiting alliances among agencies (Kramer 1981:222–24) because most are designed to serve only one type of handicap or disease entity. Our findings both confirm and disconfirm this observation. For even as specialization divides the VNPOs, it encourages other ad hoc alliances based on shared interests and goals such as those relating to income, mobility, or barrier-free access. Coalitions or trade associations composed of service-oriented organizations and umbrella organizations composed of single-issue membership agencies often have different goals. Organizations providing direct services to clients tend to form coalitions whose main purposes are to lobby, to secure government funding, and to reinforce the coalition's own legitimacy. The umbrella organizations and their single-issue membership agencies tend to be somewhat less concerned with their own public or political identity and more determined to obtain specific benefits for their disabled clientele.

The coalitions and umbrella organizations formed by the larger service-oriented agencies are ongoing institutions with multiple goals and well-developed organizational structures. In contrast, there are many ad hoc coalitions temporary alliances formed for a specific purpose, usually a single issue. In England, which reported the largest number of such ad hoc coalitions, they were reputed to be even more effective than the umbrella organizations in bringing about changes in public policy.

The Norwegian, Dutch, and British agencies' collaborative efforts to affect public policy on behalf of their clientele have many characteristics in common, not the least of which is their collective assessment that in the final analysis their influence is quite limited! Greater pluralism of representation is naturally found in England, with its hundreds of intermediary organizations, whereas one major umbrella organization serves as the primary voice of the disabled population in Norway and in the Netherlands, while this is missing in Italy. In each case, the extent and effectiveness of advocacy reflects the status of the third sector in the country and the modus vivendi of government–voluntary agency relationships. The corporatist character of Norway and the Netherlands means that the IOR between government and the voluntary agencies are institutionalized, very close, and formalized, although many contacts are made informally (Kuhnle and Selle 1990). In none of the countries was there a challenge to the right of the voluntary agency to represent a particular group of disabled citizens on the grounds that in reality, only organizational self-interest was evident. Instead, as will be seen, there is a high degree of interdependence among the voluntary agencies and between them and the government. This does not, however, preclude the existence of other kinds of IOR.

Competition among Voluntary Organizations

In all four countries, the major arena of competition among VNPOs was funding, both for governmental support and for contributions from the public. VNPOs also competed for nonmonetary resources such as new members, volunteers, and organizational prestige, but these were quite secondary to financial support. Competitiveness has become especially keen in England, and to a lesser extent in Italy and Norway, due to the rapid growth in the number of both membership organizations and service providers in a more austere budgetary environment. British voluntary agencies have also been criticized for adopting the competitive models of the market, such as in seeking a distinctive niche for themselves and striving to be the "best" and most efficient provider of services (Wilson 1992:243).

The nature of the competition for governmental contracts is largely defined by the public authorities' requirements for increasingly specific services (day care and home care, for example) for particular groups of clients. In England, the competition for public funds has exacerbated the differences between the larger agencies, which are more successful in attracting these funds, and the smaller agencies, which are at a relative disadvantage because they usually lack the staff, experience, and technical know-how to obtain contracts from the Local Authority. Because the civic culture of England is particularly conducive to the various forms of voluntarism, it is not surprising that organizational competition, including media advertising, is more pervasive there than in the other countries.

The Dutch government, citing their advantages in cost-effectiveness, has also generally favored the larger, multiple-service providers in funding the personal social services. While there is more competition among these agencies that have a broader scope of services than among the more specialized ones, this policy has reinforced the quasi monopoly of the more specialized private initiative organizations. In the long run, the inclusion of most services to the disabled in the social insurances, which are extensively regulated by the Dutch government, may reduce the amount of competition in this field.

In Italy, by contrast, there is more collaboration than competition among the larger, well-established organizations, which have learned over time to accommodate one another. Here the locus of competition lies among the newer, more specialized agencies seeking contracts for new services, such as at-home day care for the disabled. One of the few reported cases of rivalry among VNPOs in Italy occurred in Milan among cooperatives competing to provide home care assistance.

In Norway, a major focus of competition is the lottery market in which each voluntary organization strives to sell the most tickets and to offer the most lucrative prizes.

There was a general reluctance among the voluntary organizations—except in the Netherlands—to acknowledge the existence of competition among them. The realities of the "charity market" in these countries suggest, however, that elements of supply and demand affect the behavior of all organizations. Indeed, it may be that this is one of the few relatively free market economies in operation, one characterized by minimal regulation, ease of entry, and a broad range of sources of income. In sum, because collaboration and competition are not mutually exclusive, the basic relationship among the voluntary organizations could be described as *competitive interdependence* (Marin 1990).

Relations between Voluntary Organizations and Governments

Although all of the VNPOs depend on government for their legitimacy, for various resources, and for policy guidelines, their IOR with government varied greatly in terms of the degree and frequency of their interaction, level of formalization, and extent of financial dependency. The four principal types of transactions between VNPOs and their governments were fiscal, regulatory, service delivery, and political (advocacy). Though interdependence assumes slightly different forms in each country, overall, governments and VNPOs find they increasingly need each other, and cooperation and collaboration are far more frequent than conflict and competition (Saidel 1989).

England and the Netherlands have by far the strongest and oldest traditions of public-private relations. Beginning in the mid-1960s in England, a process of incremental collaboration with government developed under both Labour and Conservative regimes. Many large British VNPOs undertook gap-filling roles when statutory resources were insufficient, and later also substituted for the Local Authority as service providers under contract or as recipients of fees and grants for various forms of social care. There is also an extensive record of joint operation of service programs for the disabled in many Local Authorities, but little evidence of statutory-voluntary competition.

Because of the total financial dependence of the Dutch agencies on the state, and their role as the primary service providers, their relationships with government have been much more conflict-prone than those in the other countries. For example, the majority of the p.i.'s referred to these relationships as "antagonistic." The most recent restructuring of the funding of the personal social services included the transfer of most programs for the disabled to the health insurance system, and others to the municipalities where the traditional subsidies have been replaced by budget allocations. At the same time, government has tried to press for more coordination, set minimum standards, and prevent destructive competition. That these policy changes were preceded by a government-induced reorganization of the peak organizations of the p.i.'s, resulting in the elimination of many of them, also contributed to the rancor between them.

In Norway and Italy, in contrast, only in the 1980s was there explicit recognition of IOR between government and voluntary organizations, although in the preceding decade, there were some references to the role of voluntary organizations in the long range plans of the Norwegian government. Historically, there is a record of state subsidies to voluntary organizations in Norway beginning in the 1820s, and although somewhat "invisible," they were nevertheless embedded in public policy until their recent rediscovery in the 1980s (Kuhnle and Selle 1992a).

In Italy, the church preempted virtually all nongovernmental relationships with the state until the years following World War II. The newly emerging voluntary sector organizations have developed IOR with the government based less on ideology than on mutual benefit. Fund transfers from local governments to VNPOs have been soaring, and new legislation on voluntary action was approved in 1991.

With the exception of England, many tasks are being delegated to the municipalities, and the trend toward decentralization has altered some of the traditional relationships between government and voluntary organizations. Beginning in the early 1980s, Norway delegated new responsibilities to its 450 municipalities through the use of block grants. As in Italy, the absence of a clear policy in the central government gave greater discretion to the Local Authorities in their use and support of VNPOs. This has led to more insecurity and competition among local VNPOs, and it has been problematic for those national organizations that do not have affiliates in the community. While the Norwegian initiative to establish volunteer centers in ninety-five communities is an unprecedented recognition of the role of the third sector, its likely impact on the existing organizations is difficult to discern.

Any substantive governmental move toward greater centralization or decentralization naturally causes uneasiness and uncertainty in the third sector. In general, centralization has tended to favor the larger, more powerful voluntary organizations, while decentralization has encouraged more competition among them. In England, where the Local Authorities have lost power, ideological debate is widespread. At the other extreme, in Italy, where pragmatism is the leading trend, there is far less ideological rhetoric, and state influence has been minimal.

At the micro level, public-private relations always contain ambivalent elements. Ideologies, attitudes, and organizational behaviors are neither stable nor fully coherent. "Antagonistic collaboration" (Marin 1990) captures the flavor of these quasi-competitive, quasi-cooperative ties. The similarity of these IOR patterns in the four countries is related to the similarity of their external environment where VNPOs confront many of the same uncertainties and resource dependencies.

Regulations, Monitoring, and Accountability

Regulations governing public-private relations in the delivery of social services have increased, particularly in England and the Netherlands. While Italy has no such national regulations, many regions have adopted rules, standards, and eligibility criteria for government contracts, which are an important source of funding for many Italian VNPOs. Each region has its own procedures, but selection criteria, accountability, and public controls are usually outweighed by "cozy relations" and personal ties similar to the process of "bureaucratic symbiosis" found in other countries (DeHoog 1984). Although the reform legislation of 1991 is intended to introduce more efficiency and reduce political corruption in the use of contracting by local government, there is little optimism that this can be achieved.

The Dutch system is more consolidated and institutionalized, and in the last few years regulation has increased substantially for agencies depending on social insurance payments, as well as on the traditional subsidies from the national government. One effect of these changes has been to accelerate the transformation of the traditional private initiative organizations into semipublic agencies, which in turn has put them on a separate track from the smaller, less institutionalized, local organizations that have to deal with the "village politics" of local communities.

In between the complicated Dutch regulatory system and the loose, highly decentralized Italian one stands the British pattern. The British tradition of public-private relations is closer to the Dutch pattern, but, despite the additional, and in many cases, costlier standards that have been established in the 1980s for residential care, there was little criticism of this use of statutory authority. While the spread of contracting is viewed with considerable misgiving by many in England, the type of accountability required by Local Authorities in the past has not been considered excessive; it has been much less demanding than in the United States.

Norway is different because its VNPOs are funded more through grants and fee payments than by contracts, which vary considerably by field of service. Perhaps the absence of a contractual system contributes to a rather light-handed pattern of governmental regulation and monitoring, with greater reliance on the internal and professional sources of accountability.

Thus, although regulation by government has increased, the increase has been quite uneven. In Norway and Italy, with their markedly different political cultures and structures, governmental controls and enforcement are quite loose, and VNPOs have relatively few reporting obligations. This contrasts with the pattern in England and the Netherlands where governmental requirements for accountability are growing.

As to the VNPOs' dependence on public funding, in Chapter 6 we noted that the Italian and Dutch organizations are far more dependent on the government as a primary source of income than their British and Norwegian counterparts. Government funding accounts for more than 80 percent of the income of Italian and Dutch VNPOs, but averages less than 50 percent of the income of British and Norwegian service-providing organizations.

In sum, if we view the four countries in terms of the size of public financial transfers and the degree of governmental monitoring, we find that in Norway both financial transfers and monitoring are low; in England, financial transfers are low, but monitoring is higher; in Italy, financial transfers are high, but monitoring is low; and in the Netherlands, both financial transfers and monitoring are high. There is the possibility in the years ahead that a potential single market in the European Community will also bring about more homogeneity in these IOR as a result of the "harmonization" of laws relating to the transfer of public funds to nongovernmental bodies.

The Effects of Public Funding

Increasing bureaucratization, formalization, and functional specialization were reported along with the growth of public funding among the voluntary organizations, particularly in England, where the values of the administrative culture of managerialism were widely diffused. Reliance on public funding, however, did not seem to inhibit either VNPO advocacy and political lobbying efforts, or their self-perception as being autonomous from the state—except, as noted earlier, in the Netherlands. Financial dependence can, however, entail a loss of autonomy for VNPOs that rely on only one public source for a substantial part of their income. Obviously, diversification of funding sources can prevent a high-risk dependency, and because most of the organizations included in the study pursued such a strategy, they did not regard their autonomy as compromised by reliance on public funding. Indeed, in Italy the larger, more structured service-providing organizations—those receiving the highest percentage of their income from government—believed that they could take advantage of their quasi-monopolistic position to force local government to respond to their claims. Moreover, in all four countries it could be inferred that governments had concluded that the administrative, political, and monetary costs of more intrusive monitoring or "control" were unacceptably high (Kramer 1991).

Italian and Norwegian VNPOs did not view government "interference" as the price of public funding, and several Italian organizations declared that the advantage of public funding over private funding was the comparative laxity in the enforcement of external controls! Norwegian organizations also regarded public funding as preferable to private funding, mainly because of its stability. Despite scattered complaints about delays in cash flow and rates of payment that did not cover the full cost of services, Norwegian organizations, which do not have an anti-state tradition, saw public funding as a positive symbol of their nation's commitment to care for its most vulnerable citizens.

British VNPOs also thought the advantages of public funding outweighed the disadvantages, even though some of the accountability requirements were regarded as onerous. For the smaller community-based groups, a major problem was not so much diminished autonomy, but rather the loss of statutory support because of their inability to compete in the increasingly stringent budgetary environment of the Local Authority.

The largest number of complaints about public funding came from the Netherlands, where the p.i.'s were dissatisfied with the new financing system, the bureaucracies of central government, and the unpredictability of the municipal authorities. Budgetary restrictions and regulatory issues were perceived as posing a serious threat to organizational autonomy, particularly because of their recent inclusion in the social insurance component of the health system and its complex rules. Yet in none of these four countries, with the possible exception of the Netherlands, was there evidence that government had any significant influence on goal deflection, advocacy, or volunteerism in these organizations—a belief found among many supporters of voluntarism in the United States and England.

To understand these patterns, we return to the observations about the civic culture and administrative traditions made earlier. In Italy and Norway, public awareness of the third sector is recent, and the cultural, political, and economic "space" for voluntary organizations is still expanding. Although many components of Italy's emerging third sector are highly dependent on public funding, any potential threat to their autonomy is offset by the multiple governmental sources of their funding (municipal, provincial, regional, and national), and by the more informal style of government decision making, which relies on networks of personal relationships rather than strict, bureaucratic enforcement of eligibility and accountability requirements.

Conclusions

Interorganizational relations within the third sector and between the VNPOs and government are essentially interdependencies, although those among the VNPOs themselves often have a competitive component. To describe the IOR with government as a "partnership," however, is not appropriate because it does not take into account the vast differences in organizational, political, and economic power between them.

More extensive financial transactions with the state, however, have not led to a loss of autonomy for the VNPOs. At the same time, public policy does play a decisive role in orienting these organizations' behavior. Trends toward centralization (in England) or decentralization (in Italy and to a lesser extent in the Netherlands and Norway) have strongly influenced the tenor of VNPO activity. In England, the "contract culture" promoted by the central government can widen the resource gap between the larger and smaller VNPOs, while decentralization in the other countries is promoting greater pragmatism and modernization among the voluntary organizations.

The expansion in the number of VNPOs in the welfare states has prompted greater competitiveness among the organizations in seeking financial support and specialized staff. Apart from day-to-day cooperation in exchange of information and clients, collaboration occurs primarily through umbrella groups and coalitions that are established mainly for advocacy purposes, and much less often for coordination or planning.

As one would expect, the distinctive character of IOR in each of the four countries reflects their civic culture and traditions, as well as recent political, economic, and social realities, which will be considered in the next chapter.

9

The Distinctive Character of
Voluntary Organizations

Introduction

We have now completed our analysis of the empirical findings and comparative generalizations regarding the income, structure, governance, administration, and interorganizational relations in the four national cohorts. Accordingly, what have we learned about the nature of VNPOs in general in the personal social services? What kind of organizations are they? What can be expected from them in democratic welfare states?

In this chapter we explore some of the implications of our findings for the study of organizational behavior, and, in the next and concluding chapter, for social policy. In contrast to the cross-national comparative perspective of the preceding chapters, the focus here is on the micro or organizational level. Three topics will be considered based on our findings: (1) a series of generalizations about the distinctive character of a class of organizations—VNPOs in the personal social services; (2) the significance of the trends toward increased bureaucratization and reliance on governmental funds for the identity and autonomy of VNPOs; (3) the implications for the significance of organizational auspice, or "ownership."

In addition to our own data, we also draw on some relevant concepts, models, and evidence found in the literature of organization theory, which has, however, given little attention to VNPOs. Similarly, most of the research and theory devoted to VNPOs has been directed more to the dimensions of the sector, or to the question, "why are there nonprofit organizations?" As a result, there is a paucity of empirical data on the organizational level with which we can compare our findings; we will, therefore, refer when necessary to widely held beliefs about VNPOs.

While we share the skepticism of DiMaggio and Anheier (1990:152) about the plausibility of a general theory of nonprofit organizations, it should nevertheless be possible to develop a more empirically informed understanding of their character, role, and performance. Yet at the same time, we are somewhat hesitant to generalize from our findings to VNPOs in other fields or "industries" such as health, education, the arts and culture, the environment, and so forth. Fields of service differ in their size, core technology, external environment (such as the extent of competition), roles, and relationships to government, all of which influence the structure and performance of their VNPOs (Meyer and Scott 1983). Indeed, differences among VNPOs in various fields may be greater than those between different forms of organizational "ownership," which are increasingly blurred: "variation *within* populations (organizations) defined by legal form may swamp variation between them" (DiMaggio and Anheier 1990:149). For example, Knapp et al. (1990) found that there were greater differences in costs among VNPOs than between them and their statutory counterparts. Consequently, while the analysis that follows has implications at least for the personal social services in the broad field of social welfare, further research would be required to determine its significance for other sub-sectors.

What Do the Findings Suggest about the Organizational Character of VNPOs?

As described in Chapters 6–8, there were notable differences in and between the national cohorts on such organizational variables as size of income and staff, major revenue sources, structure, age, and extent of consumer participation. Yet, as we shall see, there were sufficient similarities among them so that we can make some generalizations about their distinctive organizational character.

The differences in size, structure, and reliance on governmental funding—except for the Netherlands—were closely related to whether the principal purpose of the organization was service delivery or various forms of advocacy. The primacy of service delivery or advocacy, in turn, reflected the pattern and locus of public policymaking and administration in the country. For example, organizations that used most of their resources for the delivery of specialized, personal social services, funded in large part by government, were invariably larger, more formalized, and bureaucratic in their structure, employing a wide variety of paid staff, including various types of professionals. They were governed by a board of directors, few of whom had the same characteristics as the disabled clientele they served; essentially, they were social agencies *for* a particular population in their country.

The organizations with smaller budgets and fewer staff were primarily voluntary associations, most of whose members had the same disability, or who were family members of the disabled, and whose efforts were directed primarily at securing services and other benefits for themselves through various forms of advocacy to influence public policy. In contrast to the other three countries, many of these organizations *of* the disabled in England also raised extensive funds on their own that were used to support research and extensive campaigns of public education.

The line between these two types of VNPOs should not, however, be drawn too sharply because the service-providing organizations also engaged in advocacy,

Figure 9.1. **The Voluntary Agency as a Hybrid Organization**

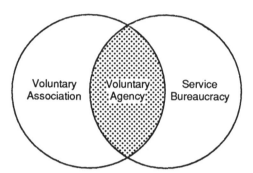

particularly in England, but much less so in the Netherlands and Norway where they were more integrated into a corporatist structure of public policymaking.

Despite these important differences, however, there were some basic commonalities among the four cohorts that suggest the unique organizational properties of VNPOs. Apart from their being subject to the nondistribution constraint and benefiting from some tax exemptions, they shared features such as: multiple, diffuse social goals, which make it more difficult to determine priorities or to evaluate performance; resource acquisition from a diversity of sources; numerous and diverse constituencies; an organizational culture that nurtures the values of both volunteerism and professionalism.

These likenesses, a form of "functional homogenization," are largely due to the similarity of their internal and external environments, which promotes isomorphism (DiMaggio and Powell 1983). It is a proposition of the new institutionalism in organization theory that organizations will become more alike under the following conditions: the greater their dependence upon, and the centralization of their resources; and the more there is uncertainty between their ends and means. Other variables conducive to isomorphism are ambiguous goals, reliance on academic credentials, and the participation of staff in trade or professional associations. These factors also contribute to the emerging institutionalization of the third sector in Europe and the United States.

The recurrent, distinguishing characteristics of VNPOs, which we found in the four cohorts, can be summarized in terms of three "M"s: Mixed, Multiplicity, and Mediating.

Mixed refers to a *hybrid* character, which combines the structural features of a service bureaucracy *and* a voluntary association, resulting in the coexistence of contrasting structures of authority, responsibility, and power, with two different organizational cultures of work norms, values, and interests (see Figure 9.1).

The bureaucratic form of a voluntary agency is most evident in its service delivery, and its roots as a voluntary association are found in its governance patterns and advocacy role. One of the distinctive features of VNPOs, then, is that there are *three* parallel lines of authority, each with its own hierarchy: one for the paid staff, another between professionals and volunteers, and a critical third one between the governing board and the executive. This condition helps account for many of the recurrent internal tensions and conflicts typically found in many VNPOs. For example, the strain between two contrasting authority structures is embedded in the often problematic relationship between the volunteers on the governing board and the paid executive of the agency (Hall 1990; Herman and Van Til 1989; Middleton 1987; Kramer 1987:244–46). This blend of lay policy control and professional direction—traditionally referred to as a "partnership"—rests on sharp differences in their social status, behavioral norms, roles, responsibilities, and power as shown in Table 9.1.

A useful distinction can therefore be made between two major types of voluntary organizations: there is the *association,* and the *agency;* the latter is more formalized, bureaucratic, and employs paid staff to provide a continuing social service to a community (McCarthy, Hodgkinson, and Sumariwalla 1992: 498–501; Kramer 1981:99–102). Billis has also called attention to this overlap between a service bureaucracy and a voluntary association, which he, too, has termed a voluntary agency (1991:60). While these two organizational forms share many values, norms, and interests with voluntary associations, when voluntary agencies enter into the world of social service provision, they become more subject to the influence of governmental policy, financing, and regulation (Fink 1990).

The co-existence of these two different organizational principles and structures was also characterized by considerable ambiguity about the boundaries between governance, management, and service delivery. Kouzos and Mico (1979) have described how each of these domains has its own structure, criteria for success, principles, and modes of work. The blurring of the boundaries between these three intraorganizational domains—rooted in the contrasting authority structures of a bureaucracy and a voluntary association—is the source of many problems experienced by community-based organizations in policymaking, financing, and staffing (Billis 1991:62).

Similarly, the differences in structure, function, and authority between service provision and advocacy organizations were notably evident in the British cohort, where nine of the national organizations, in contrast to those in Norway, were the primary service providers in their fields, and were appropriately structured as service bureaucracies. Their local branches were essentially voluntary associations, however, with a very loose affiliation to the national organization. Some of the perennial tensions reported between the national headquarters and the local affiliates could be traced to their different organizational structures. This was not a serious problem in the Netherlands, where most of the national organizations

Table 9.1

Comparison of Board Members and Executives on Six Attributes

	Board of Directors	Executive
Social status	Volunteer Trustee Employer Community notable	Professional/expert Full-time employee Director of social agency
Behavior norms	Altruism, best interests of community Proscription of self-dealing and conflicts of interests Collaborative partnership with executive and stewardship Participation in and support of the agency	Ethical, professional performance Subordination of personal interests to those of the agency and to the decisions of the board Helping relationship to board members, including leadership development
Roles	Policymaker/trustee Employer Interpreter, supporter, advocate	Multiple and diverse: enabler, guide, manager, educator, expert, etc.
Responsibility for:	Governance: policymaking/adoption Resource acquisition, allocation, control Appointment of executive, adoption of personnel policies Community relations	Implementation of policy via administration of program Appointment, supervision of staff Assisting the board, liaison between it and the staff
Responsibility to:	Community (membership, contributions, constituencies), clientele	Board of directors, clientele, staff, community, professional interests
Types of authority	Legal (formal/official) right as trustees to govern, receive and allocate funds Hierarchical—over executive	Professional expertise Hierarchical—delegated by board to implement policy (administer program), employ, supervise, evaluate staff
Power (resources for influence)	Status, authority as a corporate trustee Prestige as community notable Legitimation of organization Access to resources Personal knowledge, skill, time, energy Duration of service, intensity of commitment	Status as professional with expertise Administrative authority and responsibilities Full-time commitment; duration, continuity of service Access to organizational information Informal relationships with key persons

Source: Kramer 1987:245. Reprinted courtesy of Yale University Press.

had mainly advocacy functions, and services—as in Italy—were administered mainly by local or regional organizations.

The second "M," *multiplicity*, also refers at the same time to the *diversity* of voluntary organization constituencies, goals, accountabilities, and funding sources, which we found and which have also been observed by others (Gronbjerg 1991). In this respect, the voluntary agency could be conceptualized as a loose coalition of a plurality of various stakeholder interests such as board, staff, donors, clients, and so forth. Differences in the size, scope, and effectiveness of such organizations are closely related to the social character and resources of the interest groups they represent. For example, there are significant differences in the relatively greater development of services for the mentally handicapped compared to the mentally ill that can be traced to the social class of their major constituencies (Winkle 1989). Similarly, organizations concerned with the blind, with cancer, or with heart disease will generally have more resources because of the type of constituencies or interest groups associated with them.

In addition to the dual functions of service provision and advocacy, the mission and the goals of voluntary organizations are, as previously noted, typically diffuse. That the multiple goals of most voluntary organizations are on a high level of abstraction makes it difficult not only to evaluate their performance, but also to determine whether any "deflection" has occurred. As a result, the characteristic breadth and ambiguity of their goals makes it possible for a wide range of social purposes to be considered appropriate without having to defend themselves as abandoning the organization's mission. This possibility is aided by the considerable discretion available to voluntary organizations, which is often described as "flexibility," or its reputed superior ability to adapt to change in its environment (Powell and Friedkin 1987:180). An example of this capacity is found in Chapter 1, where we described the extensive and successful reorganizations undertaken by some of the largest, oldest, and most complex of the national voluntary agencies in England in the late 1980s (Butler and Wilson 1990:131–50). Similarly, in Chapter 2 the initiation of mergers by the p.i.'s themselves as a means of strengthening their position in the corporatist politics of the Netherlands illustrates the adaptability of these organizations to changes in their environment.

The other side of this characteristic is that while such organizations have a plurality of choices—considerably more than a governmental agency—once critical program decisions are made, they have a way of becoming institutionalized and resistant to change.

The third "M," *mediating*, refers to a voluntary organization's intermediary character on the sectoral level among state, market, and the informal social systems in the community. On the interorganizational level, voluntary agencies mediate as a buffer between the citizen and the state, donors and clients. On the intraorganizational level, the voluntary agency can be conceived as mediating between the interests of: staff and clients; board and executive; professionals and volunteers; staff for services (task) and for fund-raising (survival); and the functions of services and advocacy.

The recurrent use in the recent literature on voluntary organizations of terms like "mix," "hybrid," and "intermediary," and references to blurred or ambiguous boundaries, as well as to quangos, suggests that they all refer to the same distinguishing attribute. For example, at a European conference session in 1991, voluntary organizations were described thus:

> situated between markets and bureaucracies or hierarchies, they have to balance out the competing logics of efficient market competition, the provision of public goods—and their equitable distribution—and responsiveness to specific membership, clienteles, communities in terms of services provided and advocacy of interests. In balancing elements of community, market, and state or politics, NPOs represent *hybrids* of specific and varying mixes of informal self help, business enterprises, public agencies and special interest groups (European Group for Organizational Studies [EGOS] 1991:291–92).

This formulation raises a basic question for which there is no research data: "How does the specific mix of competing organizational principles relate to the success or failure of this mode of governance, interest intermediation, and service provision in health, welfare and social development?"(EGOS 1991). As additional evidence of their intermediary status, it is noteworthy that since the early 1970s in the United States, and about a decade later in Europe, these organizations have increasingly been called nonprofit and/or nongovernmental, even though they share many of the characteristics of government and commercial enterprise. In both instances, it is significant that the term refers to what the sector or the organization is *not* by defining it in terms of another entity. The absence of agreement concerning terminology and definitions in this field, as well as the interchangability of the various designations, is another reminder of the lack of appropriate concepts, theories, models, and paradigms for research on the fading and overlapping boundaries of the sectors (Salamon and Anheier 1992). It also explains the widespread reliance on metaphors such as third party government, the social or mixed economy, the shadow state, or indirect public administration, all of which reflect the pervasive interpenetration among the sectors.

These three clusters of distinctive elements—summarized in mix, multiplicity, and mediation—that underlie many of the dilemmas confronting voluntary agencies also pose the question of who "owns" the organization, that is, to which constituencies, and to which stakeholders, is it accountable for what? (Leat 1988; Kramer 1981:290–91). One approach to these questions is to conceive of voluntary organizations as a coalition of interest groups in both a literal and a political sense: they manifest a special, shared concern for a particular group of persons or a specific problem, which is usually expressed in a commitment to both providing specialized services for their client constituency and acting as an advocate for that constituency. In this latter capacity, like other interest groups, they try to influence public policy and they are themselves sources of power (Kramer 1981:258). Indeed, Streeck and Schmitter (1985) include voluntary organizations in their classification of Private Interest Groups (PIGs). The distribution of power among these interest groups of professionals, volunteer board and staff, and users has shifted as a result of the pressures for codetermination, on the one hand, and the reliance on centralized governmental funding, on the other. One of the consequences of the latter in the Netherlands has been the increasing displacement of the role of the board member by the professional staff, a process also found in other countries such as the United States and the UK when there is extensive reliance on contracting with government (Taylor 1992).

The inherent diversity of purposes, size, and structure of voluntary organizations is a formidable obstacle to the development of typologies as well as generalizations about them as a class. Are there models that might be useful? For example, the fact that so many voluntary agencies started out as voluntary associations might suggest that a developmental model would be an appropriate one to reflect their organizational career (Hasenfeld and Schmid 1989). Yet because of their inherent diversity, perhaps no one of the conventional organizational models will suffice; instead, depending on our purposes, several can perform a sensitizing function and contribute to a better understanding of the structure and performance of voluntary agencies (Morgan 1986). A life-cycle model, as used in Chapter 1 on England, can help describe and explain the process whereby most of the voluntary agencies became larger, more formalized, bureaucratic, and professional in the course of their organizational careers. Quinn and Cameron (1983) have integrated nine life-cycle models into one comprising four sequential stages that seems to capture the path taken by most VNPOs, except that of decline: (1) the entrepreneurial or formation stage; (2) the collectivity or development stage; (3) the formalization and control stage; (4) the elaboration of structural change stage.

Typically, voluntary agencies start as voluntary associations with a *cause* that can later evolve into a specialized service-provision *function*, one that is eligible for some governmental support (Katz 1960; Wolfensberger 1973). This model assumes that there are internal and external pressures for all public benefit organizations, especially those emphasizing services more than advocacy, to seek additional resources, to become larger, and in the process to become more formalized, complex, and "functionally specific"—for example, to separate their fund-raising and service-delivery tasks and staff (MacKeith 1992).

This view has been criticized, however, as being overly deterministic, and implying that there is little that voluntary agencies can do to shape their future because of these internal organizational imperatives (Billis 1989). However, a developmental or process model does not mean that there is a necessity for all organizations to move systematically through a particular series of phases such as community-based voluntary association to alternative agency to a formal voluntary agency to quango. What is reflected, however, is the empirical observation that this progression from informal to formal, from simple to complex, occurs very often as organizations develop over time, and that the outcomes are a response to a wide range of pressures and choices (Hasenfeld and Schmid 1989; Kimberly and Miles 1980).

Another useful perspective is to think of the voluntary agency as an open, natural system in which changes occur because of the interaction of various factors in its internal and external environment conceived as a field of forces with opposing vectors of varying strength (Scott 1981:79–101). In this model, professionalism (internal) and government (external) together serve as the "great rationalizers" of organizational processes and performance. For example, as described in Chapter 7, many of the changes in the British and the Dutch agencies were responses to both internal and external pressures for managerialism and efficiency, as well as codetermination in governance.

On the other hand, a resource dependency model seeks to explain how changes in the amount or type of funding, in interorganizational competition, or in the demand for a service can modify goals and/or structure so that the voluntary organization takes on more of the character of a governmental agency (Pfeffer and Salancik 1978; Powell and DiMaggio 1991). This model assumes that isomorphism (the tendency for organizations that interact with others in their field to resemble each other) is inevitable for weak organizations that have a vague technology and multiple, abstract goals. The same phenomenon can, however, be interpreted from an institutional or a political economy perspective whereby shifts in political and managerial ideologies in the society influence changes in structure and role in those organizations with a strong capacity to adapt to changes in their environment (Austin 1988). In addition, in a competitive environment, there may be reciprocal adoption of some of the other organization's characteristics, such as governmental agencies adopting fund-raising strategies usually associated with the voluntary sector.

These, then, are some of the distinctive attributes of VNPOs suggested by our study of the four cohorts comprising eighty organizations in England, Italy, the Netherlands, and Norway. Despite their differences on numerous organizational variables, they shared a set of unique characteristics embodied in their hybrid structure, combining the features of a bureaucracy and a voluntary association, having multiple, ambiguous social goals, and playing an intermediary role with diverse constituencies.

The Effects of Public Funding on Voluntary Agencies

As described in Chapters 1–4, the following changes occurred in most of the organizations in varying degree, regardless of their primary purposes and funding sources, although they were much more pronounced in those agencies providing direct services: (1) growth in size, scope, and complexity; (2) a parallel

increase in formalization, bureaucratization, specialization, and professionalization; (3) efforts to respond to the pressures for more efficiency, accountability,
and greater participation in governance.

Similar organizational changes have occurred to a greater extent in the United
States and the UK, where, somewhat in contrast to Europe, they have often been
viewed with alarm (Lipsky and Smith 1989; Wolch 1990; Wuthnow 1991).
Perhaps this is because of the prevalence of corporatist regimes and the different
traditions of state–VNPO relationships in Europe.

The alleged diminution of the voluntaristic character of these organizations
("devoluntarization"), the distortion or deflection of their goals (Gutch 1992),
and their growing resemblance to public bureaucracies or commercial organizations have usually been ascribed to their increased dependence on governmental
funds and/or their greater reliance on fees for service. It has even been asserted
that the greater accountability and efficiency required by governmental funding
results in "making a pact with the devil … a loss of intimacy, caring and
community" (Wuthnow 1991:291).

The belief that governmental funds are inevitably corrupting and controlling
persists, particularly in the United States and England, despite the paucity of
empirical research. In addition to the reliance on anecdotal impressions as evidence, it is exceedingly difficult to disentangle the sources and the consequences
of most organizational changes. Insofar as it could be ascertained, there was little
evidence of goal distortion or other allegedly negative impacts of governmental
funding. Analysis of the data suggests that more significant than the governmental source of funding for a voluntary agency were factors such as the number and
diversity of funding sources; the form of the fiscal transfer, that is, whether it
was a grant, subsidy, fee, or payment; and its specified purpose such as administrative, social care, demonstration, research, or facility construction.

Much of the anxiety about the future of the voluntary agency is usually based
on a pejorative view of bureaucracy. The concern about voluntary organizations'
loss of identity is often evocative of a "metaphysical pathos" (Gouldner 1955) in
which pessimism and fatalism characterize organizational models based on the
"Iron Law" of structural determinism. These models generally assume that there
is only one type of bureaucracy and that government is monolithic; hence,
bureaupathology is inevitable and it is not likely that its strains can be managed
effectively. An oppressive, Kafkaesque landscape is usually implied as the consequence of bureaucratization, which is perceived as inexorably destroying the
voluntary agencies in the United States and the UK (Smith and Lipsky 1993;
Wolch 1990), and to a lesser extent, the Netherlands.

The growth of bureaucratization, and in the size of income and staff, particularly in the service-producing agencies, did not necessarily result in inflexibility.
Others have also reported that rigidity can be reduced through an increase in
professionalism, role specialization, decentralization, and greater reliance on informal rules regarding efficiency (Rai 1983:44–58). On the whole, we found

little supporting evidence for the belief that the identity or the autonomy of voluntary agencies is inherently constrained by the processes of bureaucratization or the use of public funds.

Rather than its excess, more characteristic of many smaller voluntary organizations is that they suffer from insufficient bureaucratization (Perrow 1986:6), or the inability to manage more formalized structures. This may account for the frequent charge of amateurism or the ineffectiveness ascribed to many voluntary organizations (Salamon 1987). It is often overlooked that as a system, bureaucracy is dialectical—that which enables also disables, and for precisely the same reason. For example, greater goal specificity can lead to more focused effort or make it more difficult to change direction; greater clarity of organizational lines can lead to enhanced effectiveness or greater inflexibility. In each instance, the outcome is not predetermined, but is subject to the choices made by management and staff.

Consequently, bureaucracy per se may not be such an undesirable attribute, particularly if, as part of a trade-off, it contributes to more effective performance. As noted in Chapter 1, an incremental process of rationalization was found in virtually all the agencies in the British cohort, regardless of their size and the extent of their reliance on statutory funding. This suggests that the impact of governmental funding on voluntary organizations may be much less than is commonly believed, a conclusion supported by independent studies in at least seven countries (Kramer 1987:247). Mitigating the influence that government could exert on agencies dependent on public funds are the unacceptable political, administrative, and fiscal costs of trying to secure more accountability through additional regulations and monitoring. Other factors minimizing the constraints of government funding include the diversity of income sources, which tends to limit the control of any one funder, and the countervailing power of a VNPO oligopoly of services required by government for its clients.

What Is the Significance of Auspices?

Generalizations about the distinctive character of VNPOs have also been made by noting their formal characteristics compared to governmental and commercial enterprises, as in Table 9.2.

In an effort to get beyond such categorizations, which fail to do justice to the real world of organizations, researchers have sought to identify actual differences in costs, structure, governance, staffing, and performance between similar institutions under different forms of legal ownership. Most of the empirical research is based on hospitals and schools, although there are also a few studies on nursing homes, psychiatric hospitals, and day care for children (Weisbrod 1988; Schlesinger and Dorwart 1984). Dependent variables have been mainly cost-efficiency, service and client mix, structures, and strategies. Evaluative reviews of this research have concluded that the comparative findings are inconclusive or equivocal because of the inherent heterogeneity of funding sources, differences

Table 9.2

Some Formal Differences among Governmental, Voluntary, and For-Profit Social Agencies

	Governmental agency	Voluntary agency	Profit-making agency
Philosophy	Justice	Charity	Profit
Represents	Majority	Minority	Owners and managers
Legal basis of service	Right	Gratuity	Fee for service
Source of funds	Taxes	Contributors, fees, payments, and grants	Payments from customers or third parties
Determination of function	Prescribed by law	Selected by governing group	Chosen by owners/managers
Source of policymaking authority	Legislative body	Charter and bylaws authorizing board of directors	Owners or corporate board of directors
Accountability	To the electorate via a legislative body	To constituency via board of directors	To owners
Scope	Comprehensive	Limited	Limited to those who can pay
Administrative structure	Large, bureaucratic	Small, bureaucratic	Bureaucratic; may be a franchise operation or part of a national company
Administrative pattern of service	Uniform	Variable	Variable
Organization and program size	Large	Small	Medium to small

Source: Kramer 1987:43. Reprinted courtesy of Yale University Press.

among the organization's goals, their constituencies, and many other intangible elements (DiMaggio and Anheier 1990:147–53). Martin Knapp et al. (1990), in one of the few cross-national comparisons of different auspices for the personal social services, came to the following three conclusions: (1) it is not possible to generalize about the presence or direction of cost-effectiveness differences between the sectors; (2) there are often greater differences on any variable *within* the sector than between them; (3) conclusions reached for one industry or country are not transportable to any other.

Similarly, with respect to the social services, it has been aptly observed that "the designation of an organization as public or private, its relationship to government, and its sources of funding are not the critical variables in determining how effectively it responds to people in trouble" (Bush 1988:297). It might be hypothesized, however, that the legal form of an organization might make a difference, but that this probably depends on the institutional and ecological structure of the particular industry (DiMaggio and Anheier 1990:153).

All this suggests that sponsorship or ownership—that is, an organization's status as governmental, nonprofit, or for-profit—may be less significant in explaining organizational behavior in a particular industry than variables such as the ones we have discussed: purpose, size, age, structure, core technology, mode of governance, and so forth. This also seems to be an assumption underlying the concept of "human service organizations" (HSOs), which include all types of formal organizations working directly with people whom they seek to change, care for, or process. As an object of research and policy, human service organizations such as schools, prisons, hospitals, and voluntary social agencies share the same characteristics, such as ambiguous goals and an indeterminate technology in which staff–client relationships are the core (Hasenfeld 1983). However, the blanketing in of organizations so disparate in their auspices, size, structure, and function as if they had specific behavioral and management characteristics has been strongly criticized by Stein (1982). Nevertheless, the global concept of HSO, in which auspice is subordinated, has been increasingly used in the United States in research, policy, and management circles, at the same time that interest in the nonprofit sector has expanded. Only Austin (1988:169) has proposed the comparative analysis of human service programs by their "accountability structures" (auspices), and the proportion of governmental income in their operating budget. It remains to be seen in what ways the voluntary nonprofit aspect of some of these human service organizations will prove to be significant. For example, in one of the few studies comparing a governmental and a voluntary agency serving approximately the same type of clients, Gibelman (1981) found that the AFDC mothers received more and better services from the voluntary agency, but this seemed to be more a function of the smaller case loads than any particular attribute of "nonprofitness."

It is rare for voluntary agencies to be compared with for-profit counterparts because of the socioeconomic differences in their clientele, although substantial inroads in the field of residential child care in the United States have been made by commercial enterprises. Indeed, in both the UK and the United States, it is expected that as contracting becomes a more popular option for government, competition may reduce the market share of nonprofit organizations in many fields of service. *Who* delivers a social service may become less important than *how* the service is delivered. These considerations lead us to the social policy implications that are the subject of the next and final chapter.

Part III

Summary and Conclusions

10

Implications for Social Policy
in the Welfare State

In this concluding chapter we summarize the leading findings and discuss some of the implications of this study for social policy in the years ahead, particularly for the mixed economies in the advanced industrial democracies of Europe and the United States; the findings may also have some relevance for the countries in Eastern Europe. Although the focus is mainly on the national, sectoral level, which is appropriate for the consideration of policy questions, organizations are the link between a policy and its goals. Hence, we will refer to organizational properties of voluntary agencies as they may influence the implementation of policy. Because it is likely that increasing use will be made of voluntary agencies by government, it is important to know what can be expected from them. Most of the generalizations pertain to the personal social services, and primarily to the service provision role of voluntary agencies as utilized by government as partner, patron, or purchaser. Whether government makes, buys, or reimburses is, of course, a major policy issue. Another consideration of particular concern to the future of voluntary agencies is whether they are the primary providers, or a supplement, complement, substitute, or alternative to the government.

Following a summary of the principal findings, we will consider the major social policy issue framed as one of institutional choice in service delivery. Analysis of the changing nature of the four sectors and the welfare mix precedes a discussion of the "enabling state" as the context for social policy. Four welfare strategies are evaluated, and the chapter concludes with an analysis of their consequences for voluntary and governmental agencies, the service-delivery system, and its users.

Summary of the Principal Findings

Influenced by similar ideological, economic, and political factors in an era of welfare state retrenchment, the complex relationships between government and VNPOs in England, the Netherlands, Italy, and Norway have changed. Yet despite the differences in their histories and sociopolitical contexts, there were more similarities than differences, more continuities than changes, since the mid-1970s. This is suggested by the following trends and patterns derived from the comparative analysis of the four organizational cohorts.

The number of VNPOs increased, particularly in England and Italy, but decreased in the Netherlands because of governmentally imposed mergers in the social services, as well as those initiated by the p.i.'s themselves. The growth in the number of organizations led to more competition among VNPOs in all countries, and in Norway and the Netherlands it was also related to the decentralization of funding by the central government.

Trends toward formalization, bureaucratization, and professionalization were more evident in England and the Netherlands, while secularization and modernization continued apace in all four countries. In England, there were also notable expansions in organizational size, program diversity and complexity, and spreading commercialization. These organizational changes can be attributed to multiple internal and external factors and were not just a result of their utilization of statutory funding.

In the Netherlands, the role of board member and volunteer has continued to decline in importance since the 1970s, with more power accruing to the executive and professional staff of the organization. As in England, there was a growing emphasis on organizational efficiency and the professionalization of management, trends that also emerged in the 1970s.

There was an increased use of governmental funds, mainly for payments for social care, and an expanded use of contracting, particularly in Italy. A "contract culture" is being promoted in England as part of social policy, but it is also emerging in Italy in an unplanned way. In the Netherlands, funds for most services to the disabled have been shifted from subsidies to inclusion in social insurance where they are subject to more governmental control, even though they are administered by para-governmental organizations. Contributions as a source of philanthropic income have not expanded, but there is still active fundraising and substantial income from legacies in England. Although the 1980s are widely regarded as an era of retrenchment in governmental spending, very few of the VNPOs experienced cutbacks, and in England there was even little overall change since 1976 in the proportion of income derived from various sources.

Social Policy and Institutional Choice

Social policy includes two major components, of which only the second is directly related to this research. The first refers to basic political decisions regarding social allocation: *Who* should get *what* services and benefits in the society? The second aspect is concerned with the actual production and distribution of the service: *Who* should provide service; when and how? The latter is essentially a question of institutional choice in service delivery—whether, or to what extent should it be done by government, the market, the family, or a VNPO (Schuppert 1991).

These major institutional systems can be conceptualized in the series of "wel-

Figure 10.1. **Sectoral Relations as a Welfare Triangle**

Source: Evers and Svetlik 1991:17–18. Reprinted courtesy of European Center for Social Welfare Policy and Research, Vienna.

fare triangles" as shown in Figure 10.1, depending on the role of the state: if the state plays a central coordinating role, as it does in the Netherlands, then it should be in the middle of the welfare triangle; if it is not only central but also dominant, as in Norway, then it should be depicted as on top. The voluntary sector occupies a central place because it is mainly a mixed sector composed of elements of the other three (Svetlik 1991).

Although the social policy debate is usually cast in terms of institutional or sectoral choice, a more fundamental and practical question in social planning is: how can the delivery of public services be designed to optimize such values as access, choice, equity, quality, efficiency, accountability, and so forth (Gilbert, Specht, and Terrell 1992)? Presumably, the answers would help policymakers and administrators make more rational decisions regarding government delivering the service itself or utilizing a nongovernmental provider (Kettner and Martin 1987). Because there is very little empirical, tested knowledge that could contribute to such decision making, policy questions regarding service delivery are often resolved largely on grounds of expediency, or on the basis of questionable assumptions regarding the virtues of nongovernmental organizations (Kramer 1987).

There is, however, an alternative analytical and social policy concept—the welfare mix—whose potential role in the post-communist countries is evident in a comparative survey of care for the elderly in fourteen European countries and Canada in 1991 (Evers and Svetlik 1991). Used as a means of analyzing the changing sources of responsibility in the production of welfare in a particular field of service, it represents a step beyond the assumption that welfare problems are necessarily state problems. Situations in different countries can be compared in terms of the roles the different actors play, and the degree of integration, as in Norway, or fragmentation, as in Italy. The concept can encourage research and debate on the particular advantages and disadvantages, structural limits and potential of different patterns of shared responsibilities for policy planning, financing, service delivery, coordination, regulation, and evaluation.

For the individual needing care and his family, however, *who* provides the service is probably less important than *how* it is provided. As Svetlik (1991:14) puts it:

> The right question for social policy is therefore not the choice between one sector or another, but how to combine them most effectively in economic and social terms . . . [therefore,] [t]he task for experts, administrators, policy makers and interest groups is to find suitable forms of sponsoring, coordinating, and regulating different sectors and providers which will allow and encourage both a democratic public and effective personal control of care services.

Others, however, might want to put as much emphasis on effectiveness and efficiency as on consumer participation.

While the choice of a particular sector may be less important than the particular welfare mix, here, too, there is a paucity of information that might guide planning decisions. What do we know about these four delivery systems or sectors, beyond restating the familiar references to comingling, overlap, intermingling, mutual dependency, and so on? A search for an optimal mix between them in any particular country presupposes information and judgments regarding their respective organizational and institutional character, and their distinctive advantages and disadvantages. For example, it is probable that the state is more adept at striving for uniformity and equity, while voluntary organizations can be more responsive to cultural and religious diversity (James 1989). Perhaps organizational auspice or legal ownership *is* important; or, in David Austin's terms, "accountability structures" make a difference, although it is difficult to make a convincing case beyond the usual list of public vices and private virtues.

On the other hand, it has been asserted that "No clear or automatic connection can be made between the respective impact of a special sector and the final quality of services" (Evers and Svetlik 1991:11). In support of this generalization is the fact that most of the personal social service systems in the advanced industrial democracies, regardless of their particular welfare mix (i.e., extent of reliance on delegated nongovernmental providers from whom services are purchased), seem to have the same problems of cost and quality control, inequities and inefficiencies, as those mentioned in the introduction to this volume (Evers and Svetlik 1991; Kramer 1981; Kahn and Kamerman 1981). That this is also true in the Netherlands implies the weakness of the case for privatization, or any monopoly of service provision.

Patterns and Trends

So far, this analysis may suggest an exaggerated degree of rationality because the trend in these countries toward greater efficiency and effectiveness has not led to any significant pressures for more social planning or priority setting. The dominant operative principle is instrumental or pragmatic, as in Italy, with few attempts to formalize the relationship or division of responsibility between government and voluntary organizations. Ultimately, expediency and politics seem to be the decisive factors, not inadequate knowledge.

In any case, the question is not *whether* the voluntary sector will expand, but *how:* as part of a policy or plan, or in response to the market forces of supply and demand, and the political context? What forms will this expansion take and with what kinds of relationships to government and the other sectors, and with what consequences?

A serious consideration of these issues requires that the policy analysis move to a broader arena than sectoral choice, one that would include the multiple dimensions of the public policy process, as well as the different types of service provision relationships. For example, there still is insufficient recognition that the welfare state does not consist wholly of what government finances or does. Government is not monolithic, and many of its functions are delegated to nongovernmental bodies. Funding and the production of public goods can be separated, and we have seen how voluntary agencies played an important part in the transformation of the welfare state into the "enabling state," or what John Keane (1988) has called "l'état catalysateur." It has also been claimed that part of this process was the unplanned emergence of a "shadow state" in the UK and the United States of nongovernmental organizations highly dependent on public funding for the provision of their services (Wolch 1990).

There is no single European welfare state, but many different welfare states (Miller 1990:371; Mishra 1991), whose future has been forecast to include the following trends: very slow economic growth with continuing constraints on any significant enlargement of public spending; continuation of pressures for greater decentralization, debureaucratization, deprofessionalization, deregulation, and privatization. Also likely are the following: further erosion of universalism, with more segmentation and particularism in welfare policy, in a sociopolitical environment of considerable insecurity and uncertainty as the European Community emerges after 1992; and some destabilizing political developments in Central and Eastern Europe.

Other factors conducive to the increasing visibility and utilization of third sector organizations are embedded in the evolution of new roles and responsibilities of government in response to social changes such as the growing ethnic, political, and religious heterogeneity, and political assertiveness of minority groups; the demand for new types of more specific services for more hard-to-serve groups; and the greater capacity of communities to organize to meet their own needs. Hood and Schuppert (1988) claim that these trends have made the mass, institutionalized programs of governmental agencies much less effective, and that they help explain the growing use of VNPOs even in countries with weak traditions of voluntarism such as France and Italy.

Official recognition of the importance of VNPOs is also evident in various legislative and educational programs sponsored by the EEC in the latter part of the 1980s.

Table 10.1

Alternative Approaches to Welfare

	Function		
Approach	Provision	Finance	Regulation
Welfare state	Government	Government	Government
Welfare pluralism	Voluntary sector	Government	Government and voluntary sector "mediating structures"
New Right	For-profit sector (with a voluntary sector safety net)	Private sources	The market (through individual purchase)

Source: Taylor 1992:150. Reprinted courtesy of Jossey-Bass Publishers.

Alternative Policy Strategies

Based on the continuing viability of separating public funding from provision, the following three alternative policy strategies have been identified for England (Taylor 1992:150) and are also relevant for other welfare states as shown in Table 10.1.

The first scenario—the welfare state—is the least likely; it consists of the further concentration of service delivery as well as funding in government, a condition that has rarely existed in a pure form except perhaps in Sweden and in the formerly communist countries. Nevertheless, it is an ideal type, and is implied in many of the cross-national studies of welfare state expenditures. As a strategy, it has relatively few supporters, although it is sometimes assumed by its opponents to be the only alternative to privatization. There seems to be a much stronger national consensus in favor of other strategies, such as welfare pluralism or privatization.

As a second alternative, Miller (1990:378–83) distinguishes between two forms of welfare pluralism, both of which seek to promote various forms of citizen participation, empowerment, coproduction, or codetermination in welfare. One version stresses localism, voluntarism, and the involvement of family, neighbors, and friends. It has also been described as the "new subsidiarity" because of its emphasis on community-based, self-help, and mutual-aid associations. Advocates in England and the Netherlands on both the Right and the Left also believe that a policy of using nongovernmental organizations that promote citizen participation in the civil society can serve as an antidote to the social fragmentation, isolation, and anomie of the welfare state, as well as an alternative to its professionalized service bureaucracies (Pierson 1991:200–201).

Another form of welfare pluralism is based less on a community or grass roots approach, but relies more on the national, institutionalized voluntary sector for the delivery of social services, which are financed by legislation, as exemplified by the types of agencies included in our British, Dutch, and Norwegian cohorts. It is not opposed to professionalized service bureaucracies, and expects the state to finance most services and to provide many of them directly.

While there is much support for both forms of welfare pluralism—indeed, it is the new orthodoxy—there are serious deficiencies that deserve more attention. The first, localist strategy, is similar to the conservative populism advocated by those who mainly want to reduce public spending by relying more on volunteers and self-help as a substitute for government. This view ignores the fact that no country has found a practical replacement for public financing of most of the personal social services. Equally unrealistic is the belief derided by Robert Pinker in his dissent from the Barclay Report in 1982 in England as "a romantic illusion that we can miraculously revive the sleeping giants of populist altruism" (1985:244–45).

Attempts to replace governmentally supported programs of social care by informal social systems are subject to three sets of constraints: (1) the social networks may be nonexistent or unacceptable to the person in need of care, or vice versa; (2) the available resources may not be adequate, or the informal relationships cannot be sustained with the required competence, duration, and intensity; and (3) there are considerable data that informal networks find it very difficult to be accountable for public funds and to perform a public function (White 1981:30).

In addition to its basic lack of fiscal and administrative feasibility, reliance on localism can intensify existing inequalities and inadequacies (Knapp et al. 1990), and encourage "xenophobia, parochialism, autocracy, manipulation, segregation and narrowness" (Miller 1990:378). Also, decentralization of governmental funding can contribute to greater competition and more insecurity among local organizations as it did in the Netherlands and Norway.

Finally, the third strategy of extensive privatization, as advocated by the Right, is weakened by the lack of convincing evidence that the values and operating principles and methods of the market can be effectively transferred to the personal social services, particularly in meeting the needs of the poor, or in assuring some semblance of equality. This does not mean that there is no place for commercial providers; rather, that their role, of necessity, would be quite limited.

While the prospects of both the privatization and local empowerment strategies are rather dim, the institutionalized version of welfare pluralism will probably be ascendant during the 1990s. Based on this assumption that a policy of greater reliance on VNPOs by government for the delivery of public services is most likely, there are a number of issues and likely consequences to consider.

Issues in Service-Delivery Roles

Although historically, voluntary organizations of all types were the forerunners of the welfare state, their increased use can easily cast them into the role of a *substitute* for government. As part of what has been termed the "quangocratization of the world," the state has been able to off-load or shed unwanted, expensive, sensitive, controversial public functions, in addition to delegating the provision of public services to a wide variety of nongovernmental organizations such as the ones in our study (Hood 1991).

In serving as a substitute for government in service delivery in countries such as England and Italy, the traditional supplementary, complementary, and, some would say, innovative roles of voluntary agencies can be displaced, or at least subordinated. ("Supplementary" refers to similar services that extend those of the government; "complementary" services are different in kind from those of government). While it is not unusual for a voluntary agency to provide a mixture of services, some of which could be described as substitutes and others as complements or supplements, a form of Gresham's law may operate to drive out the latter. This process may not occur in Norway, where VNPOs have been closely integrated into the public system for many years and where, in addition, there is a low potential for any substantial increase in private giving.

In the Netherlands, the utilization of p.i.'s as the primary system for the production of the social services did not originate in a "crisis of the welfare state" or any rediscovery of the virtues of voluntarism. As a unique case of institutionalized privatization for over forty years, it constitutes the clearest and most extensive example of what can occur when voluntary agencies substitute for government as the major service provider, but not as the primary source of funds. What is a government monopoly in most countries is essentially a p.i. monopoly in the Netherlands, where a dispersed and pluralistic service bureaucracy operates in place of a more centralized and official one. The Dutch experience dramatizes the critical importance of income pluralism as perhaps the major defense against dependency and diminished organizational autonomy. As described in Chapter 3, the p.i.'s in the Netherlands are regarded as the major problem, and not the solution for the fiscal and administrative difficulties confronting the Dutch welfare state. Indeed, despite being among the most generous of welfare states, and utilizing the most decentralized, nongovernmental, and pluralistic organizational system for service delivery, the Netherlands is beset by the same dysfunctional conditions reported in the other advanced industrial democracies.

There are other problematic features associated with the use of VNPOs as a substitute. As noted earlier, there is no evidence at all that voluntary organizations in any country have the financial resources to substitute for governmental funding of the personal social services. Neither private philanthropy nor income from fees could possibly replace the latter, although it is quite likely that it may appear less costly for government to purchase certain services, rather than to provide them directly. In addition, voluntary agencies lack the organizational and legal capacity to assure that equity and the right to a public service—two of the distinguishing features of a welfare state—are attainable (Smith and Lipsky 1993).

Another possible outcome of VNPOs becoming primarily public agents could be a further weakening of the sense of collective responsibility that has undergirded the development of welfare states. This trend toward universalism has been slowed in many countries where benefits and services have become increasingly more selective and segmented. There is a greater likelihood of this occurring in England and Italy, but much less in the Netherlands and Norway where there is stronger ideological commitment to public responsibility. Although the residual philosophy of social welfare espoused by Thatcherites during the 1980s is similar to the principle of subsidiarity that underlies the Dutch welfare state, the latter, as noted in Chapter 5, is still more closely related to the egalitarian and solidaristic tendencies of the Scandinavian social democratic model (Therborn 1989).

Because Italy's welfare state, as described in Chapter 2, is already notoriously particularistic, extensive delegation of service delivery to voluntary agencies could erode even more rapidly its nominal universalism. In the political context of a weak and denigrated governmental structure as in Italy, growing reliance on voluntary agencies with their inherent limitations of scope and resources for service delivery could further undermine the legitimacy of the state and its capacity to cope effectively with social problems.

The converse side of this process is a rebound effect on the voluntary agencies, with their serving as a dumping ground where government unloads some of its responsibilities without providing sufficient resources, a prospect feared in England. Another hazard for VNPOs of a close association and dependency on government is that they may come to suffer from the growing anti-state ideology in Europe which is beginning to resemble the traditional American distrust of government.

In addition to its effects on VNPOs, which were discussed in Chapter 9, a policy of using nongovernmental providers of public services has other consequences for government, the service-delivery system, and consumers, although here there are few data to draw on. While government's performance as a public service provider is often viewed as flawed, experience shows that it may be even more deficient as a regulator, monitor, evaluator, or contractor. There are innumerable, inherent constraints in the performance of these indirect roles (J. Wilson 1989). Typically, one person's accountability is another's control that must be resisted. For government, the costs of more systematic supervision and control are often too great fiscally and politically, hence the typical lack of governmental incentive and capacity to assure adequate accountability from its private public-service providers. For example, in none of the four countries was there more than some financial reporting required on inputs, which may explain the fact that only in the Netherlands were relationships with government viewed as problematic. A major contributory factor in the Netherlands, of course, is the unique dependency on a single funding source, in contrast to the typical multiplicity of income sources of VNPOs in most other countries.

From the perspective of a service-delivery system, decentralization and the use of multiple providers may produce more flexibility in public administration, but it may also result in more unevenness, competition, inequities, and weakening of entitlements. Again, what is pluralism to one is "fragmentation" to another. Few generalizations are possible about the presence or direction of relative cost-efficiency between the sectors, except that there is constant pressure by provider agencies on government to raise the rates of reimbursement. Some research in England and the United States suggests that in the long run, any economies through the use of VNPOs disappear because their costs eventually equal or exceed those of government (Knapp et al. 1990; James 1989).

Similarly for consumers, there are virtually no data on what difference it makes to the users of the social services whether the providers are governmental agencies, VNPOs, or for-profit companies. Also, experiments in both England and the Netherlands to promote more consumer involvement in the policymaking of VNPOs have not been notably successful.

Conclusions

If the past is any indicator, the next phase of the welfare state will be characterized by an even greater use of VNPOs as public service providers. The advantages to both parties clearly seem to outweigh the disadvantages. A persuasive case can be made that even in a time of economic stagnation—if this is what lies ahead—government expenditures can be expected to increase along with the use of VNPOs to implement public policy (Pen 1987).

This seems to be quite functional, permitting the continuation of many welfare state programs and benefits that most people want, but not necessarily looking only to government to provide them directly (Taylor-Gooby 1985).

Thus, by separating funding from production, people can have their cake and eat it, too. Using VNPOs as service providers offers welfare states like the United States and other less reluctant countries an acceptable way of dealing with the decline in the legitimacy ascribed to government, and the decreased confidence in government's capacity to provide economic, equitable, and effective public services. This policy also has considerable ideological appeal because it can be presented as a form of privatization and the promotion of voluntarism, both of which are highly valued in many countries. Because there is no one welfare mix that will be suitable under all conditions, it would be desirable if there could be some experimentation on a small scale with different patterns of funding and the delivery of social services in various sociopolitical contexts. It would be useful to learn how VNPOs in different fields of service can maintain their identity, flexibility, and discretion when they are public service providers. At the same time, it would be important to study how access, equity, and accountability fare when VNPOs are used by government.

Until there is a new competing and more compelling rationale for the welfare state for the 1990s, this may have to suffice. In this way, the fate of the third sector in Europe and North America will continue to be inextricably linked to the future of the welfare state.

Bibliography

Aldrich, Howard. 1979. *Organizations and Environment*. Englewood Cliffs, NJ: Prentice-Hall.

Anheier, Helmut K. 1988. "The Public Sector and the Private: Organizational Choice and the Third Sector in Europe." Paper presented at the Spring Research Forum of the Independent Sector. San Francisco, March 17–18.

———. 1990. "Themes in International Research on the Nonprofit Sector." *Nonprofit and Voluntary Sector Quarterly* 19 (Winter): 371–91.

———. 1992. "An Elaborate Network: Profiling the Third Sector in Germany." In *Government and the Third Sector: Emerging Relationships in Welfare States,* ed. Benjamin Gidron, Ralph M. Kramer, and Lester M. Salamon, 31–56. San Francisco: Jossey-Bass.

Anheier, Helmut K., and Seibel, Wolfgang, eds. 1990. *The Third Sector: Comparative Studies of Nonprofit Organizations*. Berlin: de Gruyter.

Aquina, Herman. 1992. "A Partnership between Government and Voluntary Organizations: Changing Relationships in Dutch Society." In *Government and the Third Sector,* ed. Benjamin Gidron, Ralph M. Kramer, and Lester M. Salamon, 57–74. San Francisco: Jossey-Bass.

Ascoli, Ugo. 1985. "Welfare State e Azione Volontaria." *Stato e Mercato,* no. 13.

———. 1987. "The Italian Welfare State: Between Incrementalism and Rationalism." In *Modern Welfare States,* ed. Robert Friedmann, Neil Gilbert, and Moshe Sherer, 110–50. Brighton: Wheatsheaf.

———. 1990. "The Italian Welfare System in the 80's: Less State and More Market?" In *Testing the Limits: International Perspectives on Social Welfare Change in Nine Countries,* ed. Robert Morris. New Hampshire: University Press of New England.

———. 1992. "Towards a Partnership between Statutory Sector and Voluntary Action? Italian Welfare Pluralism in the '90s." In *Government and Voluntary Organizations: A Relational Perspective,* ed. Stein Kuhnle and Per Selle. Aldershot: Avebury.

Austin, David. 1988. *The Political Economy of Human Service Programs*. Greenwich, CT: JAI Press.

Balbo, Laura. 1984. "Tra Pubblico e Mercato, il Ruolo del Volontariato" (Between State and Market: The Role of Voluntary Organizations). *Politica ed Economica,* nos. 6–7.

Barbetta, Gian Paolo, and Pippo Ranci. 1990. "The Nonprofit Sector in Italy: Preliminary Notes on History, Definition and Statistical Sources." Paper presented at the 1990 Independent Sector Spring Research Forum. Boston, March 14–16.

Bass, B. 1985. *Leadership and Performance beyond Expectations*. New York: Free Press.

Beckford, James A. 1991. "Great Britain: Voluntarism and Sectional Interests." In *Between States and Markets: The Voluntary Sector in Comparative Perspective,* ed. Robert Wuthnow, 30–63. Princeton, NJ: Princeton University Press.

Berger, Peter L., and Richard Neuhaus. 1977. *To Empower People: The Role of Mediating Structures in Public Policy.* Washington, D.C.: American Enterprise Institute for Public Policy Research.

Beveridge, Lord William. 1948. *Voluntary Action: A Report on Methods of Social Action.* London: George Allen and Unwin.

Billis, David. 1987. "Some Puzzles and Models of Voluntary Organizations." Paper presented at the 1987 Conference of the Association of Voluntary Action Scholars. Kansas City, Kansas.

———. 1989. *A Theory of the Voluntary Sector: Implications for Policy and Practice.* Working Paper 5, Centre for Voluntary Organisation, London School of Economics and Political Science.

———. 1991. "The Roots of Voluntary Agencies: A Question of Choice." *Nonprofit and Voluntary Sector Quarterly* 20:1 (Spring): 57–70.

Billis, David, and Margaret Harris. 1992a. "Taking the Strain of Change: UK Local Voluntary Agencies Enter the Post-Thatcher Period." *Nonprofit and Voluntary Sector Quarterly* 21:3 (Fall): 211–26.

———. 1992b. "The Limits of Instrumentalism: Public Policy and Local Voluntary Agencies in the United Kingdom." Paper presented at the Third International Conference of Research on Voluntary and Nonprofit Organizations, Indianapolis.

Blau, Peter M., and W.R. Scott. 1962. *Formal Organizations: A Comparative Approach.* San Francisco: Chandler.

Borzaga, Carlo. 1991. "The Italian Nonprofit Sector: An Overview of an Undervalued Reality." *Annals of Public and Cooperative Economics* 62:4 (October–December): 695–710.

Borzaga, Carlo, and Stefano Lepri. 1990. *Le Cooperative di Solidarietà Sociale.* Brescia: Consorzio Gino Mattarelli.

Bozeman, Barry. 1987. *All Organizations Are Public: Bridging Public and Private Organizational Theories.* San Francisco: Jossey-Bass.

Brager, George, and Stephen Holloway. 1978. *Changing Human Service Organizations: Politics and Practice.* New York: Free Press.

Braithwaite, Constance. 1938. *The Voluntary Citizen: An Inquiry into the Place of Philanthropy in the Community.* London: Methuen.

Brenton, Maria. 1985. *The Voluntary Sector in British Social Services.* London: Longman.

Brown, Michael K. 1988. "Remaking the Welfare State: A Comparative Perspective." In *Remaking the Welfare State: Retrenchment and Social Policy in America and Europe,* ed. Michael K. Brown, 3–28. Philadelphia: Temple University Press.

Bush, Malcolm. 1988. *Families in Distress: Public, Private and Civic Responses.* Berkeley: University of California Press.

Butler, Richard, and David Wilson. 1990. *Managing Voluntary and Non-Profit Organizations: Strategy and Structure.* London: Routledge.

Censis 1991. *Rapporto sulla Situazione Sociale del Paese* (Report on the Social Situation of the Country). Milan: F. Angeli.

Chapin, F., and J. Tsouderos. 1956. "The Formalization Process in Voluntary Associations." *Social Forces* 34 (May): 342–44.

Charities Aid Foundation. 1982. *Charity Trends.* 6th ed. Tonbridge: England.

———. 1989. *Charity Trends.* 12th ed. Tonbridge: England.

Cnaan, Ram, Felice Perlmutter, and Chul-Hee Kang. 1992. "Voluntary Associations: Societal Variations in Response to Human Needs." Paper presented at the Third International Conference of Research on Voluntary and Nonprofit Organizations, Indianapolis, March 11–13.

Commissie Structuur en Financiering van de Gezondsheidszorg (Committee on Structure and Financing of Health Care). 1987. *Bereidheid tot verandering (Readiness to Change)*. The Hague: Distrubutiecentrum Overheidspublicaties (Distribution Center for Government Publications).

Commissie van der Burg. 1977. *Rapport van de Commissie van Advies Inzake Democratisch en Doelmatig Functioneren van Gesubsidieerde Instellingen* (Report of the Advisory Committee on Democratic and Effective Functioning of Subsidized Organizations). The Hague: Staatsuitgeverji (Government Publishing Company).

CRM (Ministry of Culture, Recreation and Social Welfare). 1974. *Rapport van de Beraadsgroep Knelpunten Harmonisatie Welzijnsbeleid en Wetgeving* (Report of the Advisory Committee on Bottlenecks in the Harmonization of Welfare Policy and Legislation). Rijswijk.

Dartington, Tom. 1989. "Management Learning and Voluntary Organisations." National Council for Voluntary Organisations, London.

David, Patrizia. 1984. "Il Sistema Assistenziale in Italia." In *Welfare State All'Italiana*, ed. Ugo Ascoli, 185–205. Bari: Laterza.

Day, P., and R. Klein. 1987. "Residential Care for the Elderly: A Billion Pound Experiment in Policy Making." *Public Money*, no. 6: 19–24.

De Ambrogio, Ugo, and Costanzo Ranci. 1989. "Volontariato in Lombardia." *Prospettive Sociali e Sanitarie*, no. 9.

DeHoog, Ruth H. 1984. *Contracting Out for Human Services: Economic, Political and Organizational Perspectives*. Albany: State University of New York Press.

De Kluiver, Harm J. 1990. "Democracy, Rights and NGO's." In the Proceedings of the 1990 Conference of the Association of Voluntary Action Scholars, vol. 1, pp. 318–20. London, June 16–18.

De Kok, A. 1987. "Savings through Innovative Care Provision in the Dutch Welfare State." In *The Changing Face of Welfare*, ed. Adelbert Evers et al., 122–37. London: Gower.

Demone, Harold, and Margaret Gibelman, eds. 1989. *Services for Sale: Purchase of Service Contracting in Health and Human Services*. New Brunswick, NJ: Rutgers University Press.

Dente, B. 1990. "Partisan Politics and Bureaucracy in Italian Social Policies." In *Discretionary Politics*, ed. Douglas E. Ashford. Greenwich, CT: JAI Press.

Dierkes, Meinolf, Hans Weiler, and Ariane Antol, eds. 1987. *Comparative Policy Research: Learning from Experience*. Aldershot: Gower.

DiMaggio, Paul. 1987. "Nonprofit Organizations in the Production and Distribution of Culture." In *The Third Sector: A Research Handbook*, ed. Walter W. Powell, 195–220. New Haven, CT: Yale University Press.

DiMaggio, Paul, and Helmut K. Anheier. 1990. "The Sociology of Nonprofit Organizations and Sectors." *Annual Review of Sociology* 16:137–59.

DiMaggio, Paul, and Walter Powell. 1983. "The Iron Cage Revisited: Institutional Isomorphism and Collective Rationality in Organizational Fields." *American Sociological Review* 48:147–60.

Donahue, J.D. 1989. *The Privatization Decision: Public Ends, Private Means*. New York: Basic Books.

Douglas, James. 1983. *Why Charity?* Beverly Hills: Sage Publications.

Dulsrud, Arne. 1988. *Frivillighet og tvang* (Voluntarism and State Power). Oslo: Institute for Sociology, University of Oslo.

Elstad, Jon. 1990. "Health Services and Decentralized Government: The Case of Primary Health Services in Norway." *International Journal of Health Services* 20:4, 545–59.

Erichsen, Werner. 1960. *Streif fra Nasjonalforeningens 50-arige historie* (From the 50-Year History of the National League for Women). Oslo: Aschehoug.

Esping-Andersen, Gosta. 1990. *The Three Worlds of Welfare Capitalism*. Cambridge, England: Polity Press.

European Group for Organizational Studies (EGOS). 1991. Tenth Colloquium: Working Group 9, "Nonprofit and Voluntary Organizations in Comparative Perspective." Vienna, July 15–17.

Eurostat Statistics. 1989. Statistical Office of the European Communities. Brussels.

Evers, Adalbert, and Ivan Svetlik, eds. 1991. *New Welfare Mixes in Care for the Elderly*. Vienna: European Center for Social Welfare Policy and Research.

Evers, Adalbert, and Helmut Wintersberger. 1988. *Shifts in the Welfare Mix. Their Impact on Work, Social Services and Welfare Policy*. Vienna: European Centre for Social Welfare Policy and Research.

Ferrera, Maurizio. 1984. *Il Welfare State in Italia*. Bologna: Il Mulino.

———. 1987. "The Italian Welfare State." In *Growth to Limits. The European Welfare States since World War II*, ed. Peter Flora. Berlin: de Gruyter.

Fink, Justin. 1990. "Community Agency Entrepreneurs: Formalization and Change in Community Based Organizations during the Reagan Era." Paper presented at the Spring Research Forum of the Independent Sector. Boston, March.

Flora, Peter, and Arnold Heidenheimer, eds. 1981. *The Development of Welfare States in Europe and America*. New Brunswick, NJ: Transaction.

Freddi, G. 1980. "Regional Devolution, Administrative Decentralization and Bureaucratic Performance in Italy." *Policy and Politics* 8(4): 383–98.

Fuglum, Per. 1984. *DNT—125 ar for alles vel* (The Norwegian Teetotalist Organization—125 Years for the Welfare of the People). Oslo: Universitetsforlaget.

Gamble, Andrew. 1988. *The Free Economy and the Strong State: The Politics of Thatcherism*. Durham, NC: Duke University Press.

Gassler, Robert S. 1990. "Nonprofit Enterprise and Soviet Economic Reform." *Voluntas* 2(1): 95–109.

Gibelman, Marjorie. 1981. "Are Clients Better Served When Services Are Purchased?" *Public Welfare* 39:26–33.

Gidron, Benjamin, Ralph M. Kramer, and Lester M. Salamon, eds. 1992. *Government and the Third Sector: Emerging Relationships in Welfare States*. San Francisco: Jossey-Bass.

Gilbert, Neil, and Barbara Gilbert. 1990. *The Enabling State*. New York: Oxford University Press.

Gilbert, Neil, Harry Specht, and Paul Terrell. 1992. *New Dimensions in Social Policy*. 3d ed. Englewood Cliffs, NJ: Prentice-Hall.

Gjems-Onstad, Ole. 1990. "The Independence of Voluntary Organizations in a Social Democracy: Governmental Influences in Norway." *Nonprofit and Voluntary Sector Quarterly* 19:4 (Winter): 393–407.

Gladstone, Francis. 1979. *Voluntary Action in a Changing World*. London: Bedford Square Press.

Glennerster, Howard, Anne Power, and Tony Travers. 1991. "A New Era for Social Policy: A New Enlightenment or a New Leviathan?" *Journal of Social Policy* 20(3): 389–414.

Gorter, Klaas A. 1988. "Zorgen voor Gehandicapte Gezinsleden, Een Landelijk Onderzoek naar Problemen en Hulpverlening binnen Huishoudens met Lichamelijk Gehandicapten" (Caring for Handicapped Family Members: A National Research Project Concerning Problems and Care in Households with Physically Handicapped Family Members). Doctoral dissertation. The Hague: NIMAWO.

Gouldner, Alvin W. 1955. "Metaphysical Pathos and the Theory of Bureaucracy." *American Political Science Review* 59(2): 496–508.

Griffiths, Sir Roy. 1988. *Community Care: An Agenda for Action*. London: HMSO.

Grindheim, Jan, and Per Selle. 1990. "The Role of Voluntary Social Welfare Organizations in Norway: A Democratic Alternative to a Bureaucratic Welfare State?" *Voluntas* 1(1): 62–76.

Gronbjerg, Kirsten. 1987. "Patterns of Institutional Relations in the Welfare State: Public Mandates and the Nonprofit Sector." *Journal of Voluntary Action Research* 16:64–80.

———. 1991. "Managing Grants and Contracts: The Case of Four Nonprofit Organizations." *Nonprofit and Voluntary Sector Quarterly* 20(1): 5–24.

Guardian. 1989. "The Cost of Caring." November 18, p. 14.

Gutch, Richard. 1992. *Contracting Lessons from the US*. London: National Council for Voluntary Organisations.

Gutch, Richard, and Ken Young. 1988. *Partners or Rivals? Developing the Relationships between Voluntary Organizations and Local Government*. London: National Council for Voluntary Organisations.

Hadley, Roger, and Stephen Hatch. 1981. *Social Welfare and the Failure of the State*. London: George Allen and Unwin.

Hall, Peter D. 1990. "Conflicting Managerial Cultures in Nonprofit Organizations." *Nonprofit Management and Leadership* 1 (Winter): 153–66.

———. 1992. *Inventing the Nonprofit Sector*. Baltimore, MD: John Hopkins Press.

Hallett, C. 1982. *The Personal Social Services in Local Government*. London: George Allen and Unwin.

Hansmann, Henry. 1980. "The Role of Nonprofit Enterprise." *Yale Law Journal* 89: 835–901.

———. 1987. "Economic Theory of Nonprofit Organizations." In *The Nonprofit Sector: A Research Handbook*, ed. W.W. Powell, Jr., 27–42. New Haven, CT: Yale University Press.

Hartogs, N., and J. Weber. 1978. *The Impact of Government Funding on the Management of Voluntary Agencies*. New York: Greater New York Fund and United Way.

Hasenfeld, Yeheskel. 1983. *Human Service Organizations*. Englewood Cliffs, NJ: Prentice-Hall.

Hasenfeld, Yeheskel, and Hillel Schmid. 1989. "The Life Cycle of Human Service Organizations: An Administrative Perspective." *Administration in Social Work* 13(4): 243–69.

Hatch, Stephen. 1980. *Outside the State: Voluntary Organisations in Three English Towns*. London: Croom Helm.

Hatch, Stephen, and Ian Mocroft. 1983. *Components of Welfare: Voluntary Organisations, Social Services and Politics in Two Local Authorities*. London: Bedford Square Press.

Hatland, A. 1986. "The Right to Care in Norwegian Social Policy." *Eurosocial*, 53–58.

Heidenheimer, Arnold, Hugh Heclo, and Carolyn Adams, eds. 1990. *Comparative Public Policy: The Politics of Social Choice in America, Europe and Japan*. 3d ed. New York: St. Martin's Press.

Herman, Robert D. 1990. "Methodological Issues in Studying the Effectiveness of Nongovernmental and Nonprofit Organizations." *Nonprofit and Voluntary Sector Quarterly* 19(3): 293–326.

Herman, Robert, and Richard Heimovics. 1989. "Effective Managers of Nonprofit Organizations." *Working Papers*, Spring Research Forum, Independent Sector, Washington, D.C.

Herman, Robert, and John Van Til, eds. 1989. *Nonprofit Boards of Directors: Analyses and Applications*. New Brunswick, NJ: Transaction.

Hernes, Helga. 1986. "Care Work and the Organizational Daily Life." *Eurosocial*, 41–52.

Higgins, J. 1989. "Defining Community Care: Realities and Myths." *Social Policy and Administration* 23(1): 3–14.

Hirschman, Albert O. 1982. *Shifting Involvements: Private Interest and Public Action.* Oxford: Martin Robertson.

———. 1991. *The Rhetoric of Reaction.* Cambridge: Harvard University Press.

Home Office. 1989. *Charities: A Framework for the Future.* Command Paper 694. London: HMSO.

———. 1990. *Efficiency Scrutiny of the Government Funding of the Voluntary Sector: Profiting from Partnerships.* London: HMSO.

HMSO. 1989. *Caring for People—Community Care in the Next Decade and Beyond 1989.* Command Paper 849. London: Her Majesty's Stationery Office.

Hood, Christopher. 1991. "The Hidden Public Sector: The 'Quangocratization' of the World." In *The Public Sector—Challenge for Coordination and Learning,* ed. Franz-Xaver Kaufmann, 165–87. Berlin: de Gruyter.

Hood, Christopher, and Gunnar Schuppert, eds. 1988. *Delivering Public Services in Western Europe: Sharing Western European Experience of Para-Governmental Organizations.* London: Sage.

Hueting, E., and R. Neij. 1991. "Sociale Zorg in Grootstedelijke Gebieden in Beleidsmatig Perspectief" (Social Care in Metropolitan Areas in a Policy Perspective). In *Maatschappelijk Werk en de Stad, Vijf Preadviezen* (Social Work and the City, Five Proposals), ed. P. den Hoed. The Hague: Wetenschappelijk Raad voor het Regeringsbeleid (Scientific Council for Government Policy).

Humble, Stephen, and Alan Walker. 1990. "Constructing a New Welfare Mix in the UK: The Role of the Voluntary Sector." In *Shifts in the Welfare Mix: Their Impact on Work, Social Services and Welfare Policies,* ed. A. Evers and H. Wintersberger, 237–67. Boulder, CO: Westview Press.

Idenberg, Pieter. 1985. "The Dutch Paradox in Social Welfare." In *Yearbook of Social Policy in Britain,* ed. Charles Jones and Maria Brenton, 123–43. London: Routledge and Kegan Paul.

Idenberg, Pieter, and P.J. Beugels. 1989. *Het Nieuwe Rotterdam in Social Perspectief: Rapport van de Commissie Sociale Vernieuwing Rotterdam* (Renewed Rotterdam in Social Perspective: Report of the Committee on Social Innovation of Rotterdam). Rotterdam.

IREF. 1990. *Terzo Rapporto Sull'associazionismo Sociale.* Napoli, Italy: Tecnodid.

ISTAT. 1990. *Annuario Statistico Italiano.* Rome.

Istituto per la Ricerca Sociale. 1990. "Research on Nonprofit Organizations in the Milan Social and Health Sector." Milan, Italy (unpublished report).

James, Estelle. 1982. *The Private Provision of Public Services: A Comparison of Sweden and Holland.* PONPO Working Paper No. 60. Institution for Social and Policy Studies. New Haven: Yale University.

———, ed. 1989. *The Nonprofit Sector in International Perspective: Studies in Comparative Culture and Policy.* New York: Oxford University Press.

Janowitz, Morris. 1976. *Social Control of the Welfare State.* New York: Elsevier Scientific Publishing.

Johnson, Norman. 1981. *Voluntary Social Services.* Oxford: Basil Blackwell and Martin Robertson.

———. 1987. *The Welfare State in Transition: The Theory and Practice of Welfare Pluralism.* Amherst: University of Massachusetts Press.

———. 1989. "The Privatization of Welfare." *Social Policy and Administration* 23:1 (May): 17–30.

———. 1990. "Problems in the Mixed Economy of Welfare." In *Needs and Welfare,* ed. A. Ware and R. Goodin, 145–64. London: Sage.

———. 1991. "The Changing Role of Voluntary Social Welfare Organizations in Britain from 1945 to the Present Day." In *Government and Voluntary Organizations,* ed. Stein Kuhnle and Per Selle, 87–107. Aldershot: Avebury.

Johnson, Paul. 1986. "Some Historical Dimensions of the Welfare State." *Journal of Social Policy* 15:4 (October).

Jolles, H.M. 1988. *Tussen Burger en Staat: Verkenningen Omtrent het Maatschappelijk Middenveld in een Tijd van Deregulering* (Between Citizen and State: Explorations Concerning the Social Intermediary Field in a Time of Deregulation). Assen/Maastricht: Van Gorcum.

Jowell, Roger, Sharon Witherspoon, and Lindsay Brook. 1989. *British Social Attitudes: Special International Report.* London: Gower.

Judge, Ken, and Jillian Smith. 1982. "The Public Purchase of Social Care: British Confirmation of the American Experience." *Policy and Politics* 10:4.

Kahn, Alfred, and Sheila Kamerman. 1981. *Social Services in International Perspective: The Emergence of the Sixth System.* New Brunswick, NJ: Rutgers University Press.

Kamerman, Sheila, and Alfred Kahn, eds. 1989. *Privatization and the Welfare State.* Princeton, NJ: Princeton University Press.

Katz, Alfred. 1960. *Parents of the Handicapped.* Springfield, IL: Charles C. Thomas.

Keane, John. 1988. "The Limits of State Action." In *Democracy and Civil Society,* ed. John Keane, 1–30. London: Verso.

Kersbergen, K., and Uwe Becker. 1988. "The Netherlands: A Passive Social Democratic State in a Christian Democratic Ruled Society." *Journal of Social Policy* 17:4 (October): 477–99.

Kettner, Peter M., and Lawrence L. Martin. 1987. *Purchase of Service Contracting.* Beverly Hills: Sage.

Kimberly, James, and Raymond Miles, eds. 1980. *The Organizational Life Cycle.* San Francisco: Jossey-Bass.

Knapp, Martin, and Helmut Anheier. 1990. "Voluntas: An Editorial Statement." *Voluntas* 1:1.

Knapp, Martin, and Jeremy Kendall. 1990. "Defining the British Voluntary Sector." In *The Nonprofit Sector (NGOs) in the U.S. and Abroad: Cross-Cultural Perspectives.* 1990 Spring Research Forum, Working Papers, Independent Sector. Washington, D.C., pp. 23–34.

Knapp, Martin, and S. Saxon-Harrold. 1989. *The British Voluntary Sector.* Discussion Paper no. 645, Personal Social Services Research Unit. University of Kent, Canterbury, July.

Knapp, Martin, Eileen Robertson, and Corinne Thomason. 1990. "Public Money, Voluntary Action: Whose Welfare?" in *The Third Sector,* ed. Helmut K. Anheier and Wolfgang Seibel, 183–218. Berlin: de Gruyter.

Kolberg, Jon Eivind. 1984. "Private og offentlige velferdskomponenter" (Private and Public Welfare Components). In *Privat eller offentlig velferd?* (Private or Public Welfare?), ed. H. Lorentzen. Oslo: Universitetsforlaget.

Kolderie, P. 1986. "The Two Different Concepts of Privatization." *Public Administration Review* 46:4 (July/August): 285–91.

Kouzos, James M., and Paul R. Mico. 1979. "Domain Theory: An Introduction to Organizational Behavior in Human Service Organizations." *Journal of Applied Behavioral Science* 15(4): 449–69.

Kramer, Ralph M. 1981. *Voluntary Agencies in the Welfare State.* Berkeley: University of California Press.

———. 1985. "Towards a Contingency Model of Board–Executive Relations in Nonprofit Organizations." *Administration in Social Work* 9:3 (Fall): 15–33.

———. 1987. "Voluntary Agencies and the Personal Social Services." In *The Nonprofit Sector: A Research Handbook,* ed. W.W. Powell, Jr., 240–57. New Haven, CT: Yale University Press.

————. 1990. "Change and Continuity in British Voluntary Organizations." *Voluntas* 1:2 (November): 33–60.

————. 1991. "Voluntary Organizations in the Welfare States on the Threshold of the 90's." In *Issues in Voluntary and Nonprofit Management,* ed. J. Butsleer, C. Cornforth, and R. Paton, 181–91. Wokingham, England: Addison-Wesley.

Kramer, Ralph M., and Bart Grossman. 1987. "Contracting for Social Services: Process Management and Resource Dependencies." *Social Service Review* 61:1 (March): 32–55.

Kronjee, Gerrit J. 1976. *Particulier Initiatief in de Gehandicaptenzorg* (Voluntary Organizations in the Care of the Handicapped). The Hague: NIMAWO.

Kuhnle, Stein. 1990. "The Scandinavian Welfare Model in the Era of European Integration." Paper presented at the ECPR Planning Session, Ruhr-Universitat, Bochum, April.

Kuhnle, Stein, and Per Selle. 1990. "Meeting Needs in a Welfare State: Relations between Government and Voluntary Organization in Norway." In *Needs and Welfare,* ed. A. Ware and R. Goodin. New York: Sage.

————, eds. 1992a. *Government and Voluntary Organizations: A Relational Perspective.* Aldershot: Avebury.

————. 1992b. "The Historical Precedent for Government–Nonprofit Cooperation in Norway." In *Government and the Third Sector,* ed. Benjamin Gidron, Ralph M. Kramer, and Lester M. Salamon, 75–99. San Francisco: Jossey-Bass.

Kunz, Christian, R. Jones, and Ken Spencer. 1989. *Bidding for Change? Voluntary Organisations and Competitive Tendering for Local Authority Services.* Birmingham, England: Birmingham Settlement and the Community Projects Foundation.

Lammers, C.J. 1983/87. *Organisaties Vergelijkenderwijs: Ontwikkeling en Relevantie van het Sociologisch Denken over Organisaties* ("Organizations Compared: The Development and Relevance of Sociological Thinking about Organizations). Utrecht: AULA, Spectrum.

Langton, Stuart. 1988. "Envoi: Developing Non-Profit Theory." In *Shifting the Debate: Public/Private Sector Relations in the Modern Welfare State,* ed. Susan Ostrander, Stuart Langton, and John Van Til. New Brunswick, NJ: Transaction Books.

LaPalombara, Joseph. 1987. *Democracy, Italian Style.* New Haven, CT: Yale University Press.

Leat, Diana. 1988. *Voluntary Organisations and Accountability.* London: National Council for Voluntary Organisations.

Leat, Diana, G. Smolka, and Judith Unell. 1981. *Voluntary and Statutory Collaboration: Rhetoric or Reality?* London: Bedford Square Press.

Leat, Diana, Sue Tester, and Judith Unell. 1986. *A Price Worth Paying? A Study of the Efforts of Governmental Grant Aid to Voluntary Organisations.* London: Policy Studies Institute.

Leduc, R., and S. Block. 1985. "Conjoint Directorship: Clarifying Management Roles between the Board of Directors and Executive Directors." *Journal of Voluntary Action Research* 14:4.

Lee, Norman, ed. 1989. *Sources of Charity Finance.* Tonbridge, England: Charities Aid Foundation.

Le Grand, Julian, and Ray Robinson, eds. 1984. *Privatisation and the Welfare State.* London: George Allen and Unwin.

Lipsky, Michael, and Steven R. Smith. 1989. "Nonprofit Organizations, Government, and the Welfare State." *Political Science Quarterly* 104:625–48.

Lloyd, Peter C. 1990. "The Relations between Voluntary Associations and State Agencies in the Provision of Social Services at the Local Level." In *The Third Sector,* ed. Helmut K. Anheier and Wolfgang Seibel, 241–54. San Francisco: Jossey-Bass.

Lorentzen, Håkon. 1986. *Mellom bevese og byräkrati. De frivillige oranisasjonenes rolle i sosialsektoren* (Between Social Movements and Bureaucracy. The Role of Voluntary Associations in the Social Sector). Oslo: Institute for Applied Social Research.

Lorentzen, Håkon, and Bennedichte C.R. Olsen. 1990. "Voluntary Organizations for the Disabled: Structure and Development 1982–1988." *Arbeids Notat* 91:4.

Macadam, Elisabeth. 1934. *The New Philanthropy: A Study of the Relations between the Statutory and Voluntary Social Services*. London: Allen and Unwin.

McCarthy, Kathleen, Virginia Hodgkinson, and Russy Sumariwalla, eds. 1992. *The Nonprofit Sector in the Global Community: Voices from Many Nations*. San Francisco: Jossey-Bass.

MacKeith, Joy. 1992. "Meeting Needs or Meeting Targets: The Relationship between Fund Raising and Service-Providing Functions in a Major British Charity." Paper presented at the Third International Conference of Research on Voluntary and Nonprofit Organizations. Indianapolis, Indiana, March 14–16.

Mackintosh, H. 1989. "Barnardo's Statutory Partnership: The Issues for Barnardo's of a Contract Culture." Master's thesis. University of Birmingham, Birmingham.

Marin, Bernd, ed. 1990. *Generalized Political Exchange: Antagonistic Cooperation and Integrated Policy Circuits*. Vol. 4. Boulder, CO: Westview Press.

Meier, Charles, ed. 1987. *Changing Boundaries of the Political: Essays on the Evolving Balance between the State and Society, Public and Private in Europe*. Cambridge: Cambridge University Press.

Melief, Willem B.A.M. 1985. "Participatie van Gebruikers, Belangenorganisaties en Actiegroepen in de Maatschappelijke Dienstverlening (Participation of Clients, Interest Organizations and Action Groups in Social Care). The Hague: NIMAWO.

——. 1986. "Gebruikersparticipatie" (Client Participation). In *Handboek Maatschappelijk Werk: Ontwikkelingen in het Beroep* (Handbook of Social Work, Developments in the Profession), ed. Erik Behrend a. o. Alphen aan den Rijn: Samsom.

——. 1991. "Functie en Plaats van het Maatschappelijk Werk in de Grote Stad" (Function and Position of Social Work in the Big City). In *Maatschappelijk Werk en de Stad, Vijf Preadviezen* (Social Work and the City, Five Proposals), ed. P. den Hoed. The Hague: Wetenschappelijk Raad voor het Regeringsbeleid (Scientific Council for Government Policy).

Mellor, Hugh W. 1985. *The Role of Voluntary Organisations*. London: Croom Helm.

Melucci, Alberto. 1991. *L'invenzione del Presente: Movimenti, Identità, Bisogni Individuali* (The Construction of the Present: Social Movements, Identity, and Individual Needs). Bologna: Il Mulino.

Meyer, John W., and Brian Rowan. 1983. "Institutionalized Organizations: Formal Structure as Myth and Ceremony." In *Organizational Environments: Ritual and Rationality*, ed. John W. Meyer and W. Richard Scott, 21–44. Beverly Hills: Sage.

Meyer, John W., and W. Richard Scott, eds. 1983. *Organizational Environments: Ritual and Rationality*. Beverly Hills: Sage.

Middleton, Melissa, 1987. "Nonprofit Boards: Beyond the Governance Function." In *The Nonprofit Sector: A Research Handbook,* ed. W.W. Powell, Jr., 141–53. New Haven, CT: Yale University Press.

Miller, Leonard, and Robert Pruger. 1990. "Efficiency and the Social Services." *Administration in Social Work* 15:12.

Miller, S.M. 1990. "The Evolving Welfare State Mixes." In *Shifts in the Welfare Mix: Their Impact on Work, Social Services, and Welfare,* ed. A. Evers and H. Wintersberger, 371–87. Boulder, CO: Westview Press.

Mingione, E. 1988. "Problems and Prospects of the Welfare State in Italy." In *Remaking the Welfare State,* ed. Michael K. Brown, 211–31. Philadelphia: Temple University Press.

Mishra, Ramesh. 1984. *The Welfare State in Crisis: Social Thought and Social Change.* Brighton, England: Wheatsheaf.

———. 1991. *The Welfare State in Capitalist Society: Policies of Retrenchment and Maintenance in Europe, North America, and Australia.* Toronto: University of Toronto Press.

Morgan, Garth. 1986. *Images of Organization.* Beverly Hills: Sage.

NOU. 1988, 1990. Norwegian Public Reports.

National Council for Voluntary Organisations (NCVO). 1986. *Relations between the Voluntary Sector and Government: A Code for Voluntary Organizations.* London: National Council for Voluntary Organisations.

———. 1988. *Into the 1990s: Voluntary Organisations and the Public Sector.* London: National Council for Voluntary Organisations and the Royal Institute of Public Administration.

———. 1989. *The Contract Culture: The Challenge for Voluntary Organisations.* London: National Council for Voluntary Organisations.

———. 1990a. *Cause and Effect: A Survey of Campaigning in the Voluntary Sector.* London: National Council for Voluntary Organisations.

———. 1990b. *Effectiveness and the Voluntary Sector.* London: National Council for Voluntary Organisations.

Noventa, Andrea, Rassana Nava, and Francessa Oliva. 1990. *Self-Help: Promozione della Salute e Gruppi di Auto-Aiuto.* Torino, Italy: Edizioni Gruppo Abele.

Olsen, Johan. 1980. *Aksjoner og demokrati* (Social Movements and Democracy). Oslo: Universitetsforlaget.

Onarheim, Gunnar. 1990. "Organisasjonar for funksjonshemma og forholdet til det offentlege" (Organizations for Disabled and Their Relations to Public Authorities). In *Frivillig organiser vered alternativ til Oentleg?* (Voluntary Services—An Alternative to State Welfare?), ed. Stein Kuhnle and Per Selle. Bergen: Alma Mater.

Owen, David. 1964. *English Philanthropy, 1660–1960.* Cambridge: Harvard University Press.

Paci, Massimo. 1984. "Il Sistema di Welfare Italiano tra Tradizione 'Clientelare' ed Esigenze di Cambiamento" (The Italian Welfare System between Traditional Political Patronage and the Need for Change). In *Welfare State all'Italiana* (Italian Welfare State), ed. Ugo Ascoli. Roma-Bari, Italy: Laterza.

———. 1987. "Long Waves in the Development of Welfare Systems." In *Changing Boundaries of the Political: Essays on the Evolving Balance between the State and Society, Public and Private in Europe,* ed. Charles S. Meier, 179–97. Cambridge: Cambridge University Press.

Pasquinelli, Sergio. 1989. "Voluntary Action in the Welfare State: The Italian Case." *Nonprofit and Voluntary Sector Quarterly* 18(4): 349–66.

———. 1992. "Voluntary Organizations and the Welfare State in Italy." In *Government and the Third Sector,* ed. Benjamin Gidron, Ralph M. Kramer, and Lester M. Salamon, 196–214. San Francisco: Jossey-Bass.

Pasquino, Gianfranco. 1980. "Italian Christian Democracy: A Party for All Seasons." In *Italy in Transition: Conflict and Consensus,* ed. P. Lange and S. Tarrow. London: Frank Cass and Company.

———. 1990. *Alla Ricerca dello Scettro Perduto* (In Search of the Lost Septre). Bologna, Italy: Il Mulino.

Patton, Rob, and Carolyn Hooker. 1990. "Managers and Their Development in Voluntary Organizations: Trends and Issues in the UK." In *Towards the 21st Century: Challenges for the Voluntary Sector.* Proceedings of the 1990 Conference of the Association of Voluntary Scholars. London: Center for Voluntary Organizations. Vol. 2, pp. 78–89.

Patti, Rino. 1987. "Managing for Service Effectiveness in Social Welfare: Toward a Performance Model." *Administration in Social Work* 11: 3,4.

Pen, J. 1987. "Expanding Budgets in a Stagnating Economy: The Experience of the 1970's." In *Changing Boundaries of the Political,* ed. Charles Meir. Cambridge: Cambridge University Press.

Perlmutter, Ted. 1991. "Italy: Why No Voluntary Sector?" In *Between States and Markets: The Voluntary Sector in Comparative Perspective,* ed. Robert Wuthnow, 157–88. Princeton, NJ: Princeton University Press.

Perrow, Charles. 1986. *Complex Organizations.* 3d ed. New York: Random House.

Peters, Tom, and Robert Waterman. 1982. *In Search of Excellence: The Leadership Difference.* New York: Harper and Row.

Pfeffer, Jeffrey, and Gerald Salancik. 1978. *The External Control of Organizations.* New York: Harper and Row.

Pickvance, Clarence. 1987. "Central Government, Local Government, Voluntary Associations and the Welfare State: Some Reflections on Opposition to Recent Public Spending Cuts in Britain." *Journal of Voluntary Action Research* 16(12): 81–96.

Pierson, Christopher. 1991. *Beyond the Welfare State? The New Political Economy of Welfare.* University Park, PA: Pennsylvania State University Press.

Pinker, Robert. 1985. "Social Policy and Social Care: Division of Responsibility." In *Support Networks in a Caring Community,* ed. A. Yoder, et al. Dordrecht: Martinus Nijhoff.

Posnett, J. 1992. "Income and Expenditures of Charities in England and Wales," *Charity Trends* 1990–91, 15:11–12.

Powell, Walter, and Paul DiMaggio, eds. 1991. *The New Institutionalism in Organizational Analysis.* Chicago: University of Chicago Press.

Powell, Walter, and Rebecca Friedkin. 1987. "Organizational Change in Nonprofit Organizations." In *The Nonprofit Sector: A Research Handbook,* ed. W.W. Powell, Jr., 180–94. New Haven, CT: Yale University Press.

Preite, Disiano. 1990. "Aspetti Istituzionali e Normativi del Terzo Settore in Italia" (Institutional and Normative Aspects of the Third Sector). In *Non per Profitto,* no. 23, ed. M.C. Bassanini and P. Ranci. Fondazione Olivetti.

Quinn, R., and K. Cameron. 1983. "Organizational Life Cycles and Shifting Criteria of Effectiveness: Some Preliminary Evidence." *Management Science* 29(1): 33–51.

Raaum, Johan. 1988. *De frivilge organisasionenes framdrif og utvikling i Norge* (The Development of Voluntary Organizations in Norway). Oslo: NOU, 239–355.

Rai, G. 1983. "Reducing Bureaucratic Inflexibility." *Social Service Review* 45(1): 45–58.

Ranci, Costanzo. 1992. "La mobilitazione dell'altruismo." (The Mobilization of Altruism). In *Polis,* 4.

Ranci, Costanzo, Ugo De Ambrogio, and Sergio Pasquinelli. 1991. *Provision Identità e Servizio: Il Volontariato nella Crisi del Welfare* (Organizational Identity and Service: Voluntary Organization and the Crisis of the Welfare State). Bologna, Italy: Il Mulino.

Ranci, Ortigosa E., ed. 1989. *Welfare State e Politiche Sociali in Italia.* Milan, Italy: F. Angeli.

Regione Lombardia, Department of Social Welfare, 1985–1988. "Spese dei Comuni della Regione Lombardia per Attività Socio-assistenziali" (Public Expenditures of Lombardy Municipalities for Social Welfare Services). Milan.

Rein, Martin. 1989. "The Social Structure of Institutions: Neither Public nor Private." In *Privatization and the Welfare State,* ed. Sheila Kamerman and Alfred Kahn. Princeton, NJ: Princeton University Press.

Rix, B. 1989. *Farce about Face.* London: Hodder and Stoughton.

Roebroek, Joop, and Theo Berben. 1987. "Netherlands." In *Growth to Limits: The Western European Welfare States since World War II,* vol. 4, ed. Peter Flora. Berlin: de Gruyter.

Rooff, Madeline. 1957. *Voluntary Societies and Social Policy.* London: Routledge and Kegan Paul.

Rossi, Giovanne, and Ivo Colozzi. 1985. "I Gruppi di Volontariato in Italia. Elementi per una Classificazione" (Voluntarism in Italy: Elements for a Classification). In *Volontariato ed Enti Locali,* ed. L. Tavazza. Bologna, Italy: Dehoniane.

Royal College of Physicians. 1986. *The Young Disabled Adult: The Use of Residential Care and Hospital Units for the Age Group 16–64.* London: Royal College of Physicians.

Saidel, Judith R. 1989. "Dimensions of Interdependence: The State–Voluntary Sector Relationship." *Nonprofit and Voluntary Sector Quarterly* 18 (Winter): 335–47.

Sainsbury, E. 1977. *The Personal Social Services.* London: Pitman Publishing.

Salamon, Lester. 1987. "Partners in Public Service: The Scope and Theory of Government–Nonprofit Relations." In *The Nonprofit Sector: A Research Handbook,* ed. Walter Powell, Jr., 99–117. New Haven, CT: Yale University Press.

———. 1989. "The Voluntary Sector and the Future of the Welfare State." *Nonprofit and Voluntary Sector Quarterly* 18 (Spring): 11–24.

Salamon, Lester, and Helmut K. Anheier. 1992. "In Search of the Nonprofit Sector: The Question of Definitions." Working Paper No. 2. Johns Hopkins University Institute for Policy Studies, Baltimore, MD.

Saxon-Harrold, Susan. 1990. "Competition, Resources and Strategy in the British Nonprofit Sector." In *The Third Sector,* ed. Helmut K. Anheier and Wolfgang Seibel, 123–40. Berlin: de Gruyter.

———. 1992. "The Voluntary Sector in Britain: A Statistical Overview, 1975–1989." In *The Nonprofit Sector in the Global Community,* ed. Kathleen McCarthy, Virginia Hodgkinson, and Russy Sumariwalla, 149–75. San Francisco: Jossey-Bass.

Schama, Simon. 1987. *The Embarrassment of Riches: An Interpretation of Dutch Culture in the Golden Age.* New York: Fontana Press.

Schlesinger, Mark, and Robert Dorwart. 1984. "Ownership and Mental Health Care: A Reappraisal." *New England Journal of Medicine* 311: 959–65.

Schmid, Hillel. 1990. "An Organizational Analysis of Profit and Nonprofit Organizations in Care of the Frail Elderly." Paper presented at the 1990 Conference of the Association of Voluntary Action Scholars. London, July.

Schmitter, Phillipe C. 1985. "Neo-Corporatism and the State." In *The Political Economy of Corporatism,* ed. Wyn Grant, 32–62. New York: St. Martin's Press.

Schnabel, P. 1988. "De Gezondheidszorg: van Immuniteit tot Publiek Domein" (Health Care: From Immunity to Public Domain). In *Outbliek Domein: De Veranderende Balans tussen Staat en Samenleving* (Public Domain: The Changing Balance between State and Society), eds. A.M.J. Kreukels and J.B.D. Simonis. Meppel: Boom.

Schuppert, Gunnar. 1991. "State, Market, Third Sector: Problems of Organizational Choice in the Delivery of Public Services." *Nonprofit and Voluntary Sector Quarterly* 20(2): 123–36.

Scott, W. Richard. 1981. *Organizations: Rational, Natural and Open Systems.* Englewood Cliffs, NJ: Prentice-Hall.

Seibel, Wolfgang. 1990. "Government–Third Sector Relationships in a Comparative Perspective: The Cases of France and West Germany." *Voluntas* 1(1): 42–61.

Slavin, Simon. 1978. "The Structure and Uses of Authority in Social Administration." In *The Management of the Social Services,* ed. Simon Slavin. New York: Haworth Press.

Smith, Stephen R., and Michael Lipsky. 1993. *Nonprofits for Hire: The Welfare State in an Age of Contracting.* Cambridge: Harvard University Press.

Sociaal en Cultureel Planbureau (Social and Cultural Planning Office). 1988. *Sociaal Cultureel Raport* (Social and Cultural Report). Rijswijk: Sociaal en Cultureel Planbureau.

Sosin, Michael R. 1990. "Decentralizing the Social Service System: A Reassessment." *Social Service Review* 64 (December): 617–36.

Spicker, Paul. 1991. "The Principle of Subsidiarity and the Social Policy of the European Community." *Journal of European Social Policy* 1: 3–14.

Starr, Paul. 1989. "The Meaning of Privatization." In *Privatization and the Welfare State,* ed. Sheila Kamerman and Alfred Kahn, 15–48. Princeton, NJ: Princeton University Press.

Stein, Herman D., ed. 1982. *Organization and the Human Services: Cross-Disciplinary Reflections.* Philadelphia: Temple University Press.

Steinberg, Richard. 1987. "Nonprofit Organizations and the Market." In *The Nonprofit Sector: A Research Handbook,* ed. Walter Powell, Jr., 118–40. New Haven, CT: Yale University Press.

Stone, Melissa. 1989. "Planning as Strategy in Nonprofit Organizations: An Exploratory Study." *Nonprofit and Voluntary Sector Quarterly* 18:4 (Winter): 297–316.

Streeck, Wolfgang, and Phillipe C. Schmitter. 1985. "Community, Market, State and Associations?" In *Private Interest Government: Beyond Market and State,* ed. Wolfgang Streeck and Phillipe Schmitter, 297–316. London: Sage.

Svetlik, Ivan. 1991. "The Future of Welfare Pluralism in the Postcommunist Countries." In *New Welfare Mixes in Care for the Elderly,* vol. 1, ed. Adalbert Evers and Ivan Svetlik, 13–24. Vienna: European Centre for Social Welfare Policy and Research.

Tarrow, Sidney. 1989. *Democracy and Disorder: Protest and Politics in Italy, 1965–1975.* Oxford: Oxford University Press.

Taylor, Marilyn. 1990. *New Times, New Challenges: Voluntary Organisations Facing 1990.* London: National Council for Voluntary Organisations.

———. 1992. "The Changing Role of the Nonprofit Sector in Britain: Moving Toward the Market." In *Government and the Third Sector,* ed. Benjamin Gidron, Ralph M. Kramer, and Lester M. Salamon, 141–75. San Francisco: Jossey-Bass.

Taylor-Gooby, Peter. 1985. *Public Opinion, Ideology and Social Welfare.* London: Routledge and Kegan Paul.

———. 1988. "The Future of the British Welfare State." *European Sociological Review* 4(1): 1–19.

Therborn, Goren. 1989. "Pillarization and Popular Movements Two Variants of Welfare State Capitalism: The Netherlands and Sweden." In *The Comparative History of Social Policy,* ed. F.G. Castles, 192–241. Cambridge: Polity Press.

Turnaturi, Gabriella. 1991. *Associati per Amore* (Joined by Love). Milano, Italy: Feltrinelli.

Tushman, M., and E. Romanelli. 1985. "Organizational Evolution: A Metamorphosis Model." *Research in Organizational Behavior* 7: 171–222.

Tweede Kamer der Staten Generaal, Parlementaire Jaar 1989–90 (Second Chamber of the Parliament of the Netherlands, Parliamentary Year 1989–90). 1990. *Werken aan Zorgvernieuwing: Actieprogramma van het Beleid voor de Zorgsector in de Jaren Negentig* (Working on Innovative Care: A Policy Action Program for the Care Sector in the Nineties). No. 21 545.

Tweede Kamer der Staten Generaal, Parlementaire Jaren 1970–1990 (Second Chamber of the Parliament of the Netherlands, Parliamentary Years 1970–1990). 1991. *Financieel Overzicht Zorg.* (Parliamentary Financial Report on Care).

Unell, Judith. 1989. "The Changing Pattern of Public Sector Support for Voluntary Organisations." In *Sources of Charity Finance,* ed. N. Lee. London: Charities Aid Foundation.

van Daal, Henk Jan. 1990. *Organizations of Volunteers in Home Care.* The Hague: NIMAWO.

————. 1990. *Vrijwilligershulp en Informele Hulp in Nederland: Een Inventarisatie van Onbetaald Werk buiten het Eigen Huishouden, in het Bijzonder op het Gebied van de Hulpverlening* (Volunteer Activities and Informal Care in the Netherlands: An Inventory of Unpaid Labour Outside the Household, in the Area of Social and Health Care). The Hague: NIMAWO.

van Daal, Henk Jan, E.M.T. Plemper, and L.F.M. Willems. 1992. *Vrijwilligersorganisaties in de Thuiszorg: Een Verkenning van Strategische Problem* (Organizations of Volunteers in Home Care: An Exploration of Strategical Problems). The Hague: NIMAWO.

van Mierlo, J.G.A., and L.G. Gerrichhauzen, eds. 1988. *Het Particulier Initiatief in de Nederlandse Verzorgingsmaatschappij, een Bestuurskundige Benadering* (The Voluntary Organizations in the Dutch Welfare State: A Public Administration Approach). Lochem: De Tijdstroom.

Wagner, Antonin. 1992. "The Interrelationship between the Public and Voluntary Sectors in Switzerland: Unmixing the Mixed-Up Economy." In *Government and the Third Sector,* ed. Benjamin Gidron, Ralph M. Kramer, and Lester M. Salamon, 100–119. San Francisco: Jossey-Bass.

Ware, Alan. 1989a. *Between Profit and State: Intermediate Organizations in Britain and the US.* Princeton, NJ: Princeton University Press.

————. 1989b. "The Changing Relations between Charities and the State." In *Charities and Government,* ed. Alan Ware, 1–28. Manchester: Manchester University Press.

Warner, Amos G. 1894. *American Charities: A Study in Philanthropy and Economics.* Boston: Thomas Y. Crowell.

Webb, Adrian, and Gerald Wistow. 1982. *Wither State Welfare? Policy and Implementation in the Personal Social Services.* London: Royal Institute of Public Administration.

Weisbrod, Burton A. 1977. *The Voluntary Nonprofit Sector: An Economic Analysis.* Lexington, MA: D.C. Heath.

————. 1988. *The Nonprofit Economy.* Cambridge: Harvard University Press.

————. 1991. "Tax Policy Toward Non-profit Organisations." *Voluntas* 2 (1): 3–25.

Wentink, Vanja. 1989. *De Toekomst van het Algemeen Maatschappelijk Werk* (The Future of General Family Social Work). The Hague: NIMAWO.

White, T. 1981. "Recent Developments and the Response of the Social Service Departments." In *A New Look at the Personal Social Services,* ed. E. Matilda Goldberg and Stephen Hatch, 3–16. London: Policy Studies Institute.

Willems, L.F.M. 1983. *Gebruikersparticipatie in de Hulpverlening* (Client Participation in Care). The Hague: NIMAWO.

Wilson, David, C. 1989. "New Trends in the Funding of Charities: The Tripartite System of Funding." In *Charities and Government,* ed. Alan Ware. Manchester: Manchester University Press.

————. 1992. "The Strategic Challenges of Cooperation and Competition in British Voluntary Organizations: Toward the Next Century." *Nonprofit Management and Leadership* 2(3): 239–54.

Wilson, James Q. 1989. *Bureaucracy: What Government Agencies Do and Why They Do It.* New York: Basic Books.

Winkle, Curtis R. 1990. "Supply Side Theory and the Role of the Nonprofit Sector: An Analysis of Two Cases." Paper presented at the Annual Conference of the Association for Voluntary Action Scholars. London, July.

Wolch, Jennifer. 1990. *The Shadow State: Government and the Voluntary Sector in Transition.* New York: Foundation Center.

Wolfe, Alan. 1989. *Whose Keeper? Social Sciences and Moral Obligation.* Berkeley: University of California Press.

Wolfenden Committee. 1978. *The Future of Voluntary Organisations.* London: Croom Helm.

Wolfensberger, Wolf. 1973. *The Third Stage in the Evolution of Voluntary Associations for the Mentally Retarded.* Toronto: National Institute on Mental Retardation.

Woolf, S. 1986. *The Poor in Western Europe.* London: Methuen.

Wuthnow, Robert, ed. 1991. *Between States and Markets: The Voluntary Sector in Comparative Perspective.* Princeton, NJ: Princeton University Press.

Young, Dennis, and Stephen J. Finch. 1977. *Foster Care and Nonprofit Agencies.* Lexington, MA: D.C. Heath.

Index

I

ICAN (England), 38
Income of voluntary organizations,
    130–39
  autonomy and, 138–39
  changes in sources of, 133–37
  England, 23, 25–26, 29–30
  government funding, proportionate
      size of, 4
  growth of, trends in, 131–33
  Italy, 54–56, 63–65
  national patterns, 137–38
  Netherlands, 73–77
  Norway, 93–97
  public funding, effects of, 167–68,
      178–80
  sources of income, changes in, 133–37
Institutional care (Italy), 57–59
Intermediary character of voluntary
    organizations, 175–76
International comparisons, 125–26,
    127
Interorganizational relations, 158–69
  advocacy patterns and, 161–63
  collaboration, 158–60
  competition, 163–64
  England, 38–40
  with government, 164–66
  Italy, 62–63, 65–66
  Netherlands, 83
  Norway, 103–5
  public funding, effects of, 167–68
  regulations, maintaining, 166–67
IPAB. See Istituti Publici di Assistenza
    e Beneficenza
Istituti Publici di Assistenza e
    Beneficenza (IPAB), 49, 58
Istituto dei Ciechi, 58
Italy, voluntary organizations in, 12,
    48–66, 195
  advocacy activities, 161
  Church–state relations and, 49
  government funding, 2, 137–38
  growth rate, 113–14

Italy, voluntary organizations in,
    (continued)
  for handicapped, 55–66
    advocacy agencies, 59
    autonomy, 65–66
    community care, 56–57
    funding and income, 54–55, 63–
        65
    governing structures, 61–62
    institutional care, 57–59
    interorganizational relations, 62–63,
        65–66
    sheltered workshops, 60
    structural changes during 1980s,
        60–61
  ideology of, 160
  income growth, 131
  income sources, 133, 136
  lack of competition among, 164
  local-national relations, 145–47
  political decentralization and, 52–
      54
  postwar developments, 50–52
  public funding, 167–68
  recognition of third sector and, 110
  role of religious affiliation, 149–50
  structure, 142–44
  trends, 66

L

LASSDs. See Local Authority Social
    Service Departments
League for the Rights of the Disabled
    (LEDHA), x, 63, 161
LEDHA. See League for the Rights of
    the Disabled
Left, attraction of voluntary
    organizations for, 1–2
Lega Lombarda, 53
Legislation in Netherlands, 84
Local Authority Social Service
    Departments (LASSDs)
    (England), 12, 19, 21–22, 27,
    32, 36–37, 39–40, 45–47, 163,
    168

Third sector *(continued)*
  as term, 10
Typology of third sectors, 125–26,
  127

U

UILDM (Italy), 60
United States, 2

V

Verzuiling. See Pillarization
Voluntarism
  England, 20
  Italy, 50–52
  Netherlands, 70–71
  Norway, 88–89
  types of, 2

Voluntary Action Act (Italy), 54

W

Webb, Beatrice, 5, 20
Webb, Sidney, 5, 20
Welfare pluralism, 21, 123, 124, 192–93
Welfare state
  alternative policy strategies for,
    192–93
  crisis of, 1–2, 111–12
  disillusionment with, in England, 21
  separation of public financing from
    service provision in, 3
Welfare triangles, 188–90
White Paper on Community Care
  (England), 22
Wolfenden Committee, 21
Wolfenden Report, 43

About the Authors

Ralph M. Kramer, DSW, is Professor Emeritus of Social Welfare at the University of California, Berkeley. He is the author of over seventy articles on citizen participation, social planning, and the voluntary sector in the U.S. and Europe. His books include: *Voluntary Agencies in the Welfare State, Participation of the Poor, Readings in Community Organization Practice*, with Harry Specht, 3rd ed. and *Community Development in Israel and the Netherlands*. His books and publications in scholarly journals have been translated into Italian, Dutch, Spanish, French, Hebrew and Hungarian.

Håkon Lorentzen is Senior Research Fellow at the Institute for Social Research, Oslo, Norway. He was the coeditor of the journal *Sosiologi Idag (Sociology Today)* from 1977–1987 and has edited two books, *Privat eller offentlig velferd? (Private or Public Welfare?)* and *Sosialpolitisk Forebygging (Social Prevention Theory)* and published several articles on relations between public authorities and voluntary organizations.

Willem B. Melief, DRS, a sociologist and social worker, is Senior Researcher and Project Manger at the Netherlands Institute for Social Work Research (NIMAWO) in the Hague. He is the author of numerous research monographs, and has edited and contributed chapters in books published in the Netherlands on research methodologies, social policy and the professional practice of social work.

Sergio Pasquinelli is a sociologist, working as a research associate at *Synergia*, Milan, Italy. He is also a member and collaborator of the Istitutuo per la Ricerca Sociale in Milan. He has published several articles on the Italian third sector, and is coauthor of the book *Identita e Servizio*.